A Field Guide to

Awkward Silences

A Field Guide to

Awkward Silences

Alexandra Petri

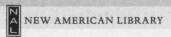
NEW AMERICAN LIBRARY

New American Library
Published by the Penguin Group
Penguin Group (USA) LLC, 375 Hudson Street,
New York, New York 10014

USA | Canada | UK | Ireland | Australia | New Zealand | India | South Africa | China
penguin.com
A Penguin Random House Company

First published by Signet, an imprint of New American Library,
a division of Penguin Group (USA) LLC

First Printing, June 2015

 REGISTERED TRADEMARK—MARCA REGISTRADA

LIBRARY OF CONGRESS CATALOGING-IN-PUBLICATION DATA:
Petri, Alexandra.
A field guide to awkward silences/Alexandra Petri.
p. cm.
ISBN 978-0-451-46960-1 (hardback)
1. Petri, Alexandra. 2. Journalists—United States—Biography. I. Title.
PN4874.P455A3 2015
070.92—dc23   2015001217
[B]

Printed in the United States of America
1   3   5   7   9   10   8   6   4   2

Set in Dante MT
Designed by Spring Hoteling

PUBLISHER'S NOTE
Penguin is committed to publishing works of quality and integrity. In that spirit, we are
proud to offer this book to our readers; however, the story, the experiences and the words
are the author's alone.

For Mom and Dad and all those times you turned to me and whispered, "That would make good material."

I hope you weren't kidding.

Contents

A Field Guide to

Awkward Silences

How Not to Be Awkward

1. I have no idea.
2. Well, how about this? Don't do any of the following.

Flopper

I am afraid of many things. Drowning, fire, the disapproval of strangers on the Internet, that I'll be hit by a bus without having had a chance to clear my browser history, that one day everyone else on the subway will suddenly be able to hear what I am thinking and turn on me. You know, the usuals.

One thing I'm not afraid of? Looking like an idiot.

See, I knew I was a writer. That was protection. No matter where I went, no matter what I did, I could turn it into a story. Fall through a hole in the sidewalk? Story. Make the worst Final Jeopardy! wager of all time? Story. Anger the lord of the ocean, stab a one-eyed guy, and get very, very lost on my way home to Ithaca? *Epic* story.

Those were the two things I knew about myself: that I was a writer, and that I didn't mind looking stupid. Growing up, you figure out pretty quickly which of your friends is the person who doesn't mind looking like an idiot, and that was me, hands down. I was the one going over to strangers and asking if the mothership had landed. I was the one standing in an airport with a giant foam cow hat on my head, accordion open, ready to greet friends as they landed, and not even because I'd lost a bet. Mortification was a poison to which I had built up immunity after years of exposure. Besides, it was much less embarrassing to *be* me than to have to stand next to me and admit you were *with* me.

And the writer in me had noticed that the bigger of an idiot you appeared to be, the better the story was. Nobody wants to hear, "And everything went smoothly, just exactly according to plan." Something had to go wrong. You had to trip up. That was where the excitement lay.

I collected experiences the way some people collect old coins or commemorative stamps.

One year, for fun, I called the ExtenZe male enhancement hotline every day for a month, with different voices, just to see what would happen. (What happened, if you want to know, was that Phoebe, who worked the dinner shift, got annoyed when I identified myself as Franklin Delano Roosevelt (a fun fact about the ExtenZe male enhancement hotline is that they make you identify yourself before you start your call) and threatened to transfer me to the police.)

All of this seemed to be leading to some kind of grand adventure. I sat there, glumly, waiting for a wizard to drop by the house and invite me to steal dragon-gold, or a wise old man in a brown hoodie to offer to teach me the ways of the Force. But no one showed. I would have to strike out on my own.

What was a field in which a willingness to look foolish might come in handy?

Of course! Reality television.

Like anyone growing up after 1980, I always had the dim, nagging sense that I was supposed to be famous for something. A certain measure of fame just seems like our birthright these days, next to life, liberty, and the pursuit of happiness. Food, shelter, Wi-Fi, and the sense that someone's watching; these are the modern requirements for survival. The only thing more terrifying than the feeling you're being watched is the feeling that you're not. Privacy is just an uncomfortable reminder that you're not a celebrity.

My portion of fame, I knew, was waiting somewhere, neatly labeled in a holding facility. To claim it, all I'd have to do would be to fill out some sort of form and show up in the designated audition city. And until that moment it was my right, as an American, to stare at the television and mutter, "I could do that."

If I were being really honest with myself, these people I saw competing on television all possessed skills that I lacked—whether on *American Idol* or *America's Got Talent* or even *America's Most Wanted*. I could hold a tune, but only the way you hold a stranger's cat: not closely and not long (not to mention the strange yowling noises). I Got some talents, all right—excellent grammar, for one—but they weren't the kind of thing that would exactly sing on the national stage. Whenever I tried to "smize," model-style, people asked if I'd been possessed by an ancient and evil spirit. I had never murdered anyone, to the best of my knowledge, and if I did I would certainly not elude capture for long.

But there are always two ways of making it on the air: to be spectacular, and to be spectacularly bad. The second group was more fun to watch anyway. Why be Kelly Clarkson or Carrie Underwood or that one ventriloquist guy whose puppets all seemed oddly racist (get new dummies, Terry Fator! Then you won't have to sit there with a pained expression while they rant about the people taking our jobs), when you could be short, sweatshirted William Hung, wrangling his painfully earnest way through "She Bangs!" or Leonid the Magnificent, dropping his equipment as the big red X's buzzed above him, weeping profusely and promising that "next time, I will be perfect"? Sure, on one path lay Kelly's international fame and Terry's bucket-loads of gold, but on the other lay William's

Christmas album, *Hung for the Holidays*. Now *that* was what I called a career trajectory. *That* was a story!

And that was going to be my way in.

I was going to seek failure out—on the national stage, with a glowing neon X attached.

The plan was simple. I just had to become dramatically, unquestionably, horrifically bad at something. I had to get myself in front of the judges and flop like no one they'd seen before.

Maybe, if I worked hard, I could become just as earth-shatteringly terrible as my idols and wind up on the air. It certainly seemed like my best shot.

My trouble was that I'd had little practice failing. I came up during a very specific era of child-rearing in which everyone seemed to believe that if Little Sally ever failed at anything, ever, she was going to be completely wrecked for life. Dutifully they set about sanding off the sharp edges of existence and childproofing all possible scenarios against hazards of choking under pressure. Trophies for everyone! A part for everyone in the school play. No failure. No rejection. You are a golden snowflake. Have a sticker.

For someone who hoped to make a career of rejection, this was a considerable setback.

I had no opportunity to pursue failure in high school either, where, distressingly, I kept succeeding at things. By senior year, I had been appointed president of four clubs and had mysteriously become captain of the volleyball team, even though I never left the bench. As a flop, I was a failure.

College was a different story. With a clean slate and thousands of people who didn't know that I was doing it on purpose, I could begin my training for the big bomb.

I began collecting rejections.

There is an art, as I quickly learned, to flopping. You can't just be bad. Half the art is knowing how to go too far. You must keep a straight face. If you're auditioning, you must sing badly, but feelingly. You must put the emphasis on the wrong syllable, read comedy as tragedy and tragedy as comedy. Overact, overgesture, pause for no reason midsentence and open and close your mouth like a bewildered carp. You must, in a word, turn in a whole performance.

I began my training in my freshman year, auditioning for plays under a false name. You could be more convincingly terrible, I discovered, when you had a backstory, so I crafted a character. Her name was Gloria Nichols. She had recently lost a lot of weight, loved to make bold gestures where no bold gestures were called for, and was polite to excess, striving to please an unseen vocal teacher who told her she had great promise.

"Any talents?" the student directors asked.

"I have heart!" I wrote. "And kidneys!"

Gradually, I broadened my scope. I auditioned for the Women in Science Players Ensemble. It was the first audition I'd seen listed that was on campus but involved no one I could conceivably ever have met. For my monologue, I recited Yoda's death scene from *Return of the Jedi* in its entirety, doing all the voices. It was a natural choice; as a *Star Wars* fan, I already had the dialogue memorized.

"Lu-uke," I croaked. "There is another s—ky—wa—kk-errr."

When it was over, they looked at me. They seemed to be deciding whether to be angry or confused.

"What possessed you to choose this as your monologue?" they asked.

"*Star Wars* is science," I said.

It was a start.

Later that fall, when I saw a Craigslist ad for Halloween Dancers,

I knew it was directed at me . . . even though my dance experience was restricted to the five miserable years of ballet that gets foisted on every girl of a certain demographic too timid to play soccer.

To give you an idea of how good I was at ballet, when we performed *The Nutcracker*, I played the Girl with the Butterfly Net. There is no such character in *The Nutcracker*. After each scene of the real ballet was finished, I ran across the stage holding a butterfly net.

The Craigslist ad was for "Pussycat Doll–Style Dancers." As far as I could tell, it did not require prior experience, and it paid.

The audition was all the way out in Quincy, Massachusetts. I took the subway there from Cambridge, since I somehow had the naive idea that everything in Quincy was located conveniently on top of the T stop. This turned out not to be the case. Having decided to look the part, I found myself walking along Massachusetts State Highway 3A in leopard-print leggings and a tank top. Cars kept slowing. I waved them on.

The ad listed the audition location as My House, which I assumed was a bar because of the capital letters. But bars usually don't have doorbells.

Another thing I realized when I finally arrived was that I had forgotten to choreograph the requested five minutes of dance. The only song on my iPod of more than four minutes was "Will You Be There" by Michael Jackson. That would have to do.

Despite the doorbell, My House was, in fact, a bar. (I can tell you this definitely only because I Googled it later, but there were some clues on arriving.) The overall aesthetic inside was sort of like a gentrified barn, whose previous cow occupants had all been forced to become leather couches or leave. Everything was dark wood. The main room gave off a vaguely baffled vibe, like it didn't quite know whether the party theme was Hip Happening Club Scene Place,

Man Cave with Leather Chairs, or Old-Timey Stage Set, and was trying to split the difference.

On getting inside, I discovered a large stage area cleared away. There were a few unenthusiastic colored spotlights on the ceiling that seemed to have been laid off from a job at a strip club to which their talents had been much better suited. Near the dance floor, at a table, sat two judges, a black man and woman who looked to be in their mid-thirties, both of whom seemed friendly and encouraging.

"I'm here for the dance audition," I told them. They gave me a still-friendly but mildly perplexed look, the kind of look I assume you would give someone if you crawled out of the desert starving on hands and knees and someone handed you a jar of pickles. It was the kind of look you get when that person unwraps your gift, and there's a longish pause, and then the recipient starts to tell you that it was a Really Lovely Thought.

"I brought my own music," I added.

Five minutes is a much longer time than you think it is. Having run through my entire repertoire of dance moves in the first minute, growing from a seed into a tree and then back, Flowers-for-Algernon-style, I decided that I would repeat each movement eight times while turning slowly counterclockwise.

This was when the male judge burst into smothered laughter and darted from the room.

When the music finished, the remaining judge suggested I try something "more upbeat." I gyrated futilely to Justin Timberlake while she made notes. On my way out ("Don't call us. We'll call."), I leaned over her notebook and glimpsed the phrase "Good enthusiasm."

They didn't call.

But that was perfect. I had flopped, big-time, with earnestness and a straight face!

I was ready to move on to bigger pastures.

That summer, I signed up to audition for *America's Next Top Model*. It has always been my unwavering conviction that I would make a great After model. I'm okay looking, but if someone told you I had just lost sixty pounds, I would look *incredible*. This, I figured, would be my "in."

In order to appear on *America's Next Top Model*, you have to fill out a thirteen-page form detailing such things as "Have you ever been so angry you threw something?" ("My back out, one time," I ventured.) "What would bother you most about living in a house with nine to thirteen other people?" ("Not knowing more specifically the number of people in the house.") "What in the past do you regret?" ("The Holocaust.")

The audition itself was brief, but the afternoon entailed a *lot* of waiting around in heels. I befriended one fellow auditioner who had also failed to print out her demo shots in time, and we commiserated at the Rite Aid as we tried to coax the digital printer into submission. I had had some friends take shots of me posing in what I hoped was a model-like fashion the night before, but when I tried to print them out on my parents' printer, it did that thing that printers do where they insist that they Absolutely Physically Cannot Print Unless All the Colors Have Been Loaded, Because Black Just Doesn't Feel It Would Be Right to Take This Big Step Without Cyan Present.

It was unnerving to be waiting for my prints to come next to someone who actually wanted it. She kept talking about her strategy for winning, pointing out the flaws and weaknesses of the other girls in line. I couldn't see any flaws or weaknesses, other than maybe that they were too skinny and attractive and might blow over in a high wind. I couldn't tell her I was there to lose. Instead, I stood there smiling amiably and murmuring that everyone "looked like a model," which seemed safe.

When you got in front of the judges you had to walk your model walk, which, since I was in heels, was difficult. In heels, I always look like something that is walking on land for the first time—less Ariel than some kind of recently evolved amphibian. I teetered boldly from one end of the designated Walk space to the other, trying to be Fierce like Tyra said. I handed them my photos.

They asked us to tell a video camera the craziest thing we'd ever done to win a contest. I told them about the time I had crashed a dog show and run the agility course myself. "It wasn't really about winning the contest," I admitted, "but it certainly seemed to un nerve the other dogs." (This had occurred in Bermuda and had, I realized, been good practice for making an idiot of myself. As a general note, if you ever want to run a dog agility course, just tell the organizer that you need to do it in honor of your deceased dog, "Topanga." This was what I did, and to my total surprise, they cleared the dogs off the course and let me run it. It may have helped that I was wearing a helmet at the time. I had recently gotten off a moped, but the organizer had no way of knowing that and it probably looked to her as though something ominous was the matter with me. P.S. Dog agility courses are hard, especially if you are not entirely sober.)

They seemed pleased by the story, but months passed, and I heard only silence. They get in touch with you only if you make the show. Otherwise, you just find yourself on several e-mail lists of Style Products and Promotions. I still get e-mails from time to time with New Way to Add Volume to Your Hair and New People Eager to Judge Your Outfits.

But I was getting pretty good at this whole rejection thing.

Finally my moment arrived: the auditions for *America's Got Talent*.

I signed up to audition with a spring in my step and a slight twinge of remorse at having to use my own name. This was something for which I had not been entirely prepared.

Most of my practice (*America's Next Top Model* auditions aside) had been under the guise that I was someone else. One of the advantages of this system was that I got to weather rejection after rejection, flop after flop, without ever feeling the sting of actual failure. Every time, I was venturing out under a protective shell. Everyone else was climbing out of trenches to face the barrage unprotected, but I was neatly secluded in the turret of a tank.

I was putting myself out there, all the time, without actually putting myself out there at all. I was, in fact, putting someone else out there. She had her own name and e-mail address and everything. And if I failed, well, that was because I was trying to fail. Not because I wasn't good enough. It was a neat system, really.

None of these baffled judges had ever seen me trying my best. They had no conception of what that would look like. So I could preserve the illusion of myself intact.

I don't think I'm alone in believing that I secretly carry a really wonderful person around inside me at all times. This person is genuinely good and smart and talented and kind enough to do all the things that real me fails at. This person is a bang-up performer and stays in touch with all her friends and puts together coordinated outfits and when she writes the sentences that sound perfect in her head land on the page just right and she uses the correct bins for glass recyclables and doesn't say "uh" or wave her arms around when talking.

You would think I would be a little concerned that she has never once appeared in twenty-six years, but I feel convinced she's in there somewhere, just waiting for her moment. The only difference between her and Failure Gloria is that people have actually seen Gloria.

It had seemed courageous, before, this bold determination to fail, as splashily as possible. Now it felt a little cowardly. What if my worst wasn't bad enough? Then I'd just be on record as an actual failure.

What if, all this time, I should have been trying to be my best instead?

No. I was prepared. My training would pay off. I was going to be so wincingly bad that I'd make it on the air. I was going to join my idols. All I had to do was seem sincere. As the saying goes, if you can fake that, you've got it made.

I pondered my shtick. I would be a performance artist, I decided. Gloria had tried this once before at a Christian talent agency, offering a triple-threat combination of mediocre monologues, bad song, and worse dance. "Come back to Earth, Gloria," the organizers had gently urged as I aimlessly roved the stage, staring off into the middle distance. This approach seemed ripe for a broader audience.

I would rap and mutter and speak in tongues and shout the names of the Founders and sing snippets of "I Dreamed a Dream." I drilled myself into the wee hours of the morning, then waited in line all day, going over the routine.

It was almost, a nagging voice suggested, as much work as developing a real skill.

I smothered this voice quickly.

I glanced around the roomful of hopeful people waiting to audition at the Ronald Reagan Convention Center. Either they were serious, or they had taken the pursuit of rejection to a whole new level.

A young man with a melon-shaped head and diminished interpersonal skills approached me and sang a few snippets of Usher, spitting into my face. Old men plied their banjos, ineptly. A girl and her entire family waited in front of me, humming "Grenade" by Bruno

Mars, thumbing her iPod in flagrant defiance of the rule against singing to recorded accompaniment. A tiny young rapper got stage fright after the organizers formed a circle around him and tried to make him rap for the camera. One man cornered me and told me about his plans for an evangelical book set on another planet where everyone had more than five senses.

They had glanced over my application form and decided, for some reason, that I belonged with the Vocalists. I saw myself as more of an all-around threat, i.e., Russia rather than North Korea, but I dutifully joined the line.

When I got into the audition room, I gave it my worst. I sang. I twitched. I shouted. I turned in what would have been the performance of Gloria Nichols' lifetime.

I didn't stand a chance.

As I flailed and gyrated—"I dreamed a dream in time gone byeeee . . . Aaron Burr Aaron Burr"—I caught the woman judge looking at me. We made eye contact, and I could tell she knew.

So *that* was what actual rejection felt like.

My worst wasn't bad enough.

All this time, working hard to be terrible, and—nothing.

"If there is one thing I've learned from this afternoon," I typed on my phone, after Melon-headed Spit-Singer asked for my number and offered to pray over me, "it's that no amount of concerted effort can make you seem weirder than people who are just being themselves."

I'd been overlooking one thing, I realized. The best bad movies aren't the ones that try to be bad. They're the ones that try to be good.

If I really wanted to fail spectacularly, I should have been trying to succeed. For the most spectacular rejections of all, you have to believe. You have to go out there and give the performance of your life.

Only then does the ax really fall.

Failing, it turns out, is easy. You don't have to be *trying* to fail. It's a part of life. It sucks. It will come and find you whether you seek it out or not, like women who want to talk to you on long airplane flights.

I'd always thought I'd be all right because I was a writer. Words were a bright thread that could lead me out of any labyrinth; I just had to keep them pinched carefully in my fingers as I walked. Nothing could hurt me as long as I kept hold of the thread. I could seek out anything—awkward, odd, novel, even a little dangerous—and cage it up in sentences, put it on display, its teeth still sharp, maybe, but the bars too thick to bite through. But in trying not to be hurt, I was missing the real story. I was still afraid of jumping. I didn't want to fail for real. I wanted to be a secret success.

All this time I thought I was becoming a master of flops, I'd been safe inside my turret. Where was the adventure in that?

I knew rejection was supposed to be a part of life. Failure, rejection, flopping, embarrassment, all of this.

So why was it so frightening?

Easy.

Historically speaking, I have no problems. We have no problems. We live long lives surrounded by indoor toilets, penicillin, air-conditioning, birth control, smartphones. Everyone has great teeth. Consider that everything that George Washington accomplished in his life, he accomplished while experiencing horrible tooth decay. I have had toothaches once or twice in my life and they left me completely incapacitated for *days*. I could barely do laundry. Meanwhile George lost all his teeth and managed to win a war and start a country.

You would think that this lack of actual complaints would make us happier and more confident. But no. Instead, we have become allergic to things that didn't used to bother us at all. We're acutely focused on minor inconveniences. We're terrified of commitment the way our ancestors used to be terrified of mammoths. I have never seen commitment spear anyone on a tusk and leave him to bleed out slowly in a corner of the cave while wind howls around him. No matter. It scares us just the same. Embarrassing ourselves in front of strangers is literally one of the worst things that can happen to us. It's in the slot where polio used to be. Awkwardness, rejection, missing out. We've conquered everything else and these constants of human life are all that remain to bedevil us.

Once you get rid of all the biggest problems, once you realize you can avoid them, you start to think you can inoculate yourself against the minor ones too. Phone calls are awkward? Just text all the time. Going up to people and asking them on dates is mortifying? Don't worry—now there's an app for that! Not only don't we have to deal with scurvy on a daily basis, but we don't have to actually speak to another human in order to order a pizza.

No wonder we think there must be some way to get out of life's inherent awkwardness, scot-free.

But how do you vaccinate yourself against failure?

One way is to court it. Use irony. Try without really trying.

I'm not the only one I know who grew up doing this. Dancing around awkwardness is something we do. We are vigorously, painfully self-aware princesses waiting to call out the pea under the mattress. Look at all those earnest people throughout history! Hippies, flappers, Napoleon! Look how idiotic they were! We would never look so stupid, unless it was on purpose.

We call attention to awkwardness as soon as it flares up so we can't be accused of being oblivious. We keep announcing to the world how little we've studied so we can't be called dumb. We put ourselves down before others can get the chance. Whenever anything seems like it's on the verge of becoming earnest, we come blasting out with snark.

Don't be too earnest. Don't look like you care. Then you're vulnerable. Life is full of opportunities for rejection, and if you start really trying, you're going to start really failing. Hard. And it'll hurt.

So we put on dopey glasses and grimace so no one can tell us we're not pretty. We drink lousy beer so no one can accuse us of having bad taste. We look stupid on purpose out of fear of looking stupid by accident. We don't even *try* to dance. Anything to postpone the moment when we are actually going to have to stand up, put ourselves out there, and be told it's not good enough.

The result of all these carefully assembled layers of irony?

We get to feel that, if we look like idiots, it's because we meant to. That we never failed, because we never actually tried. They never saw the real us, lurking inside, the ones who could have done it, if they'd wanted to.

But after a point that's a pretty thin satisfaction.

And the trade-off is brutal. You never get to know if you would have made it or not. Maybe you wouldn't have looked stupid. Maybe you'd have been incredible.

So why not take the leap? We're all weird. We're all awkward. We're all bound to fail from time to time. It's in our DNA as human beings . . . along with a certain innate wariness of mammoths.

Five Uneasy Pieces

Some are born awkward. Some achieve awkwardness. Some have awkwardness thrust upon them.

In my case, it was all three.

I am not boasting when I say this. I am simply stating a fact.

Just to give you a general sense of my Supreme Capacity for Awkwardness, here is a casebook of five of the most awkward things that I have ever done. What strikes me about these, in retrospect, is that in every case I was genuinely trying to *avoid* awkwardness. I remember looking at each of these situations, as it began. "This is going to be awkward," I said to myself each time. "I had better think of a clever way around this."

That was the key to all of these scenarios. I really thought I was making it better.

I was not.

Problem: Couple having public fight directly in front of me.

Awkwardness Level: 3

Solution: Pretend to be insane.

I was standing in line to get frozen yogurt. There was a couple fighting. Loudly. I couldn't help noticing them. Possibly I was staring, just a little.

The man noticed me. "You see?" he said. "People are staring."

"I don't care if they *are* staring," the woman said.

"I'm so sorry you have to witness this," the man said, turning to me directly.

I froze. Well, I thought. I have two options. I can engage with them, or I can pretend to be an insane person.

I fixed my eyes on the middle distance. "Reuben," I said, distinctly, "Reuben, send the cattle home."

It was at this point that I realized that they were in line in front of me and we would be stuck together for some time. I could not, I reasoned, abandon ship now. I spent the next ten minutes repeating, at intervals, "Reuben, Reuben, send the cattle home."

I was committed. There was clearly no other option. I could not simply return things to the pre-Reuben-send-the-cattle-home status quo. So I went with it.

It was a very long ten minutes.

Problem: Want to ask someone out.

Awkwardness Level: 7

Solution: Have a robot do it.

In high school, I took it into my head to invite my friend Mark to a dance. Too intimidated to call him in person, I decided it would be easier to use text-to-speech software to ask for me. All I'd have to do was hold the phone up next to the computer, and a reassuring mechanical voice would request Mark's presence at the winter formal.

I figured there was no way that this plan could possibly go wrong. The one thing I had not planned for was that Mark's father would answer the phone instead of Mark. The instant someone picked up, I hit PLAY.

"Greetings. This is an automated message on behalf of Alexandra Petri to request Mark's presence at the National Cathedral School winter formal—"

"What's going on?" Mr. Parker said into the phone. "Hello? Hello?"

"—dance on Saturday, December the—"

"Hello? Who is this? Hello?"

"Please indicate your acceptance or refusal by saying—"

"Who are you? What is this?"

This was not going as I had intended. I allowed the message to conclude, then hung up the phone, in disarray. I steeled myself to call back to explain what was going on.

"Don't worry, Mr. Parker," I said. "That creepy machine you just heard was actually me! It's Alexandra, from youth group! I just thought it might be a more efficient way of asking Mark to the formal. You know, like you do."

It took me a while to explain my logic. I kept stressing the "convenience" and "efficiency" of my technique. There was less risk for everyone! If anyone got rejected, it wouldn't be me! It would be the robotic Dance Invite voice. That made perfect sense. Nobody's feelings would get hurt if a robot intermediary was used!

Mark wound up attending the dance, but only after I had apologized to his parents for having a robotic voice call their house to demand their son's presence, something I now realize is a total hostage nightmare that gets visited only on Liam Neeson characters in movies.

Problem: Want to *avoid* going out with someone.

Awkwardness Level: 8

Solution: Sabotage date.

A guy on whom I was not particularly keen had invited me on a second date. Just saying no seemed rude, somehow. And I'd heard the Gradual Contact Fade was frowned on. How to avoid this?

"I know!" I said. "I should go on this date, and I should just be as awkward as possible, so he'll be able to reject me instead! No hard feelings for anyone!"

I put it in my calendar as Sabotage Date.

"That is a terrible idea," my friends said, not for the first time. "Just say 'I'd prefer not to go on a second date with you, but I would like to be friends.'"

"NO!" I said. "This will be easier. Trust me."

I showed up at the Thai restaurant an hour late.

"It's okay," he said brightly. "I read Wikipedia in the car."

My plan of attack was simple. I would demonstrate enough nervous tics to alarm a yak. "Who is this strange, gesticulating bundle of terror?" he would murmur to himself. "Check, please!"

I began adjusting the silverware and tapping everything. Adjust place mat. Tap. Move plate. Move plate back. Tap. Tap. Avoid eye contact. Mumble frequently about badgers.

He seemed unfazed. He remained unfazed. We were almost done with the meal and he'd barely batted an eye.

"This is probably a good time to tell you," he said. "I have Asperger's."

"Ah," I said. My strategy of using social awkwardness as a wedge between us was clearly backfiring. Plan collapsing in ruins around me, I darted into the restroom to regroup.

"You can quit now," I told my reflection. "Or you can level up."

I looked around for props. There was nothing but hand soap. I dabbed a healthy portion on my face and did not wipe it off, strolling back into the restaurant with a pearlescent smear on my cheek and as much nonchalance as I could manage.

He seemed unfazed. "Let's get ice cream," he suggested.

We strolled out into the street. Pearlescent white liquid trickled slowly down my face. Upon arriving at the Häagen-Dazs, I again darted into the restroom to regroup. I wiped the soap off my face and stared, again, at my reflection.

"You can quit," I murmured, "or you can level up."

I cast about me for anything that might prove useful.

Finally I landed on it, and came darting out of the restroom with a plunger clutched in my hand. "I must have this plunger!" I shouted. "We've made the bond! Quick! To the exit!"

The man behind the Häagen-Dazs counter shot me a strange look. "Ma'am," he said. "Give me the plunger."

Because I am, fundamentally, law-abiding, I handed it over to him. It is always at moments like this when my nerve deserts me. "Er," I said, "I will pay you good money for this plunger. I feel as though we've really bonded."

"That's all right, ma'am," he said. I got the sense he wanted me to leave.

When I got to the sidewalk, my date was waiting. "Don't worry," he said. "I'll buy you a plunger of your very own."

I was about ready to give up. But never let it be said that a Petri gave up without a fight.

"I can quit," I thought to myself, "or I can level up."

I frowned. What did men find off-putting? Weird sex things, right? Men traditionally disliked strange sex things, I bet. That would scare him off immediately. (Dazed by my prior failures, I was not, I confess, thinking entirely clearly.)

"Gee," I said out loud, "you're nice, but—I am only capable of erotic attraction to badgers. And members of the Beatles. You know, in tandem. Doing, you know. Doing . . ." I struggled to elaborate. My explanation quickly devolved into a series of nervous hand gestures, which looked sort of like reaching into a jar where you think there might be spiders.

Finally I lapsed into silence.

He walked away. I'd done it! I thought. He had rejected me! I'd made it! We'd all go home feeling better about ourselves.

Then I saw him looping back around. He stopped right in front of me. "That's the sexiest thing I've ever heard," he breathed.

I was defeated. There was nothing for it.

I bowed to him and darted away.

Afterward, I ignored his calls. "I should have done that in the first place," I told my friends.

"No," they said, wincing. "No, that's not really a good strategy either."

Problem: The world is full of injustice.

Awkwardness Level: 5? This is not really "awkward" so much as "unjust" or "bad."

Solution: Become a one-woman vigilante.

Growing up I watched *America's Most Wanted* religiously each week, hoping I would see a fugitive and be able to make a difference. Saturday nights at nine were sacrosanct.

COPS would end. The "Bad Boys" credit music would start to play. ("Bad boys, bad boys, what you gonna do?") and then—whoosh! Zoom! Onomatopoeic noises!—a Big Shield with an Eagle on It would come flying in.

"Welcome to *America's Most Wanted*," John Walsh would say, dignified in his leather jacket and gray hair. "Tonight we're continuing our fight. We're on the MANhunt for some wanted sex traffickers."

"Eeugh," my mother would say. "Eeugh, how do you watch this?"

"Shh," I said.

On the screen, a naked tearful woman was running down a highway as cars swerved and honked. She had just escaped from a kidnapper's van, using courage and ingenuity. (Never, John Walsh reminded us, try to sell your wedding dress in the classified ads. This is what will happen.)

"I hate this," my mother put in. "This is awful."

"No," I would say. "This is REAL LIFE. This is AMAZING. We are going to make a difference."

On the TV, John Walsh talked compassionately to a man who was convinced that his vanished daughter had become a stripper. The man now spent all his days walking down the Vegas streets handing out flyers. Some footage of this followed. The passersby seemed somewhat baffled.

"Please," the father said into the camera. "Crystal, just come home. We don't care what you've done."

"You realize this is Saturday night at nine," my mom said. "Are you sure there isn't a high school party with alcohol and boys you would rather be attending? I could drive you."

"That's not the POINT," I said, folding my arms. "I'm going to make a difference. Like that hotel clerk last week who identified the bank robber."

We fell silent as the screen showed us a reenactment of an elderly Indian mother being mowed down by a white van on the morning of her son's wedding. Much of *America's Most Wanted* is basically anti-van propaganda.

"I can't stand this," my mother would say for the sixth time.

"Then why are you watching?"

"We're bonding." To be fair, this was how bonding worked in our family. We would find some activity that only one of us enjoyed and all three of us would do it. Bonding was not supposed to be fun.

"Shh," I said, "they're doing the Fifteen Seconds of Shame, profiles of wanted fugitives. I've got to commit their vital statistics to memory so I can call them in."

That was the dream. I wanted to be on *America's Most Wanted*. Not as a criminal, of course. I used to prison tutor and I am positive I could not make it behind bars, because my tattoos would all support concepts like "grammar" and "the Oxford comma," and those don't really bring much gang backing. ("Nice tear tattoo!" "Actually, it's a comma.")

No. I wanted to make a difference. I would spot a criminal, like that vigilant hotel clerk had, and I would call 1-800-Crime-TV. Remember, John Walsh said, you CAN remain anonymous!

As we drove down to visit my grandparents in Florida that Christmas, I checked out all the wanted fugitives along our route on the *America's Most Wanted* Web site. "Could we stop in Miami?" I suggested, timidly. "There's a bouncer with prominent barbed wire tattoos that I think I've got a very good visual handle on."

My father shrugged at my mother, who gave him the parental look that translates to "What's going to happen when she gets out of the house?"

I knew what would happen. I was going to get my man.

When I got to college up in Boston, I soon fell into my groove, watching *America's Most Wanted* on the dorm TV on Saturday nights, staying sharp and vigilant, like a knife that is also vigilant.

And then, one afternoon, I saw him.

He was walking down the cobbled street looking for all the world like another law-abiding citizen among dozens of other law-abiding citizens. But I knew who he was. I knew what he had done.

I can still remember the reenactment footage of him going on a murderous rampage, putting his daughter into a plastic bag and tossing her in the river. There he was with that toothy smile, the thinning brown hair that looked sort of like the top of an eggplant, that corrugated wrinkly forehead.

I followed a few steps behind him, hoping he wouldn't notice, but he gave me a look, casually, like a "You following me?" sort of look. I tried to give him a look back that said, "Hell yeah, I followed you because of your raw sexual magnetism," instead of the Inspector Javert–like Glower of Justice I was currently sporting.

I looked forward to calling the hotline to announce: "I have seen the man—what's his name—the murder guy—with the bag—and the face—and I'm a tipster and a hero now!" And they would totally know who I was talking about. And they would tip off the local police department, where a rugged old sergeant with a mustache who was all but retired except he couldn't let this one case go would sit bolt upright at his desk and he would say PARTNER, CALL THE TEAM. WE'VE GOT A REAL 3-9, and they would show up outside the dorm and surround it and take out the creepy man in handcuffs and everyone would say "What's all this commotion? Was it really him? He seemed so quiet! We never suspected!" and I'd shrug and say, "Yeah, just a little thing I like to call Making a Difference," and then *America's Most Wanted* would call me up and I'd get to be on the air (but with my face obscured in case the guy came busting out later seeking vengeance) and John Walsh would shake my hand and say, "Tell me about your courage," and I'd say, "Well, John, I have been watching *America's Most Wanted* for the better part of my life, and I just knew I could make a difference." And then I could go off somewhere and die contented, and all those nights I'd spent watching *America's Most Wanted* instead of familiarizing myself with nineties culture like everyone else wouldn't have been a big old waste because I'd brought CLOSURE to a FAMILY.

All this in my mind.

But as I followed my suspect into what I realized with horror was my dorm's cafeteria it struck me that maybe calling in and saying, "I have the guy, the murder guy, with the bag," might not be maybe exactly a hundred percent the best idea of all time. Maybe I should get the name, just so I wouldn't sound like an idiot on what was sure to be the first of many lifesaving calls.

When I got to the cafeteria, my friends were no help. I nudged them, trying to avoid drawing attention.

"Doesn't that guy there look like the murder bag guy on that recent episode of *America's Most Wanted*?"

"Dude," they said, "A, no one watches that but you. B, no one watches that but you. No one. And C, that's the prelaw tutor."

"No," I said. "No, that's a lie, that's a falsehood, that's an alias! I'm going to go look this up on AMW.com, and you are going to see who is vindicated and who is not. Keep a visual on him."

I rose in a blaze of glory and climbed the stairs to my laptop to visit the AMW Web site and try to find the actual name of this Wanted Felon.

I found his name, all right.

I found the picture. I found the details of the case—the bag, the daughter. And he did look just like I remembered.

There was only one problem.

The crime had happened in 1970. It was unlikely he looked exactly the same thirty years later, unless of course he were some kind of warlock, in which case we had a much bigger problem on our hands.

So that was awkward.

You begin to see the pattern.

Every time I thought I was out, I was only dragging myself deeper in.

But maybe that was all right.

It was one thing to have people around you staring and murmuring and pointing at you. It was another to throw yourself into the awkwardness, wholeheartedly, and see where you could get.

If you leaped into it with both feet, arms flailing wildly, you were invincible, like someone in a video game who had stepped on one of those flashing stars.

But I hadn't quite figured that out yet.

I couldn't keep away the nagging sense that all this would have gone so much better if someone else had been writing it. I had more experience with books than people. And when people in books did things like this, they always turned out a little bit better. Logan Pearsall Smith said, "People say that life is the thing, but I prefer reading." Logan Pearsall Smith was onto something.

My favorite book growing up was something called the *Penguin Dictionary of Modern Humorous Quotations*. It was given to me at a formative age and I read it cover to cover. It was an anthology of humorous quotations taken completely out of context, a sculpture composed entirely of elbows.

Do you want to know what Oscar Wilde said about smoking? I can tell you without even turning on my phone. ("A cigarette is the perfect type of a perfect pleasure. It is exquisite, and leaves one unsatisfied.") Do know want to know what George Bernard Shaw said about self-plagiarism? "I often quote myself. It adds spice to my conversation." You want P. J. O'Rourke's advice about when to send funny cards? "Save them for funerals, when their cheery effect is needed." I've got all of this at the tip of my tongue.

Now it makes a kind of sense.

But back then it didn't.

I read it cover to cover, over and over. I read all the naughty sections, where I learned everything that I knew about sex, drugs, and rock 'n' roll. "Sex is bad for one, but it's good for two," I quipped. "For three, it's fantastic." I didn't realize why some of it was naughty or why much of it was funny. But I knew that, on the occasions listed, those would be the words called for.

I had the words all ready to go. All I needed were the opportunities to use them. If I discovered love, I was supposed to agree with P. G. Wodehouse, that it "seems to pump you full of vitamins. I feel as if my shoes were right and my hat was right and someone had left me ten thousand a year."

The quips were like bread crumbs strewn through literature for me to find. As I read along, there, in the middle of the page, would be a quotation that I recognized, beckoning me forward. There was that thing Oscar Wilde had said about marriage. There, on page 89, that Evelyn Waugh quip about sex and dentists. ("All this fuss about sleeping together. For physical pleasure I'd sooner go to my dentist any day.") All of it made a little more sense when I saw where it fit.

The picture filled in, slowly. The words weren't always right. They didn't always defuse the situation with a laugh, the way I'd hoped.

There is a certain awkwardness inherent in coming at life book-first.

Life was a word whose definition I knew but I had never seen used in context.

That tends to lead to mispronunciations. And then someone has to take you aside and say, "No, it's not Penile-ope, it's Penelope." "It's Rafe Fines, not Ralph Fee-yennis." (I'm pretty sure that one is on him, though.)

I had all the dictionary knowledge I could have wanted. What I needed was context. I had to go out there and live. I had to use all these words in sentences.

Reality comes on with a jolt. The way you imagine that things will be and the way they actually are go gliding toward each other like the *Titanic* into the general vicinity of an iceberg. Growing up is the process of watching them collide.

And that's plenty awkward.

The only way I could handle it was to turn back around and feed it back onto the page again. On the page, marshaled in words, it made a kind of sense. On the page, I could almost see a logic to it. It had themes. It was awkward but it was also all the other things that life is—beautiful in unexpected ways, full of those strange gifts that the universe sends you on mornings that are otherwise rotten, when you walk past a statue that is supposed to be a majestic lion and notice it looks constipated instead, when you spot an unexpected purple house, when you hear a favorite character's name being called out over the PA system at an airport and it feels like a private joke. The trick was to notice these parts and save them from the wreckage.

So. I swam out to the lifeboats, and began dragging the words onto the beach, shuddering, with towels around their shoulders, and waited to see what they'd look like when they dried.

Ten General Rules

- Nobody who actively enjoys middle school is a good person.
- Never wear a T-shirt with a picture of someone more attractive than you on it.
- "Live like you're dying" is bad advice. You would never stop skydiving and telling people you loved them.
- Nobody saw that.
- There is nobody whose browser history, if published, would not fill the world with shock and horror.
- "I'm not a [noun], but . . ." = "I'm a [noun]."
- Never compare anybody to Hitler.
- It's hard to pass the Bechdel test at brunch.
- The smaller and more esoteric the online community, the nicer the comments.
- Never read the comments.

How to Talk to People

A Handy Guide Arranged by Age

Talking is awkward. Not always, but most of the time. Not knowing what to say is even worse. At their worst, conversations can feel like a horrible countdown to the inevitable moment when you and the other person have both run out of things to say and, for want of anything better, are forced to start describing the scenery around you and reading, word for word, the signs you pass. Sometimes one or two ideas for things to talk about are the only difference between silence (awkward) and years of lasting friendship. And that's where this guide (arranged by age) comes in!

Babies: You can tell if someone is a baby because that person is next to you on an airplane emitting sharp ninety-decibel bleats. If you aren't sure if it's a baby, try to pick it up. If it won't come with you, or claws you on the shin, it might not be a baby.

Sometimes people treat their dogs or cats like babies, dressing them up in little Future Princetonian sweaters and buying them expensive organic food. This can be confusing. It is best not to go by how the human charged with their care behaves but to judge the baby itself. If it barks, it might not be a baby. If it wears a leash and collar, it could be your friend's lover, Dean, although it is considered a little gauche to wear these things out in public.

The key to talking to a baby is not to act like you're talking to a baby. Speak frankly and use adult words. One advantage of talking to babies is they seldom want to interrupt you with stories of their own, so you can wax eloquent to your heart's content.

One-year-olds: One-year-olds look like babies, but larger. If one tries to engage you in conversation, "How 'bout that object permanence? Far out, right?" is a safe response.

Two-year-olds: These are called "the terrible twos." Just to be safe, address them as you would a work colleague, avoiding controversial political topics that might set them off.

Three-year-olds: The difference between a three-year-old and a two-year-old is that three-year-olds scream less—unless they make a habit of listening to a lot of talk radio. They don't remember much at this age, so it is still safe to insult them witheringly, as long as you keep your tone friendly and use polysyllabic words ("that ensemble is far from pulchritudinous, and you are NOT callipygian, not that I would notice, because that would be creepy, hey, you know what, never mind").

Four-year-olds: Four-year-olds start to have personality. Some of them can read. They actually remember things that happen, so don't insult them or say anything sick that might stick with them and warp their development.

Five-year-olds: Like four-year-olds, but louder and a little more mobile. This is the paper birthday. Or is it tin?

Six-year-olds: Don't baby-talk to them—not because six is too old for baby talk, but because you should never baby-talk to anyone ever. Someone might overhear you speaking with a rising inflection and think you are unfit for a promotion, especially if you happen to be a woman.

Seven-year-olds: Just old enough to develop lingering resentments over not winning the class spelling bee or being typecast as a rock in school plays. Should be able to read, but it may be difficult to find a book you're both interested in discussing. A safe topic is how they are *nothing* like first-graders and clearly developmentally well advanced.

Eight-year-olds: They should be in third grade. Remember the rule: Age minus five equals grade! (The other rule is that whenever you apply this rule, it will be wrong. See also: when you are *ninety* percent sure you remember someone's name and use it to address him.)

Nine- to Eleven-year-olds: Ask if they've "written any good books lately." If my own experience is anything to go by, most kids this age have written something that they feel is a good book.

Twelve-year-olds: Middle school. Commiseration is called for.

Thirteen- to Sixteen-year-olds: Some gnawing obsession is devouring this person, infecting her Internet presence and eating the inside of her locker. Figure out what it is and you won't need to say another word for the remainder of the conversation.

Seventeen-year-olds: Whatever you do, don't ask about college. (Naturally, this will be the only thing you can think of to ask about.) Instead, try a less sensitive subject like, "Do you still respect your parents?" or "And your sexuality, do you feel that you've got a handle on it?")

Eighteen- to Twenty-two-year-olds: There is something about being confronted with a recently minted adult that fills you with the overpowering desire to offer life advice. Try to resist this urge if at all possible. If you can't, just quietly murmur, "As Dear Sugar says, don't be afraid to break your own heart," as you say good-bye.

Midtwenties: Quick, they are just on the cusp where joking about getting old is funny rather than Too Close to Home. Hangovers still manageable. Complain about yours.

Thirtysomethings: Before you can talk to a thirtysomething, you must identify him or her as a thirtysomething, a feat I have

never excelled at. For women of a certain █████████
like a good signifier, but it's hard to predict. █████████
to see when they go to bed. Yawn and say, "█████████
turn in!" and see what the other person does. █████████
thirtysomethings include "So, do you still feel █████████
and "When Mozart was your age he was still aliv ████ you
I'd avoid any suspicious antimony-based powders."

Fortysomethings: When people turn forty you are supposed to address them entirely in reassuring slogans in the formula "[noun] is the new [noun]," at least if Hallmark cards are anything to go by (are they anything to go by?). Forty is the new thirty! Forty is the new orange! Forty is the new cupcake! Note that this will get old quickly, so you may be better off searching for common interests.

Fiftysomethings: Say, "How's your back?" Once people hit a certain age, it is always safe to ask about their backs.

Sixtysomethings: This is about the age when all the technology in the house will turn on you, and cease to turn on for you. Address them accordingly. If you want to rile a sexagenarian, ask him to install something on your TV.

Seventysomethings: The best thing to do when talking to a septuagenarian is to quote, verbatim, the contents of any ominous-sounding forwarded e-mail of dubious veracity that you have recently received. They just love e-mail forwards of dubious veracity. This is about the age when you start to unquestioningly believe e-mails that are forwarded to you. Otherwise sane people will start telephoning their children out of the blue to ask if they know about The Horrible Lizard Thing the Masons have replaced the president with. Be careful that you are talking to a septuagenarian before you begin, though. Seventysomethings often look deceptively young. As a class, they are generally fairly spry, as long as you don't ask too much of their hips.

somethings: They know what they like, and what they
s bowls of salted nuts, purses full of tissues, and listening to TV
at a high volume. A fun conversation to have here is to urge one of
them to retell you the plot of a movie he or she just saw part of on
TV.

Ninetysomethings: Good things to say to ninetysomethings are
not hard, as long as you speak slowly. If you've made it to ninety, you
are indestructible, for a given value of indestructible. These émi-
nences grises tend to avoid ice, high winds, and places where there is
loud background music. Don't try too hard to dazzle. Most conversations devolve quickly into volleys of nodding and shouting. You
shout and she nods; then she shouts and you nod. Sometimes silence
is best.

Hundredsomethings: Don't ask about the competition for Oldest
Living Person. It's bound to be a sore subject.

Three Hundred Plus: This person is either a brain in a jar or a
vampire. Which one is the case should be obvious. Modify your remarks accordingly.

Tuesdays with Hitler

I have a strange affinity for old men. Not "older men," the type who are fortyish but still in their prime, men like Mr. Big, who notice that you are stumbling along the sidewalk and stop their limousines to offer you six seasons' worth of excitement and trying not to fart in bed.

No, not older men—*old men*. I must exude an oddly specific musk, like mothballs and racism.

I guess you could say this is my superpower. I can't fly or freeze things with my breath (unless I've eaten *lots* of garlic), but I can summon elderly men from great distances. For instance, every Monday afternoon for months, I managed to attract visits from an octogenarian named Mr. Oliver.

Mr. Oliver and I met laboring under the same misconception. My high school history teacher had telephoned me and insinuated that Mr. Oliver would "get me on Broadway." As an aspiring playwright, I thought this sounded amazing! Eagerly I awaited the arrival of this Mr. Oliver, whom I pictured as some kind of old-timey theater magnate, chomping a large cigar. "It ain't Noël Coward," he would say, perusing my first script, "but I think it's the real Tabasco, kid!"

Instead, what I saw when I came down to the lobby of the *Post* was an old man wearing shorts with a Band-Aid over his forehead at a rakish angle. He was carrying a large bag of old newspaper clippings.

"I hear you're going to get me onto Broadway," he greeted me.

It took us several meetings to sort out this confusion, and by then it was too late. We had gotten into the habit, and, more important, the lady at the front desk had become convinced that he was my long-lost grandfather and would buzz me immediately whenever he showed up.

"What do I do?" I asked my friends. "How do I get this to stop? Do I just wait until he's too feeble to travel? That could take years!"

The thing about very old men is no one ever questions them. No one says, "Hey, should he be let into the building?" They just assume that the man in question is your grandfather. When I am old, I intend to use this situation to my advantage.

"My grandson doesn't like to acknowledge me in public anymore," I will say, clanking down hallways after celebrities who have piqued my interest.

Mr. Oliver turned out to be quite an accomplished gentleman. A retired lawyer, he had written dozens of plays, one about Hitler (a light comedy entitled "How Much Time Do We Have!?!"), one about a happy housewife who talked some sense into Simone de Beauvoir and another one about how, as far as he can recollect, everyone in his college fraternity was gay but no one thought anything of it at the time.

The basic plot of the Hitler play was as follows. Hitler and Eva Braun managed to escape to South America, after a lot of yelling about his trouble performing in the sack. He blamed Eva for making him feel emasculated. Finally she wanted to go sunbathe topless. Hitler did not want her to. Then someone shot him. Goebbels narrated. Also at one point a number of children were killed onstage?

Tonally, it was all over the place, but I think it was supposed to be a comedy. It was *Springtime for Hitler* but not on purpose.

In fact, the Hitler play, I discovered at Mr. Oliver's eightieth birthday party, had been a cherished dream for some time. He introduced me to his family. "This is my son," he told me. "When we did the reading, he was Hitler."

"Ah," I said.

"This is my other son," he added, waving. "He played Goebbels."

A female friend of his sat down. "And how do you know her?" I asked.

"She was Eva Braun." He grinned and nodded. "A dead ringer, wouldn't you say?"

Mr. Oliver insisted on reading his works aloud as we sat at a coffee shop frequented by my work colleagues. "I forget everything after I write it," he informed me, every time. "And then I look and I think, hey, this guy, he's pretty good, the guy who wrote this play!" He chuckled, sounding pleased, yet phlegmy.

Another of his plays featured lengthy confrontations between Marilyn Monroe and Arthur Miller and he especially enjoyed performing those ("Now listen to me, Arthur, you just like to have me, Marilyn Monroe, a beautiful shiksa, on your arm, don't you, Arthur Miller? You like to prove that a skinny nudnik can wind up with a girl like me, Marilyn Monroe!") as I winced and pretended I had wound up at the table by accident and had no idea who he was. Which was hard to do convincingly, given that we went there every week. It was like *Tuesdays with Morrie*, except that instead of inspirational messages about loving one another and affirming life, I got diatribes about Hitler. There was also the occasional confrontation between Woodrow and Edith Wilson, from his play *Versailles*. ("Edith: Woodrow, don't lie to me! You had a stroke, didn't you? When were you planning to tell me? Woodrow: Gaaaaargh.")

In turn, I told him about what I was working on. "This one's called *Social Suicide*," I said. "It's about a girl who wants to get revenge on all the people in her life by killing herself in the middle of a dinner party."

"That sounds awful," Mr. Oliver said. "That's a downer! Yuck! Yuck!"

"I'm also writing a children's show in which the Beatles are forest creatures," I added. (This one actually got produced!)

Mr. Oliver, evidently mistaking this for a joke, gave me a funny look and started laughing.

He kept telling me that he was on the verge of a major production. This seemed improbable. "I got an e-mail from the theater asking for the next stage of the script," he would tell me. " 'We request the next stage of the script,' it said."

"No!" I would gasp. "No, you didn't!"

Finally, grinning, he would produce a printout of the e-mail. It would say, "We have received your script. Please do not send us anything further unless we request the next stage of the script."

I kept hoping against hope that this situation would turn into my own personal version of *Tuesdays with Morrie*. Mr. Oliver would become a font of wisdom and start spewing words of inspiration. Instead, he kept creating situations in which I came within inches of mailing people pictures of Hitler. (To wit: He once gave me a picture of Hitler and Eva Braun with "HOW MUCH TIME DO WE HAVE?!?" written on it in large black letters. It got mixed in with some papers I was carrying to mail and had disappeared into an envelope before I realized my mistake. Fortunately I was able to pry it out in time; otherwise this story would be entitled, "How I Got Fired from Everything, Ever." I had a panicked vision of the recipient opening what she thought was a polite letter from a young journalist, only to discover a totally context-free image of Hitler with the words HOW MUCH TIME DO WE HAVE?!? scrawled on it in terrifying old-man handwriting. Then I would get an intense, angry call: "What is the meaning of this? Do you think this is some sort of a *joke*? Are you the ZODIAC KILLER?")

Then again, his were far from the worst plays I had read. There was fierce competition for that title. I was a member of two writing groups. The first one was comprised of professionals who had taken jobs in DC but felt, secretly, that they had a screenplay or a novel lurking and festering deep inside them, somewhat like a tapeworm. We met every two weeks at a fancy downtown office with large glass walls and a buzzer at the door and flags of multiple nations in the hallway. The man who ran the group was a successful published novelist in England only which seemed like it might resemble having a beautiful girlfriend in Canada only. He had written several novels about the Crusades. His advice was all filtered through this lens, making it somewhat less than universally applicable. "Write the parts you want to write first," he said. "Like if there's a big beheading, or an encounter with Richard the Lionheart, definitely write that first, then outline the other parts."

Evelyn, a former journalist who was working on what she described as "a darkly comic screenplay about a bunch of elderly people who find out that the plane they are on is about to crash, so they decide to have a good time," emitted a baffled sigh.

Every week the moderator fought with the woman whose office we were using, who insisted that she had worked in the publishing industry and that "sorry, Brian, that's not how it works." Sometimes she would just shake her head with a wise, knowing look in her eyes, but mostly she barked, "Nope. Nope. No, Brian. No. That's wrong. I'm sorry. That's wrong."

Fortunately there was wine. We needed it. One of the first writers to present was a middle-aged Indian gentleman named Anup who had written what he called an "environmental thriller." The script revolved around a banker whose son was killed in the Amazon. The banker was seized with the desire for vengeance, worked out a couple of times, and suddenly became capable of a Rambo-level expedition into the jungle, where he and a nubile young lady managed to defeat everyone standing in the way of their sweet, sweet vengeance. This could have been fine if it were not for the fact that every few pages there was an X-rated sex scene, complete with throbbing and pounding.

"Anup," we said, when we gathered to discuss the script. "Um, nice, nice script you got there. Uh. So. Uh. How do I put this: What was up with all the sex?"

Anup's brow furrowed. "I was worried," he said, "that the main character was too much of a 'goody-goody.' I thought that it would humanize him if he enjoyed rough sex!"

I choked a little on my wine and made eye contact with Tina (Mystery Novel Set in a Ballpark) and Greg (Screenplay, Then Novel, Then Screenplay, Then Novel About the AIDS Crisis). The three of us had formed a drinking group in order to cope with the excesses of the writing group. Greg was nice but was also trying to make several personal catchphrases happen. "I'm pressing my OnStar button!" he would exclaim, at intervals. "Clutching my rosary! I've brought my oxygen tank and I need to take a big inhale!" And these were the ones whose company I sought out!

Things kept going downhill. The lady who Knew Publishing handed us her own screenplay. It was nearly three hours long and consisted mainly of voice-overs, accompanied by "She'll Be Coming 'Round the Mountain."

"What IS this?" we asked, as gently as possible.

"Don't worry," she said. "They're already making it in China, so I don't really need to make edits to it."

Greg poured himself another glass of wine. "OnStar," he whispered.

The second group met at a public library. I was the only member of the group who did not have liver spots. The first week I went, the group moderator was tearing into a play about a mysterious man named William Ruske Lancier (Ruske, the author hinted, means "shake," and "Lancier" means "spear") who insisted on speaking only in Shakespearean verse, even though he lived in a modern-day apartment complex.

"The thing about this play," the author explained, as what looked like tears started to form in his eyes, "is really, you have to read it right, with good actors, to get the full flavor of it. If he'd read it bet ter it would have sounded better."

"Why is he rhyming?" the moderator—grizzled, balding, and peremptory—asked.

"That's the whole mystery of the play!" the playwright exclaimed.

"You need to make it clear he's not some kind of dangerous weirdo. He says he met this woman's son. Okay. So that's grounds for thinking he's not a weirdo, you know, he met him, they chatted, he didn't strip him bare and suck him, so, okay, he can be trusted, you should work from that."

Strip him bare and suck him, I thought. That's—that's an oddly casual way of describing that.

"I'm telling you," the playwright wheedled, "to understand why he speaks this way, you need to read the whole play. It's revealed. It makes sense."

The moderator shook his head. "No. I'm telling you. You have to listen if you want it to be better. Okay, Henry, what do you have?"

What Henry had was a play about St. Augustine of Hippo.

Norbert, whose face looked like a foot, had written a play about two people on a balcony. "I don't know what it's about," he said. "But if you like it, I can keep on writing and maybe we can figure out what it's about."

David was writing a cop thriller. He had, it appeared, been writing it very slowly and painstakingly over the course of decades while technology had completely passed him by.

"Hang on one second," his character said, "while I feed some more carbon paper into this typewriter. Then you can tell me what you know."

"We can get him on tape," another character proposed later. "Just take this pocket cassette recorder and secure it somewhere on Bernie's person."

"No can do," another cop responded. "He's in the building already. We have no way of communicating with him."

"When is this set?" the moderator asked.

"The present day," David said, looking baffled.

Actually, compared to these crews, Mr. Oliver seemed downright normal. He was conviviality itself. One upside of our extended acquaintance was that we figured out that neither of us really wanted to be drinking coffee at four in the afternoon, so we came up with a new system where we went to a bar and drank four beers apiece and agreed with whatever the other person was saying because the music was too loud to hear over. It was much better. We gave up the pretense of wanting to get plays on Broadway and instead I just downed a Sam Adams Seasonal while he told me the things President Obama was doing wrong and brought me his print copy of the *New Yorker* with several unflattering paragraphs about Hillary Clinton circled in ballpoint pen that I ignored as politely as I could.

There's a kind of relief that comes from hanging out with the elderly. With them, I no longer needed to pretend that I watched *Boy Meets World*. With people my age, I'd been doing this for years, and it had started to become a strain. "Oh yeah," I say. "*Boy Meets World*. Loved it. He met the heck out of that world, didn't he? Topanga! Topanga!" If Wikipedia ever makes an error in its plot recaps, my entire social life will collapse.

I started looking forward to it. "Do you want to come out on Monday?" my other friends would inquire.

"I can't," I would say. "I'm going to be getting drunk with an old man."

For a while, during the vampire craze, being an old-person magnet began to seem like an asset instead of a liability.

"This whole *Twilight* mania is just about being obsessed with pasty immortal creatures who have been around for hundreds of years and don't go out in the sun. Octogenarians are the next best thing! They're immortal, so far. And they don't go out in the sun very much, except to renew their prescriptions. If I can hang with them, vampires will be easy."

"I thought you hated *Twilight*."

"There's no better way of protesting *Twilight* than showing people what it would *really* look like," I suggested.

What concerned me was that Mr. Oliver didn't seem to think of himself as an old man. Superficially, he knew his type. He had once walked over to a church that was putting on *A Christmas Carol* and volunteered his services as Scrooge. (They didn't cast him.) But on the inside? I wasn't so sure. On our Monday evenings, Mr. Oliver sat there making off-color jokes and downing beers like any of my other friends. Did he think we were on the same plane? Sure, I'd never claimed to be hip, but at least I'd never had a hip replacement.

Would this be me in a few years?

Being cool in the present was something I barely managed at the best of times.

For years I was the person adding "Songs of World War I" to class playlists. Jenna would contribute "Bohemian Rhapsody" and Kat would contribute "Sweet Child o' Mine" and I would contribute "Belgium Put the Kibosh on the Kaiser." This is an actual song. I can sing it for you now, but I won't, because you have done nothing to deserve it. I curse like a sailor . . . who died in 1840. "Gadzooks! Heavens to Betsy! Land o' Goshen! Oh, for the love of Pete!"

In sixty years, I'll be hopeless.

Maybe this friendship was a form of insurance. If I was willing to hang out with Mr. Oliver, maybe, someday in the future, when I'd crested the ridge of seventy, someone would be willing to sit there with me and pay for three rounds while I complained about how the government had gone downhill. I certainly hoped so.

Old people are just people, after the vigorous application of time.

And I know how fast obsolescence comes on. I once owned a BlackBerry.

I expect every morning to climb out of bed obsolete. I know how it will start. I will suddenly be very interested in the weather. My joints will ache. I will flip, instinctively, to the obituaries. I will discover that I am helpless when confronted with the latest technology. The thought will occur to me that something terrible has happened to popular music. I will spend my days meticulously planning visits to the grocery.

I do what I can to forestall this. I do everything short of lurking outside middle schools, grabbing students as they emerge, and shouting, "The trends! Tell me the trends!" I spend a good hour every day worrying about ways that people from the future might consider us racist and deciding whether or not to endorse robot relationships. I even listen to dubstep.

But already I can feel myself growing outdated.

Not to say that I have an old soul. People who tell you they have "old souls" usually are jerks who just got back from a trip to somewhere in the Andes that Really Changed Their Outlook. I don't have an old soul. I just understand my place in the culture, and it's next to the Metamucil.

I'm especially worried because I'd always had the idea that Old Age was really more of a place than a time. You arrive at seventy, and they welcome you with a Werther's Original and a record player and replace all your kitchen fixtures with blue Formica. When I finally hit that point, after years and years of being fifty or sixty-odd years behind the times, I was going to have an edge, for once.

So I remember vividly the terror that gripped me when the Oldies station I'd been listening to switched from songs of the fifties, sixties, and seventies to "Classic Rock." The past wasn't supposed to *move*. It was supposed to wait for me.

Meeting Mr. Oliver had only confirmed me in my terror. He wasn't the vampire. I was. The only way I was ever going to get my fix of hanging out with old people who liked what I liked was if I did it now. And that would only put me further behind.

Maybe you get the Morrie you deserve. Mitch Albom got an inspirational old geezer who said things like "If you hold back on the emotions—if you don't allow yourself to go all the way through them—you can never get to being detached, you're too busy being afraid. You're afraid of the pain, you're afraid of the grief. You're afraid of the vulnerability that loving entails. But by throwing yourself into these emotions, by allowing yourself to dive in, all the way, over your head even, you experience them fully and completely" or

"It's like I keep telling you—when you learn how to die, you learn how to live."

I frowned at the notes that I had compiled of things Mr. Oliver said to me. "Mr. Oliver? I'm not a Mr.! I'm a Sir!"

"Take a look at my class photo: Wouldn't you say 'Young Jack Kennedy'?"

"Have A Lolly, Dolly! Love, Olly!" (This was a handwritten note I received at the office.)

"What do I think of Woodrow Wilson? How can you even ask that? I hate him! Hate him. Yuck. I think he's just awful. Worse than that guy we've got now."

"Alexandra? Thank God! Thank God you're alive! You didn't pick up the phone, and I was worried you were dead."

Trust me to wind up with the old man who, instead of dousing me with wisdom about what the Buddha said about detachment, all the while dying in a picturesque and heartrending manner, told me off-color jokes about Marilyn Monroe, repeated that Bowdoin was superior to any other place on earth, stayed healthy as a kickboxing horse, and made me pay for our drinks.

But gradually, as we got farther and farther away from the plays, it got nicer and nicer to have someone to talk to. What would I have done with Morrie? He would have bored me stiff. You can only take so much inspiration before you want to run outside and scream.

One day Mr. Oliver showed up looking particularly jolly.

"I went to the doctor today," he said. "My nurse—a male nurse, we've forged a real connection, he's a Filipino, he says he's leaving to go to Florida, which I'm just so upset about, but he says—guess what?"

"What?"

"He says: I give you twenty years."

"Huh?" I said, temporarily nonplussed.

"He gives me twenty years! Isn't that great news? I'll be a hundred years old!"

"Wow," I said. "Twenty years!" Twenty more years of his odd cackling laugh and his somewhat mangled retellings of the lives of famous writers. Twenty more years of squinting at his hand-scrawled manuscripts because the woman at the library who used to type them up for him had finally gotten fed up. Twenty more years of Mr. Oliver. "That is great news!" I said.

And the strange thing was, I meant it.

Go Whistle for It

Maybe anyone can whistle. (All you have to do, I hear, is put your lips together and blow.) But I felt like the world's biggest impostor.

I was sitting in one of the front rows of the Franklinton Baptist Church as the pastor, a tall man with short graying hair who looked like a cheerier version of the magician Penn Jillette, worked himself into a lather.

"Whistling," he was saying, "is an expression of pure joy. I whistle when I feel joy, and I always feel joy when I hear someone whistling. And we are just so blessed, truly blessed, to have a whistling champion here with us today."

Oh no.

Please stop, I thought. That is more than plenty.

"A champion who has come all the way from Washington, DC," he went on, "to share her amazing gift with us."

The assembled parishioners sat up a little as I shrank down still farther in my pew. Maybe I could melt slowly away and vanish, I thought, like an embarrassed polar ice cap or a damp Witch of the West. Maybe I could just vanish deep into the earth.

"Please welcome—"

Oh no.

"Alexandra Petri."

I should probably start from the beginning.

I was in North Carolina for the Fortieth Annual International Whistling Convention.

I like whistling the same way I like farting: I enjoy doing it myself, but I don't get any particular pleasure when other people do it around me. My idea of a good time is certainly not driving miles and miles down the East Coast to listen to strangers fart.

But in the interest of journalism, I trucked down to Louisburg for the Fortieth Annual International Whistling Convention to see what the fuss was about.

The history of this event, as I understand it, is that on a lark they had a whistling contest at one town festival. Then word spread. The contest mushroomed. One morning they woke up and there were contestants coming in from everywhere to demonstrate their whistling chops. Spain. Israel. China. Japan. New York City. California. You name it, they'd sent a whistler. Without return postage, if possible.

Whistling has a long history. As long as people have been capable of making funny noises on purpose, it has been part of the rich vocabulary of music. However, it didn't really achieve success as an art form until the turn of the twentieth century.

I learned all of this at Whistling School, conducted by a woman I'm going to refer to as Doris because that was the vibe she gave off.

To say that the International Whistling School (I have my graduation certificate sitting around somewhere) gave us an exhaustively thorough account of the history of whistling would be a gross understatement. We started with the whistling of the Greeks and Romans and worked gradually through the highlights up to the present day.

The biggest problem with doing a history of whistling is that it is a noise we have been able to make ever since we evolved to have the proper equipment. But documentation is lacking.

Doris lamented the fact that in so many ancient cultures the word for "hissing" and the word for "whistling" were the same. In the Bible, for instance, it was impossible to tell whether God wanted us to "whistle at the ends of the earth" or "hiss at the ends of the earth," one of the numerous Bible-translating problems that are bound to lead to a certain amount of awkwardness when we come to the Day of Judgment. "What's this about being in subjection to owl husbands?"

(Yes. There's actually a Bible from 1944 that says women should be in subjection to their "owl husbands," but this is a typo.)

Because of this minor verb confusion, you couldn't tell which one people were doing until you got all the way to Chaucer's *Canterbury Tales*, where a young squire was described: "Syngynge he was, or floytynge, al the day." Floytynge could have been whistling or playing the flute, but Doris thought it was probably the former.

Whistling really started to Happen in a big way after the Civil War. There were whistlers before that—Samuel Pepys, the famous English diarist, reported hearing someone who could whistle like a bird—but it took vaudeville to turn it into a massive fad, when George W. Johnson, a former slave, climbed up the charts. Unfortunately, because everything used to be terrible, his top-selling tracks all had names like "The Whistling Coon," but at least he seemed to make a decent living out of it.

Up until this point whistling was mostly an activity for men alarmed by prices they had just heard, birds, or birds alarmed by prices they had just heard. But then along came Mrs. Alice Shaw.

Alice Shaw was the most famous lady whistler of the nineteenth century.

In addition to being the most famous lady whistler, Alice was definitely the most uncomfortably sexy.

"All beholders held their breaths as the broad expanse of snowy decolleted bosom heaved gently," wrote the Des Moines *Mail and Times* in 1889, "the handsome head and face uplifted, the rich ruby lips puckered kissably, and a soft, sweet, silvery trill shot forth, at once electrifying the audience and suggesting the presence of an impossibly cultured canary."

Yes, really. I did some more research into Alice Shaw, just to see if her whistling was always that sexy, and the short answer is that it was not.

"Certainly it cannot be claimed that whistling is the most dignified and important form of art," the *Musical World* of November 3, 1888, noted, describing Mrs. Shaw's performance. They did not mention the heaving décolletage or rich ruby lips, instead contenting themselves with observing that "There is but one Mrs. Shaw; we shall not be charged with discourtesy when we hope that, for her sake, and our own, there may not be another" because "a generation of whistlers is an appalling thing to imagine."

Whistling sprouted and blossomed and became ubiquitous over the following decades.

There was even a radio show in the forties called *The Whistler*. It was like *The Twilight Zone*, but with more eerie, high-pitched pucker whistling and less wrestling with moral issues using the framework of science fiction. "I am the Whistler," the voice on the radio intoned. "And I know many things, for I walk by night. I know many strange tales, many secrets, hidden in the hearts of men and women who have stepped into the shadows. Yes, I know the nameless terrors of which they dare not speak." I don't know how he found this out while whistling. I would have assumed that the people with strange tales and secrets who stepped into the shadows would have heard him approaching from a long way away. But I guess it was a different time.

There is something of a schism in the whistling community over different types of whistling. Pucker whistling is the kind you picture when you picture whistling.

Palate whistling, on the other hand, comes out high and pinched through the teeth and includes a sound like a moon-bounce slowly deflating. It seems to be a little more versatile than pucker whistling in terms of the number of notes you can produce per minute. It is the best for summoning cabs, by a mile.

If Pucker Whistlers are the Jets, Palate Whistlers are the Sharks. They could have the world's least threatening rumble. And for whatever reason—depending on whom you listened to, it was Judge Favoritism or Sheer Merit Because Pucker Whistling Is Simply More Pleasing to the Ear—Palate Whistlers tended to place lower in competition than Pucker Whistlers.

Finger Whistling is not even permitted in championship competition. The use of fingers puts it into the category of "allied art," which is whistling while doing something else. Your work, for example.

There was a whole phase of popular culture in the mid-twentieth century where every movie or TV show seemed to have a whistle or two in its opening credits. *The Andy Griffith Show. The High and the Mighty.*

But then it began fading out until it was just Sitters on the Docks of Bays, Dwarves Who Work in Mines, and Cartoon Characters Trying to Act Nonchalant.

There's been a pop resurgence of whistling in recent years— "Pumped Up Kicks," Flo Rida's inventively titled "Whistle," "Moves Like Jagger," among numerous others. It would, however, be hard to say that whistling is back in the mainstream, especially if you looked around you at the whistlers' convention. The audience consisted of the whistlers themselves, their somewhat beleaguered-looking families, a few local thrill seekers, and some elderly people who had been bused over from their retirement home to take it all in.

The first performance I heard was the Vassar a cappella whistling group. This was their big off-campus trip every year. I'm sure it was a big inducement. "Join the whistling a cappella group!" posters probably proclaimed all over campus. "Spend spring break in a place actively worse than where you are right now." Not that there was anything wrong with Louisburg. There wasn't. It was a lovely place, and everyone there seemed nice. I liked all the stoplights. There was a good coffee shop/bookstore that had a nice display out to celebrate Gay History Month, which, in my naive way, was not what I had expected of Louisburg, North Carolina.

Doris crept onstage with a harp. Her demeanor at all times was that of someone trying to avoid waking a person sleeping in the next room.

She plucked the harp. Twang dinkle twangle twang-tringgggg twingle. (That was my attempt to write how the harp sounded. William Shakespeare, eat your onomatopoeic heart out!) "Do you hear the Autoharp?" Doris asked. Twingle tring tring tring tringggg.

"Yes," we said. We heard the Autoharp. Doris proceeded to whistle a lugubrious French song, tinkling along on the Autoharp. It had that characteristic of obscure French songs of seeming to go on a lot longer than it actually did and having no discernible tune. I mean it in the best possible way when I say that her whistling sounded like a seasick theremin. I think that was what she was going for.

By the time it was over I felt a faint buzzing at my temples. This, it turned out, only intensified as the three days of whistling got under way. There is a very, very specific kind of headache that only comes from three days of whistling, similar, I assume, to the kind of hangover you get from drinking only single-malt scotch. You have to really seek it out, but it's a doozy.

It wasn't that the whistling was bad. It was that there was so much of it. Also, some of it was bad. Some of it was awful, actually.

To really immerse myself in the experience, I had decided to compete. To prove you were serious, you had to send in an audition tape. I recorded mine in the women's restroom at the *Washington Post*, where the acoustics were almost great. I say "almost" because the toilets were motion-operated. If you got particularly emotive, they flushed, instantly ruining the recording. Also people kept coming in. I wonder how they explained to themselves the sound of someone slowly and intently whistling "Princess Leia's Theme" in the end stall, followed by the sound of flushing, then a voice saying, "Not again!"

Eventually I managed to cobble together a whistling sample that didn't have flushing noises on it, which I mailed in. When I heard that I was accepted, I guessed that the bar must be pretty low.

When I arrived I was positive.

There was, for instance, one guy with sharp, pointed fingernails who showed up at the Allied Arts competition in one of those newsboy caps that old men wear to disguise or advertise the fact that they are balding, shut his eyes, and proceeded to whistle tunelessly for several minutes to the accompaniment of what sounded like spa music, flapping his arms in a soulful manner.

"Your performance was really something," I told him, afterward.

"Thank you," he said. "I call it the Nightingale in Paradise. It is a Baha'i allegory."

"Oh," I said. "I see. Why were you flapping?"

He smiled coyly. "Oh, that just came to me. Choreo."

If you ever find yourself in Louisburg during whistling season, I recommend without a moment's hesitation that you go to the Allied Arts competition. There were people who whistled while playing the guitar, people who whistled while folding origami, people who whistled while fighting with ninja throwing stars, people who whistled while feuding with a large woodwind. I am not making any of this up.

The real star of this event was a guy named Roy. Last year, everyone said in hushed tones, Roy had dressed up as Lady Gaga in full lace Red Queen regalia and played the piano while whistling. There was no telling what Roy would do this year. Roy was expected to escalate. Roy was a wild card. We knew he would be whistling, but that was all we knew for sure!

Roy showed up with something that resembled a gigantic James Bond poster. He proceeded to whistle and play piano and sing to a long medley of Bond songs, donning an Adele mask and firing a plastic gun—one of those fake guns with "BANG!" on a flag that comes out of the muzzle. It was definitely something. Roy won.

I tried to make friends with the other whistlers, but every time I thought I had a handle on them as characters they would turn around and pull the rug out from under me. One woman was there from Canada. She seemed friendly. We both admitted we had never done this before on a professional level and were "just here for fun."

(There was a white-haired lady sitting next to her. "Ah," I said, "you must be the WHISTLER'S MOTHER."

She gave me a blank look. "What?")

I was proud that I had isolated and identified at least one other normal person. Then she stood up at the Whistlers' Dinner and announced that "I hold the Guinness World Record for the highest note ever whistled, and for the longest time whistling a single note— almost 24 hours!—which my swami encouraged me to do as a test of my mettle and a quest of self-discovery."

Oh good, I thought. Yes. Well. Good.

The other normal person was named Maggie. She was from Indiana and could befriend anyone at the drop of a hat. At some point in your journey from childhood to adulthood, usually somewhere on the childhood end, someone sits you down and says something stern about Not Talking to Strangers because Who Knows What Might Happen, Maybe They've Got a Trunks Full of Axes, Maybe They're Skinwalkers Who Have Faces with No Eyes or Mouths but They Can See You.

Or, in my case, they administer the lesson in two blows: a Berenstain Bears book about Stranger Danger called *The Berenstain Bears Learn About Strangers* (Brother Bear almost gets into a stranger's car to see his "model plane"!) and another book called *You Can't Be Too Careful*, which consisted entirely of shortened newspaper accounts of gruesome accidental deaths. Neither of these had really sunk in, in my case—just a few months earlier, I had given my number to someone with a neck tattoo, named Galaxy, whom I met at a bus stop.

But at least someone had *tried*. With Maggie it seemed that this had never happened. She greeted people at the neighboring gas station/convenience store like long-lost friends. She talked to some policemen as we crossed the street and somehow we wound up whistling "Amazing Grace" to them. She was the Midwesterner foreigners imagine all Midwesterners are like but most of us can only dream of being.

My other friend, Lars, was a mustached paterfamilias with a full rack of shoulder-chips. He was still upset, he told me, that a palate whistler had been denied the title a few years earlier. That man had been incredible. That man had been so good that Lars had rushed the stage and mobbed him before the man's wife could even get there. That man had whistled "Free Bird." That man had been robbed, robbed! It was because the judges were biased. That man's whistling was unlike anything you had ever heard or would ever hear again.

The host of most of the festivities was a New York whistler who seemed to have traveled directly from the Borscht Belt sixty years ago, without stopping to update his jokes. "He's from Tsingtao," he said of the Chinese contestant. "Where they make the beer." He introduced a Japanese contestant as "one of our ninjas." This seemed to be exactly what everyone expected. People got a real kick out of his joke about how he, a whistling champion, hailed cabs. ("Taxi!" he mimicked, raising a hand. "Taxi!")

He stalled for me while I tried to get my music ready. There are few places left on Earth that still require you to use a CD to play music, but the International Whistlers Convention is one of them. I had not come prepared. Instead, I had the tracks on my iPhone, and the sound guy could not get them to play.

I had decided to whistle "Singing in the Rain" because after attending Whistling School I realized that I was way, way out of my league and needed something that didn't have too many notes in it. Still, it took a lot of rehearsal. I sat in my hotel room at the Motel 6 whistling over and over again until my neighbor started to bang on the wall. Staying in a Motel 6 is bad enough under ordinary circumstances. ("Didn't I see this room on *COPS*?" I asked myself. "Surely not. They would have advertised that fact, right? 'As Seen On TV!'

Or is being featured on *COPS* as the location of a violent standoff with state officers the kind of thing you advertise?") The last thing you want is a whistler like me dragging her way through "Singing in the Rain" on the other side of the wall.

"For God's sake, stop," I could hear the person in the next room thinking to himself. "Surely this is hell." The walls were so thin I could literally hear the person's thoughts. Later he spent a lot of time missing his cat and being excited by the free soaps.

Then again, if the walls were that thin, maybe that really *was* the original pattern of the comforter. That was reassuring. My assumption had been that someone had been disemboweled on it. But you couldn't possibly murder someone when noise carried like that.

My actual whistling went, I thought, okay; the judges thought, terribly. I came in, I think, thirty-seventh out of forty whistlers. (However, men and women got judged separately, so I was only something like ninth out of ten where ladies were concerned. (Yay, gender disparity!))

Usually at a contest or convention like this, you can get everyone together to go drinking and break the ice. But alcohol is apparently bad for your whistling muscles. So is coffee. So is anything salty. ChapStick and water, that's the deal. (Also, you're not supposed to whistle with your eyes closed, the judges informed us. You might think it made you more soulful, but you should use your eyes to connect with the audience.)

It was hard to bond with anyone over ChapStick and water.

Trying to do it made me exceptionally glad I never belonged to a dry sect or lived during Prohibition. I wouldn't have known where to begin. How did people socialize before alcohol? I know sitting around as a family and reading the Bible aloud used to be big, but I can't imagine it was much good when it came to bonding with the group of strangers around you.

This is why people who don't drink are always having to go to Couples Cooking Classes or play extremely involved board games or go bowling. With drinking, you can just sit. You either sit somewhere loud or sit somewhere quiet, and you drink. Gradually you feel wittier and more attractive and generally fonder of everyone around you.

A glass or two in, and you are shouting in all caps. "I FEEL SO MUCH CLOSER TO ALL OF YOU ALREADY," you boom. "LET'S BE BOON COMPANIONS—I WOULD GIVE YOU MY LIVER. I HOPE YOU KNOW THAT. BECAUSE I KNOW THAT, BUT I HOPE YOU KNOW."

Then you fall over a lot, and later you feel awful, but in the interim, it's bliss.

Not that I'm an alcoholic, by any means. I can state this definitively because I once took a test to make sure. "Do you ever drink alone?" the test asked. "No," I replied, indignant. "I'm always surrounded by people. Sure, they're like, 'Petri, it's nine o'clock in the morning!' 'Why do you have a flask?' 'This is a staff meeting.' 'Is everything okay at home?' but I'm not *alone*. That would be weird and sad." "Has drinking impacted your relationships negatively?" "Negatively?" I asked. "Alcohol is entirely responsible for my ability to get along with my extended family."

When we finally did get around to bonding, the convention was all but over. It was karaoke night. We no longer had to worry about keeping our whistles dry, so it was time to party down. They'd even brought a wind-guard for the microphone in case someone wanted to whistle "Dock of the Bay."

Except nobody wanted to whistle "Dock of the Bay." Everyone just wanted to sing. "Come on," the woman who had organized us kept saying. "Come on, this is the only time all year when it's normal to whistle! Come on! This is your chance to let it out! Nobody will silence you, like usual! Whistle, people! Whistle!"

I looked around me and, not for the first time, felt like an impostor.

"It's so nice to be among fellow whistlers," everyone said.

"Yes," I murmured, trying to nod convincingly. "Isn't it!"

In an interview with *The Village Voice*, the MC said coming to the whistling convention for the first time was "like coming out of the desert after forty years and finding your tribe."

But I thought—Tribe? How can this be? What can whistlers feel guaranteed to have in common with one another? All they can say for sure about their fellow whistlers is that they are able to make a certain sound by blowing through their mouths. At a *Star Wars* convention, at least you know that the people you meet will agree that Han shot first.

Then again, sometimes you misjudge how close a hobby will bring you to another person. Once, I started a Meetup group for people who love airports, based on the logic that everyone I'd ever met who confessed to enjoying spending time in airports was a great human being. The people who showed up to our first meeting (in the TGI Fridays of Reagan National Airport, just outside security) were not what I had envisioned at all. Conversation quickly fizzled. "Let's meet at a train station next!" one of them suggested.

I bristled. "I don't think you understand the ethos of this organization."

There was one other impostor at the whistling convention. She was there because she'd heard about it on NPR and wanted to know what it was all about. We recognized each other on sight.

"You're a journalist," she said. "Do you go to this kind of thing often?"

"Yes," I said.

"Is it always like this?"

I thought it over. "Yeah," I said. "Basically."

Do you ever have the feeling, driving through a strange town, stopping at a strange restaurant, seeing strangers laughing at the corner table—what if? What if this were my table, what if these were my old friends, what if that waiter knew my order? What if this were home?

That's how it felt.

Proust said one of the startling things about aging was how you started to see people you knew everywhere you went. There's Kat's laugh. There, right there, coming out of a stranger's mouth. There's the face of someone you knew in middle school, riding the bus on top of a strange body. There's your old chair in a stranger's living room. There's your old coach. There's your grandfather sitting in someone else's living room sipping iced tea. Life keeps reassembling people. There are only so many tunes you can play on these strings of DNA.

Every friend group has a Karen, and if you don't know instantly who it is, it's you. Every e-mail list has the same squabbles. Every class has the same people—the clown, the brain, Dave. Every horoscope is true.

Depending on when you catch me, this is terrifying or not. All the effort you put into living your authentic life, and it all works out much the same.

That was the depressing thing about whistling: It was so fundamentally identical to every other pastime. It was weird being on the outside, for once, peering in.

The convention was like spending a weekend with someone else's grandparents. It was nice. On some level, all grandparents are the same. "Here is some food," they say. "Now, it is time for us to watch TV at a high volume."

But it didn't feel like it was mine.

When I got home and told people where I'd been all week, they all gave me a shocked look.

"You whistle?" they asked. "I had no idea."

"Well," I said, "I don't whistle *well*, but I do whistle. I can make whistling sounds come out of my mouth. It could be worse."

Not much worse, though.

Which brings me back to where we started: Franklinton Baptist Church.

On the contest application form was a box you could check if you wanted to go whistle at area churches after the competition was over. The way it was worded led me to picture a large gaggle of whistlers, standing in neat rows, soberly whistling "Amazing Grace." I was up for that.

"You're still up for it?" an elderly man with a large yellow pad inquired, the day before.

"Yes," I said. "Absolutely."

"Great. And you're staying in Franklinton, right?"

"That's right," I said, wondering where this was going.

"Good," he said. "We'll have you at Franklinton Baptist, okay?"

"Great," I said.

"Amy can't make it—will that be a problem?"

"Shouldn't be," I said. Dimly I began to wonder why he was telling me this.

· · ·

The next morning, a little hungover from our karaoke revelry, I drove to the Franklinton Baptist Church, parked, and wandered in. I was wearing my Whistler Participation Ribbon to look festive. I glanced around. I didn't see any other whistlers.

The preacher came barreling over to me. "Are you our whistler?" he asked.

Whistler, I thought. Singular.

"Yes," I said, "I guess I am."

"We are just so thrilled to have you," he said. "Do you have music, or anything?"

I swallowed. "No," I said. "Just the whistling."

He nodded sympathetically.

"You know," I mumbled, "purity."

"Sure."

"Purity of sound. I pucker whistle. I'm a pucker whistler. Not palate. BOOOO palate."

"Well, we can't wait." He handed me a sheet of blue paper and a pen. "Do you have an intro you'd like for yourself?"

I frowned at the paper. Did I have an intro? What was my intro? "Hello there, Franklinton Baptist! Alexandra is not actually a whistler! Well, she's a whistler, but she's not a good whistler. She is so sorry about all this." "Hello there, Franklinton Baptist! Wow. I hope I make the mouth-noise you are expecting!" "Hello," I finally wrote. "Alexandra is just blown away by how nice everyone is. She is honored to be here today, in this nice place, where people are so nice."

Then I got into the pew and started to think frantically about what I might whistle. Something patriotic, I thought. Something short. Something with not too many notes in it.

The choir filed in. Parishioner after parishioner filled the pews.

Who knew this church held so many people? I thought, frantically. Good God. It's like a reverse clown car. I mean, er, not that,

Lord. I mean a respectful metaphor, er, Lord. It's like a very—beautiful—Eden-place. Er, listen, Lord, as long as we're chatting, could You let me actually make some kind of sound that resembles a whistle? I'll give You my firstborn. No, wait. You've been known to take people up on that. I'll start flossing. I'll—uh—I'll—start going to church. No, wait. Something realistic. I'll—give up—soft cheese. No, hard cheese. No, soft cheese. No—"

The pastor took his place at the lectern. I applied some more ChapStick and took a sip of water. I wished for something stronger.

"We are so, so lucky to have a whistler with us today," he said. "A champion. All the way from Washington, DC! She says thank you for being so nice. Come on up here."

With nervous, slow steps, I approached the microphone. The congregation leaned forward expectantly. Something patriotic, I thought. Something short. How about "My Country, 'Tis of Thee"?

I very slowly and breathily whistled "My Country, 'Tis of Thee." It was not the most impressive thing that has ever happened. I also knew a song called "When I Get Back to the USA" that dated back to World War I and seemed to have roughly the same tune, and midway through, I discovered that I had somehow switched to whistling that instead. The tune ended and deposited me on the other side, like someone who has gotten momentarily distracted at the end of a moving walkway. I nodded at the audience and scuttled back to my seat.

"Thank you for that," the pastor said.

I felt like the Emperor's New Whistler. Everyone still sat forward with a baffled expression, like maybe if they thought it through a couple more times what I had just done would be impressive. A man got up and started leading us in prayer. He thanked the Lord for sending me to whistle "Let Freedom Ring."

Maybe *that's* what I whistled.

. . .

As soon as the service was over, I hightailed it out of there, breezing past congregation members who came up timidly to say, "I wish I could do what you do."

"You can!" I tried to tell them. "Did you hear that? I'm not a whistler. I'm an impostor. You definitely can do what I did. Anyone can. All you have to do is put your lips together and blow. It's not like I'm Alice Shaw."

"Alice who?"

"You know, the famous lady whistler, with the decollet—"

A blank look. "I don't know these whistler things."

Whistler things. Oh God. Maybe I'm one of them, after all.

How to Join a Cult, by Mistake, on a Tuesday, in Fifty-Seven Easy Steps

1. Make sure it's Tuesday.
2. Schedule yourself a somewhat boring evening. Make sure all the other events on your list are things like "Attend a Friend's Experimental Theater Production of a show called People in Deconstructed Cars Who Are Having Sex Doubts."
3. Walk down the street in Harvard Square. Another square will do, in a pinch.
4. Look friendly and approachable as you walk. Avoid the Head-Down-Eyes-Down-Hands-in-Pockets walk that you would do if you were a ladybug and someone had just told you your family was dying in a fire, or the Head-Up-Elbows-Out-Darting-Swiftly-Among-the-Passersby like a lady gazelle on the way to an important board meeting. I recommend the jaunty I-Have-Nowhere-of-Pressing-Importance-to-Be-So-I'll-Smile-Indiscriminately-at-Everyone walk.
5. When a cluster of women on the corner ask you if you want to learn about the Woman Image of God in Scripture, smile and say, "Yes."

6. Listen as they explain the book of Genesis with a lot of pointing and exclamations. Wonder what country their accents are from.

7. Say, "Wow," a lot. As you look at the Bible, realize that it's been a long time since you went to church. Ponder the fact that this isn't because you actively Lost Faith, but rather because you keep sleeping through Sunday morning with a hangover that feels like a Greek god is about to come pounding her way out of your skull. Feel dimly remorseful about this.

8. When they ask if you want to come to Bible Study with them, say, "Yes."

9. Wonder whether saying, "Yes," was actually a good idea when they all say, "Really?" like this has never happened before.

10. When they ask your name, tell them it's Gloria.

11. Follow them to their car as they repeat, "You're the first person to say yes. You must not be from around here."

12. When asked where you are from, admit that you're from Wisconsin. Climb into the car. Reassure yourself that nothing says, "We won't rape you" like "We're a bunch of women going to Bible study."

13. Buckle your safety belt, because being safe is important.

14. Drive a little bit farther out of town than you were expecting and pull up outside a massage parlor with a neon sign. Reassure yourself that all the best churches probably got their starts above massage parlors. Realize that this is an obvious lie. Console

yourself with the thought that "Hey, I've never been upstairs at a massage parlor before! That's probably where they keep the happy endings!"

15. Climb up the stairs to a nice carpeted hallway above the massage parlor.

16. Answer an enthusiastic "Yes" when the women ask if you want coffee. Hand them your coat. Smile when you meet their "Deacon," a dark-haired man with an equally mysterious accent.

17. Join him and a recent female convert for Bible study in a small room with a table and a whiteboard.

18. Make the mistake of disagreeing with him when he asserts that the Emperor Constantine was actually Satan and we know this from the Book of Daniel.

19. Point out that all of his decoding of hidden biblical meanings—"It's not 'communion'! Communion is a lie made up by Constantine/Satan!"—seem to be based on this specific translation, and you are pretty sure that the Bible was originally written in Hebrew and Greek.

20. Realize that he won't move on until you admit that he is right. Glance nervously at your watch and realize that it is getting to be later than you thought.

21. Decide the best way to get a ride back to Cambridge is to agree with everything the Deacon says.

22. Get through the remaining scriptural points in record time.

23. Make a nervous noise that sounds like a cat coughing up a hairball when the Deacon says, "So, do you want to be baptized?"

24. Say, "No, no, rather not, think I'll pass, actually, but I'm, you know, flattered and everything."

25. Watch as the Deacon's face falls. "You know, the last person who agreed that all of this was true and didn't accept baptism . . . she got hit by a bus."

26. Admit that baptism sounds a lot more appealing when you put it that way.

27. Make another hairball noise when the Deacon says, "Great. We'll get everything ready. Go put on your robe."

28. Stare at yourself in the bathroom mirror. Realize that your great idea to barricade yourself in the bathroom while you call a friend with a car is not going to work, because your phone is in your coat and not in the bathroom with you.

29. Apologize to God. Apologize first for the fact that you are in a bathroom, putting on a robe, about to be baptized into a church of people of whom you know nothing other than that they think Constantine was Satan and they like to hang out on sidewalks. Apologize for how the majority of your prayers happen when you think you have lost your wallet or cell phone and usually take the form of a kind of look-I-know-the-universe-operates-by-certain-rules-but-couldn't-you-possibly-make-a-small-exception-in-my-case bargaining. Promise that if you make it out of this you will straighten up and fly right. Admit, somewhat ruefully, that this was exactly what you promised last time on the condition that you found your wallet. Promise that this

time will be different. Admit, somewhat ruefully, that this was what you promised last time too.

30. Hear singing.

31. Put on your robe. Reflect that, historically, people who put on robes had something bad in store for them. Jesus? Gandalf? Hugh Hefner? Cross. Balrog. Old age and, probably, syphilis. My point is, it never ends well.

32. Walk into the chapel. Kneel in the baptizing tub. Reassure yourself that this probably isn't a cult because everyone seems so polite. Besides, aren't cults supposed to revolve around charismatic leaders? You have yet to see anyone who possesses more charisma than a slice of whole-wheat toast. Also: zero pentagrams so far. And hey, no one has painted "DIE PIGS" on any walls in blood yet. Realize that you are grasping at straws here.

33. Say "Amen" when the Deacon tells you to say "Amen", as they pour water over you.

34. Emerge from the bathroom to a large cluster of people singing and addressing you as Sister Gloria.

35. Accept your head-covering. Point out, timidly, that no one said anything about a head-covering. "Yes, of course they did," the Deacon will tell you. "Paul said that for a woman to pray with her head uncovered is just as shameful as if her head were shaven."

36. Take "Passover." Listen politely as the Deacon explains that the only true time to take "Passover" is on January fifteenth at twilight, but that this is a temporary Passover that will cover you in the eyes of God if you are hit by a bus between now and

then. Wonder why being hit by a bus is becoming such a big theme of this evening.

37. Listen politely as the Deacon explains the rules for your new life. "Three big ones," the Deacon explains. "First, no eating food that has been sacrificed to a false god." (That will put a big damper on Thanksgiving.) "No eating the meat of an animal that has been strangled to death." (This sounds fine, since you don't even know where to begin to find an animal that has been strangled to death.) "No drinking blood." (Well, there goes Sanguine Saturday!)

38. "Also, no sexual immorality Do you know what that means?"

39. Say, "Goats?" in a timid voice.

40. Watch the Deacon pretend not to have heard you. "No. It means you're married to Jesus now."

41. Say, "Aha," in what you hope is a reassuring tone.

42. Stay for a supper of hot soup and logic puzzles, specifically one of those puzzles where you have to rearrange matches to form a perfect square. Now that you are married to Jesus and prohibited from drinking blood, you have a lot of such wholesome evenings to look forward to!

43. Finally get your ride back to campus!

44. Listen carefully to their warnings that your Passover is only good until January fifteenth at twilight. Promise to come back for more Bible study. Bid your new sisters good-bye.

45. Climb the five flights of stairs to your dorm room. Smile propitiatingly at your roommate when she

asks, "Why is your hair all wet?" Explain that you may have just accidentally gotten baptized into a cult.

46. Google the Church of God that you just joined.

47. Realize with growing alarm that there are numerous Web sites for Churches of God and that they all claim that the other Churches of God are agents of Satan in disguise.

48. Hope you didn't join the one that's an agent of Satan!

49. Avoid Harvard Square for several days.

50. If you have to walk through it, use the Eyes-Down-Head-Down Ladybug Family Emergency walk. Tell your friends to watch out for people addressing you as "Sister Gloria."

51. Later tell a somewhat altered version of this story to your mother, who quite reasonably panics because, as an only child, you are her sole reproductive investment and this story makes you sound like a total idiot who is just a few brain cells short of being sexually attracted to fire. Patiently field her questions by shouting, "Look, it seemed impolite to just get up and leave, and they were women!" in response to everything she says, including but not limited to: "How did you know they were women? They might have been witches! How did you know?"

52. Admit that this is what you should have been worried about. That they could have been witches. That was the big concern here.

53. Months later, after your Passover has expired, you have graduated from college, and the whole inci-

dent is only a distant memory, spend an afternoon ravaging the carcass of a Borders bookstore for cheap books.

54. Freeze as a cheery female voice asks, "Have you heard of the Woman Image of God in Scripture?"
55. Emit a startled yelp.
56. Say, "Oh yeah, I'm familiar."
57. Walk away.

Teen Jesus

Once, in high school, I was Jesus.

I don't know if it helped on my college application or not.

Then again, you can never really tell what is going to help with a college application. I once spoke to the head of the Harvard admissions department for a story and she told me that, as "supplemental material," somebody had mailed in a taxidermied squirrel. The reason this did not help the person's application was not, as you might expect, because it was a taxidermied squirrel, but because it was not a *well*-taxidermied squirrel. It started to fall apart in the mailroom. So the takeaway here was not, "Don't mail a dead squirrel to the Harvard admissions department" but actually, "If you're going to mail a dead squirrel to Harvard, make sure that you taxidermy that thing correctly."

But people will try anything.

That wasn't why I was Jesus, though.

I was doing it because I was in a church youth group, it was Easter season, my church was doing a tableau of Stations of the Cross—all the spots Jesus stopped on his way to getting crucified—and there were no other volunteers.

Really, that last reason was why. It wasn't the most stringent church youth group in the world—we were Episcopalian (as Robin Williams liked to say, "Catholic Lite—all of the pageantry, none of the guilt"), where church is really more of an excuse to wear a bow tie once a week than anything. Some people say they're spiritual but not religious—we were religious but not spiritual. All Christ Church asked was that we show up once a week, sometimes for pizza and a movie with Spiritual Implications like *Lord of the Flies* or *Dead Poets Society*. We also sold pancakes, Super Bowl chili, and holiday wreaths—well, Christmas wreaths; I guess selling wreaths with your church group is one context where it's definitely safe to say "Christmas" instead of "holiday"—and saved the money to go on pilgrimage. We sold a lot of pancakes, so we flew to Ireland. A previous group that had not really had their act together had gotten only as far as Canada, and I think they had to go on foot.

Among the many great facets of Episcopalianism— besides choral music and never having to feel guilt—is that women in the church can do all the things men can. You can't be pope, but then again, neither can anyone else. So when nobody else volunteered to be in our Station (we were supposed to depict Saint Veronica wiping the face of Jesus with her handkerchief), I got the gig.

Veronica was portrayed by my friend Michaela. We were the two least cool members of youth group. During the pilgrimage to Ireland I bought books and she read them. Everyone else got sucked into a vortex of drama because one of the couples in our group had decided to break up and wanted us to take sides. Horribly complicated alliances formed and dissolved wherever you looked. It resembled the lead-up to World War I. (The fact that I suggested it resembled the lead-up to World War I tells you just how cool I was.)

When it came time to be Jesus it was a bright warm spring afternoon. I put on a white robe. Michaela and our deacon very carefully drew a thick beard on me with face paint and eyebrow pencil.

I tried to look beatific. If there was ever a time to look beatific, I reasoned, now would be it. It was harder to look beatific when I was outside toting a large wooden cross down the sidewalk, to the excitement of onlookers, but that seemed about right for the part. The good thing about being Jesus was that if people reviled you and muttered all kinds of evil against you, you could argue that you were just doing your job.

I staggered over to Michaela in what I hoped was a stately but pained manner. She wiped my face with her handkerchief. In the actual story, there was an image of Jesus left in the handkerchief and it became a sacred relic. In our rendition, there was a big brown smudge from where my beard had rubbed off. It wasn't really the sort of object you wanted to make into a relic. Then again, people made relics out of knee bones and things, so you could never be sure. Maybe it would have been exactly the ticket.

"Bless you, my child," I said. (That was my one line.) I might also have said, "Please, I'm thirsty."

I handed the cross off to a member of the congregation and staggered beatifically offstage.

Being Jesus was not actually that hard. This surprised me, given all the literature. If all you had to do to make it into Heaven was walk in the footsteps of Jesus, I was going to be a shoo-in.

A few years passed.

Heaven slipped a little out of mind, to be replaced with more practical concerns. Like college.

College and Heaven seemed to have a lot in common. Everything I had heard about college suggested that it was an earthly paradise. You could drink and lie around all day, surrounded by a minimum of seventy-two virgins. Probably more, if you took advanced math. You would never have to work again. There would be free wings, on Wednesdays, anyway.

The only trick was getting there.

Having religion had prepared me well for the college application process. There was a kind of religious warfare between different approaches. You could take the puritanical approach—make your children as miserable as possible for as long as possible by forcing them to wear drab uniforms and banning fun. In the end, it turned out that the whole process was random and the only people who were rewarded were the members of a tiny, preselected elite.

Or you could try to buy your way in with costly indulgences. ("The gymnasium is named after me! And I donated this relic of a thighbone! Junior's getting in for sure.")

I read somewhere that the emperor Charlemagne used to be followed around at all times by a monk, ready to baptize him at a moment's notice if he ever showed the slightest sign of being about to die, so that he could go straight to Heaven with a clean conscience. These days, this approach is called helicopter parenting. People hover just over their children's shoulders, feeding them SAT words, shredding incautious birds in their rotating blades.

If you're not sure your kid is amassing enough virtue just sitting at home studying for six to eight AP's, you can always send Junior off on a children's crusade to wage holy battles abroad. Access to lepers is preferable.

There are some doubters and heretics who don't believe in life after high school, of course. But everyone else picks up a backpack burden and makes his pilgrim's progress through the Slough of Deadlines and the Vanity College Fair as best he can. Then, senior fall, he stands at the gate, hearing his virtues and sins read off, trying to figure out where to get a letter of recommendation to enter the Celestial University. (Wow, *Pilgrim's Progress*–based puns don't really pay off, huh? Hi, one old man just outside Phoenix laughing hysterically, alone. I'm sorry, everyone else.)

"What about all these church activities?" our college counselor asked, looking at my sheet.

I had more church activities than you would expect, which is to say, I was still engaged in any church activities at all. Youth Group had disbanded a while ago, but I was still lurking around. There were free doughnuts, and I needed something to do during the hour before children's choir practice. I was no longer, strictly speaking, a child, but the choir director was desperate to keep me because I was one of two members of the choir who did not cry and try to eat the sheet music. The other one was the choir director's son. And his voice was changing, a fact that she refused to acknowledge and that made us especially pleasant to listen to. It was a little embarrassing to be the only person in the choir taller than four feet, but the alternative, Mrs. Harris assured me, was too horrible to contemplate. They would have to switch entirely to handbells.

To pass the time before practice, I offered to teach Sunday school. This was a sort of futuristic Montessori hybrid Sunday school where you were supposed to let the children discover Jesus on their own initiative. My function was to sit at the edge of the room and look encouraging. In order to do this, I had to attend several training sessions. During one of these sessions the woman instructing us accidentally dropped a small toy Jesus that was made out of wood. Then she apologized to it.

After this I decided that maybe Sunday school teaching was not my line.

"Do you think you could get one of these people to write you a recommendation?" our school's college counselor asked.

I shrugged. "I could try."

This was how I wound up with a letter of recommendation from our church deacon that started, "Ever since I saw Alexandra take on the role of Jesus, I have been convinced that she would be a good fit for your university." I didn't really think my Jesus had been that memorable, but when Deacon Jane got going, she really got going. Apparently I had been the Golden Jesus Standard by which all others were to be measured. The admissions department would be lucky if I didn't get taken up into the sky on a trailing cloud of glory before their letter reached me. Such was my commitment to the role that I was probably out right now tending to a leper.

I frowned at it. Applying to college tends to make you question your motives anyway. Here you had thought you were just studying Ancient Greek because you wanted to know Ancient Greek or being Jesus in a church pageant because, well, *someone* had to be Jesus in your church pageant. But it turned out that college had been lurking at the back of your mind all along, hadn't it? Were you being good because you wanted to be good? Or were you being good because you hoped that you'd be rewarded? You were just as bad as the meek, sidling around being meek all the time just so they could inherit the earth away from the rest of us. Those sneaks.

It was a catch-22. The trouble was that the best way to fake genuine enthusiasm was to be genuinely enthusiastic. But then were you trapped in a long con? Were you genuinely enthusiastic because you knew that this was the best way to get what you wanted? So that you could say, "No, I'm real, not like the others. I don't care about the point value! I'm not grubbing for indulgences."

It was the sort of thing that probably kept John Calvin awake at night.

Why was I walking around trying to impersonate Jesus, anyway?

I began to feel some serious doubt. I couldn't be an atheist. I don't like lots of bumper stickers. I couldn't be an agnostic. I don't like admitting there are things I don't know. What did that leave? What was I supposed to do?

At least for college, my suspicious Jesus activity had its intended effect.

Like Heaven, college is a consequence-free zone full of robes. It does't prepare you for life. It barely prepares you for the workforce. College actively makes you less fit for most jobs than you were during high school. You stop being required to show up in places at specific times, a skill that is useful for adults to have. Instead, you develop an uncanny ability to cook noodles in settings where, frankly, you should not be cooking anything. The workforce needs you to be able to do basic math? Nuts to you, workforce! Here is a course called "How to Befriend a Number" that counts toward your math requirement. (Seriously. I once took a science course called "Nanothings," whose entire message was, I quote, "Small things are different." For my final project, I wrote a play about a ray of light that could not decide if he were a particle or a wave.) The workforce wants you to be able to arrive at work at nine a.m.? Oh, Workforce, that's cute. At college we learn to say the phrase "I do most of my best work after one a.m." with actual conviction. Why not? There is seldom class before noon, if you pick the right major.

And then it turns out there's a Beyond after all, outside the gates. And this time, you're completely unprepared.

So forget life after death. I'm barely figuring out life after college.

Maybe I should get a monk to follow me around, though. Just in case.

Your Prize Came

When I got to the mailbox and opened it up, I was startled to find that it contained nothing but trophy after trophy. And they were for you! See, trophies did not cease being awarded when you turned eight and stopped playing soccer. You've been secretly getting them all your life! They just had the wrong address for you.

Your prizes finally came for:

- Letting it go
- Not telling a story even though you had a really good story that was going to blow everyone out of the water because it was clear the evening was winding down at that point
- Letting that lady into your lane
- Intending to give up your seat on the bus but then somebody else did but still you totally would have
- Arriving at brunch on time
- Offering *everyone* your gum even though that meant you went from a whole pack to no gum in a few seconds
- Writing that thank-you note

- Having only one drink and sipping water the rest of the evening
- Exercising
- Actually not telling the secret you promised not to tell, but not (as usual) because you forgot what the secret was
- Thinking nonjudgmental thoughts about that mother on the bus whose baby kept crying and crying and crying the whole way
- Being right on the Internet
- Going to your friend's improv show
- Being a good loser
- Breaking up in person
- Taking out the trash
- Finishing Proust's entire *In Search of Lost Time*
- Finishing Proust's entire *In Search of Lost Time* and NOT bringing it up every chance you get, which shows real restraint
- Buying, cooking, and eating a vegetable
- Ordering salad
- Cleaning the bathroom
- Stepping on that cockroach for your roommates while they screamed and screamed
- Putting that spider under a glass and letting it out very carefully
- Filing your income taxes
- Fixing your parents' computer
- Fixing your parents' computer that other time
- Waking up early
- RSVP'ing
- Holding the door

- Not holding the revolving door
- Taking a taxi to the airport with that credit card your friend left in a bar so she was able to get on her plane and go to a job interview
- Cooking her that dinner
- Listening to your friend hem and haw and agonize and carry on about this guy she's seeing who might be right but might also just be her idea of what's right but how can you really know and what's love anyway and is that the last beer do you mind if she has another beer?
- Doing the dishes
- Cleaning up after yourself
- Not crying
- Crying

They all came here and they are waiting for you. Let me know where to send them, and I will.

The Naked Pun

Being the world champion of something isn't usually an instant social liability.

When Miss America arrives at your dinner table, you don't sigh and throw up your hands and say, "Great! Now she's going to smile and change into an evening gown, and our whole evening is ruined!" Actually, quite the opposite. When another guest confides that she is a member of the World Champion luge team, no one expects her to begin luging then and there. (Besides the simple fact that it would be rude, it would require a lot of specialized equipment that it is hard to carry with you to parties.)

Not so with punning.

Saying that you are a champion punster is like announcing that you are a world-class leper. "Oh," everyone says, giving you a look as though you have just casually dropped an ear into the bean dip. "Well, congratulations," they add, in a tone usually associated with the phrase "You should probably get that checked out."

"Thank you," you say.

"Well, do you want to make some puns for us, or what?" someone says, and everyone else glowers at him.

Punning is not a *skill*, their gimlet glances seem to say. Punning is a *condition*. Punsters should be treated gently, with kid gloves, and you should give them that firm, polite, too-bright smile that these same people give when walking their children past cup-shakers on the sidewalk. "Don't look away," you can hear them murmuring, "but don't stop, either. On no account stop."

And as long as we're being honest, these people may well have a point.

It's a disease. We can't help it.

Punning is a kind of Midas Touch. Everything you touch turns to puns, even if all you really want to do is eat a sandwich in peace and quiet:

"We would enjoy this sandwich, if you'd lettuce."

"You mayo."

"I'm not the one getting jalapeño face about it."

"Give me some time to ketchup."

"But I just mustard a lot of good puns!"

"Stop it! Just stop it!"

"Oh, 'just top it!' Good one!"

It's like nuclear escalation. You can't stop before the other guy does, or there'll be fallout. (That wasn't actually a pun, but it was close.)

Fran Lebowitz said that the opposite of talking isn't listening— the opposite of talking is waiting. For punsters, the opposite of talking is waiting to make a pun.

Just recently, I was having a perfectly nice brunch when someone said, "I love lychee," and with horror I heard myself saying, "I Love Lychee was my favorite 1950s sitcom."

"Whyyyy?" everyone groaned, and I shrugged and shrank down in the chair and tried to explain that it wasn't me; it was the condition.

It is the condition. It's a sickness. It's a disease.

My favorite quote about punning is from Stephen Leacock, who noted, "The inveterate punster follows conversation as a shark follows a ship."

If so, this explains why sharks have so few chums.

(You see?)

Hearing nothing, understanding nothing, waiting only to make a meal of a carelessly dropped word, the punster follows, dogged and ineluctable in his pursuit, like Captain Ahab but leggier.

And now I've got the badge to prove it. Well, the trophy. Well, three trophies, if we're staring at my rack.

I wasn't born with it. It isn't a thing you're born with, like a silver spoon or a caul or synesthesia (I *wish* I had synesthesia! Right now, if I want to taste the rainbow, I have to buy a bag of Skittles) or a cool mutation that allows you to light things on fire with your thoughts. It's learned.

I know when I learned it, too. My parents, worried that I might become popular at school, got me a book of puns at an impressionable age.

It worked like a charm. Puns were my anti-drug. They were my anti-social life. My social circle shrank to those who could tolerate long, rambling jokes that concluded with a triumphant "AND THAT'S WHY PEOPLE WHO LIVE IN GRASS HOUSES SHOULDN'T STOW THRONES." No chance of falling in with a bad crowd who would introduce me to Boys and Liquor and Jazz—but, hey, as the fern liked to say, with fronds like these, who needs anemones?

The book my parents gave me, *Pun and Games* by the eminent punster Richard Lederer, taught you how to take any conversation you were faced with and turn it into a pun. It was the wordplay equivalent of a manual on how to build bombs from common household materials. It came complete with sets of pun-problems for you to fill out with a pencil or pen.

There were lots of other wordplay games, too, like decoding vanity plates for various professions. NML 10DR was a zookeeper. 10SNE1 was a tennis pro. And those are just the ones I remember off the top of my head.

I learned about inflationary language, whereby "wonderful" became "twoderful" and "I don't know what you ate that for" becomes "I don't know what you nine that five." It didn't make sense to anyone who wasn't me, but so what? That was the story of my life.

I learned about Spoonerisms. William Archibald Spooner was an Oxford don who gained fame by inadvertently swapping around the beginnings of his words. "Three cheers for our queer old dean!" he once toasted, raising a glass to Queen Victoria. "Mardon me, Padam, you are occupewing my pie," he told a lady at church. "May I sew you to another sheet?" During World War I he commented, "When the boys come back from France, we'll have the hags flung out."

He wasn't useful in average conversation, but he was great if I ever got into a situation where a cutting retort was called for. "You," I would sneer, "are what William Archibald Spooner would have called a shining wit."

No one ever seemed to notice how biting this was. Again, this was the story of my life.

By the time I had worked my way through all the exercises, learning along the way that "the man who hated seabirds left no tern unstoned, while the talented masseuse left no stern untoned," I was unstoppable.

I hadn't been a shark before, but now my eyes were opened. I saw pun potential everywhere. I began to follow conversations, sniffing for blood in the water. It was like one of those hideous transformations in a superhero movie. I walked into my room a normal person, was bitten on the ankle by a radioactive punster, and came staggering out a monster, spewing puns everywhere I turned.

With great power came great power to annoy.

And this state of things persisted.

When I got to college, everything changed. One of the first friends I made was someone who said, "Did you hear about the lady who shaved her legs and rectum?"

I nodded, feeling that sudden hot sensation that floods through your body when you experience true love or sit on something sharp.

"That's my mom's favorite pun," she said.

And then I knew I was in the right place. We went on to be roommates and write several shows together, and after that she became a famous person whose Facebook updates I have to keep Liking. No, I'm kidding; we're still friends. I think. (Call me?)

College was a parallel universe where punning was actually celebrated, in the form of the Hasty Pudding Theatricals, which I can best describe as a group for drinking, putting on an elaborate drag musical while drinking, and making puns while drinking. For a few halcyon years I breathed the rich, supersaturated air of people who could not see a word ending in "er" without tacking on "I hardly know 'er!" (To give you a sense of the level of wordplay involved, there was a show called "Acropolis Now" set in Ancient Greece, with a character named Hades Pantsaretight. I say "there was a show" like I didn't cowrite it and take full responsibility for that pun.)

Then, gasping like a fish, I was decanted from college into the real world.

In real life there are few such safe spaces for puns. You cannot turn to someone during, say, an earthquake at your church and murmur, "Christ Church Parish? More like Christ Church Perish!" It just doesn't get the reception you'd hope, like a disappointing wedding or [INSERT NAME OF YOUR CELL PROVIDER HERE!].

(You see what I'm talking about. It's a disease.)

These days I work at a newspaper, where, in theory, there is plenty of room for puns. What are headlines, if not pun-Dumpsters? "WEINER HANGS OUT, EMBARRASSES CANDIDATE."

But that was before the dark times. Before the Internet.

The Internet has given us punsters much—Twitter, for one—and I am grateful. But it has also paved over many of the pun's time-honored stomping grounds. Newspaper headlines, which used to be safe spots where young puns could roam freely and graze at will, now have to be written to attract as much traffic as possible. A great headline pun, like "At Convention, Female Spiderman Spied Her Man" (okay, a passable pun) becomes "Six Unbelievable Tricks for Finding Love That Are Tangentially Related to Miley Cyrus in Some Way and Also Pornography! (Pornography)" or "This Article Made Me Cry for Six Reasons Beyoncé Beyoncé Beyoncé," or no self-respecting search engine will ever point you toward it.

(For anyone reading this in the distant future, Miley Cyrus and Beyoncé were two basically amiable carbon-based life-forms who were very good at making mouth-sounds and for some reason everyone felt the need to talk about them ALL THE TIME. (Those Earthling meatsacks, am I right??) Also, hi, future reader! What's an advanced life-form like you doing with a book like this? If you are near humans, please don't hunt them and convert their parts into scrap!)

Without the headline as a pun dumping ground, I had to console myself by hunting down the pun in literature and history and spreading the Good News, with the kind of nervous tenacity generally reserved for people who want to give religion to you or get drugs from you.

"Jesus used to make lots of puns," I told people on the bus. "That was how you could tell he had tremendous personal magnetism. He went up to Peter and said, 'From now on, your name will be 'Rock,' because on this 'Rock' I build my church!' And Peter actually followed him, instead of groaning and running away!"

"That's nice."

"You want miracles? That's a miracle right there!"

"Oh look, here's my stop," my seat partners would say, getting off at a deserted reservoir several miles from any parked cars or people.

"Jesus also had a great one about how 'you are fishermen now, but I will make you fishers OF men' that you really have to hear in the original Greek to get the full flavor of!" I yelled cheerily as the doors closed.

Of course, people punned long before Jesus. Aristophanes was way into puns, doing clever and untranslatable things with "proktos" (butt) and "protos" (first). Cleopatra made a famous pun to cheer up her lover Mark Antony after their troops lost the town of Toryne to Emperor Augustus. Toryne means "ladle." "What danger can there be from a ladle falling into his hands?" she asked. Ha-HA!

I look forward to cheering up a lover in a similar way. I know a lot of puns about disease, so I am well-fortified against any possible bad news. "Hip dysplasia?" I will say. "That must displease-ya!" "Yes we cancer!" "Acute appendicitis? I think it's just okay-looking." "Lou Gehrig's Disease? Sorry, uh, that—you're on your own there."

And history had plenty more. "Not Angles, but Angels!" said Pope Gregory, seeing some Angles for the first time. "Oh no," the Angles said. "Oh God. Leave." (They also said this for unrelated reasons.)

Aside from spreading the Good News, I tried to work puns into my daily life, with mixed results. Even when things got serious, I couldn't stop. "I see your father's retiring," a coworker told me.

"Well," I said, "he's always been pretty retiring."

Groan.

Story of my life.

And then I discovered the O.Henry Pun-Off.

Every week, as part of my duties at the *Post*, I host a chat, which mostly consists of my talking to strangers about bacon and fending off the advances of one man with a Philly IP address who wants to know if I've gotten my "birthday spanking" yet. Noting my fondness for puns, they suggested that I try the Pun-Off, and in May of 2012, I did.

I had been traveling a fair bit that year—Iowa! South Carolina!—but I was instantly enchanted by Austin. I had never been to Texas before, and I thought that everything there was going to be cartoonishly large. I would get off the plane and all the road signs would be large enough to swat a mammoth with. All the mosquitoes would be the size of butterflies. Butterflies would be the size of hardcover books. There would be a big beltway comprised entirely of large Bibles. Everyone would have jangling spurs and go swaggering around leading giant blue oxen behind them.

But instead there was just a bit of traffic from the airport, a couple of clean-looking, well-lighted strip clubs, a giant park full of food trailers hung with fairy lights, and some buildings that resembled big crayons. If your idea of Heaven is anything like my idea of Heaven—which is to say, lots of weirdos, corn dogs, and cheap beer—Austin is the place for you.

The O.Henry Pun-Off was preceded by dinner at a Mexican restaurant called Opal Divine's. I sat down at the table and instantly felt at home. On the table was a whole worksheet of Punny Names for Cocktails. It was just like *Pun and Games* all over again. "Your neckwear." Mai Thai. "Citizen of the galaxy"? Cosmo-politan.

I was as prepared on the subject of puns as I was ill-equipped when it came to O.Henry, the pen name of William Sydney Porter. All I had read of O.Henry was "The Gift of the Magi," a short story about why you should never go out of your way to give somebody a thoughtful gift. "William Sydney Porter is buried in North Carolina," said one of my dinner companions, a man with a mustache who resembled a worried moon.

"Great!" I said. "Is O.Henry buried nearby?"

He laughed as though I had made a hilarious joke, and I realized my mistake.

First came the tribute to the punster of the year, then everyone got up and told stories with pun punch lines, then the MC brought in a bin of objects and we all lined up to make puns on them. It was heaven.

"Being a punster can be hard," one contestant confided. "Someone told me his wife had a stroke and I said, 'That's terrible! Three strokes, you're out!' and he didn't think it was funny."

I nodded sympathetically. "Story of my life," I said.

Kurt Vonnegut coined the term "karass" in *Cat's Cradle*—it means, basically, people who are on your kickball team at life. Punsters were my karass. We kept the party going at the birthday festivities for the friend of Miranda, another punster. She was one of those perfect-looking smart people who speak literally six languages and have beautifully toned upper arms. We wound up at a hip downtown bar and started punning on lightbulbs while her friends looked on in commingled delight and horror. "I'm sick of this topic. Let's switch." "Does someone have a mint? I'd like to fill a mint." "Did you hear about that cannibal inventor of the lightbulb? Yeah, Thomas Alva Et His Son!" (I didn't say they were good puns, just that they happened.)

I felt like I was home.

. . .

The next day was the actual competition. The format of the Pun-Off is simple. There is the long-form, prepared Punniest in Show—a run of puns lasting no more than two minutes on a topic of your own choosing—and Punslingers, a grueling several hours of competitive wordplay that pits one punster against another on a randomly chosen topic like "Celebrity names as questions!"

"Do you know where Shelley Winters?"

"Is it okay to Pat Sajak?"

"Is Terry Gross?"

Repeat one, and you get a strike. Make a dubious pun that isn't a pun but a play on words, you get a strike. Fail to come up with one in three seconds, and you're out. It takes all afternoon. It's serious business. You can spend months training, if you want to, and some people want to. Don't bring a life to a pun fight.

For my two minutes of prepared material, I had decided to make puns about philosophers. At the last minute, I suddenly panicked that people might not know all the philosophers to whom I was referring and decided to print out a series of paper slides identifying them.

This resulted less in "greater clarity for the audience" than in "lots and lots of philosophers flying off into the wind, never to be retrieved." Still, it had its moments.

"I need to stop drinking with philosophers," I started. ". . . I always wind up getting illogically propositioned. . . . Paris Hilton was pretty drunk. You should have seen that heiress tottle (Aristotle) . . . I always Schopenhauer later than I'm supposed to . . . It was one of those bars where I don't think Descartes anybody."

It was all like that, better in parts and worse in parts. I think I came at it from a lot of good Engels and left Marx on the judges' memory. They said to one another, yeah, Heidegger.

(DO YOU SEE WHAT I'M SAYING? IT COULD BE LIKE THIS, IN YOUR MIND, ALL THE TIME.)

Even with the wind taking the great thinkers away, I still came in fourth overall. The guy who had told me the thing about "three strokes, you're out" reassured me that this was a very solid performance, and as high as he'd ever placed.

I was elated.

Then came the Punslingers.

I got eliminated pretty quickly, mainly because I ran out of units of distance. ("King's arm?" I tried.)

But then I got to sit back and enjoy. It is no exaggeration to say that watching the Punslingers competition was a magical, transcendent experience. It was a boxing match. It was a concert. It was two people sparring and dancing together and making something beautiful. It was opera, in the sense that it went on and on and on and most people would consider it torture.

It was like seeing the face of God, if your idea of the face of God is twelve solid minutes of farm puns.

"Holy Plow!"

"There was a lady contestant in this, but we had to bumper."

"Sow?"

"Well, come on, reap between the lines."

"I have a lot of plants in the audience."

"Somebody bale me out of this!"

"Hay!"

"A dog won't help you farm, but a cattle."

"That pun was an udder disgrace."

And so on.

For me, this was heaven. For you, this might be somewhere on the scale next to waterboarding or attending someone's child's recital.

I didn't want it to end. Fortunately, there was an afterparty where I signed up for everyone's mailing lists of daily puns. The celebration continued well into the morning.

I boarded the elevator at the Airport Howard Johnson (as a general rule, if you are a hotel and your main selling point is your proximity to the airport, you are not a nice hotel) with a spring in my step and a smile on my face.

There is a certain undeniable camaraderie to hotel elevators at four in the morning. We've all done *something* that got us there.

The elevator smelled like a Febrezed ashtray. Its other occupant was wearing a too-short dress and too-tall strappy shoes in a yellowish color. The dress fabric looked like something you would regret upholstering your couch in. "Hey!" I said. We sort of gave each other the Howard Johnson four forty-five a.m. elevator once-over. "Hey!" she said.

"Living the dream!" I said.

I understand that there is a certain irony in shouting "Living the dream!" to the other occupant of the Airport Howard Johnson elevator, but in my case it was true, or as close to being true as you ever get with realized dreams. I really was.

She fiddled with her black, stringy hair. "I'm hungry," she said.

There was the real world I remembered.

I had to come back.

Next year, I'd have a plan.

The 2012 champion and I had agreed that the way to go next year would be some limited, elaborate category of puns with a lot of weird syllables in it that the judges would know.

When we arrived at the 2013 competition, we discovered that we had both picked the same category: books of the Bible.

Fortunately, I went before he did, and also fortunately, I was doing mine in order, which offered a certain advantage. He later told the *Wall Street Journal* that he could not defend the title his second year because "It's like a band's second album . . . You start getting into the experimental material."

"Baby, I want to get biblical with you," I told the audience, launching into a series of puns on books of the Bible in order. ("Remember when they threw the Republican nominee into that pit of freezing grizzlies? I hated seeing what those NUMBERS DEUTEROMNEY.") I got thirty-nine points out of a possible forty, tying with the pun legend Zeb (he'd placed third the past year, and had been a Punslingers champion), who had a routine about spices entitled "Seasonings of Love." It came down to a clap-off. He won, but I was thrilled with my performance.

Then came Punslingers. And instead of just watching, I somehow made it all the way to the final four. All I can say is that the spirit was on me.

It didn't hurt that "religion" was a category and I could go straight back into my routine. ("Look Obadiah!")

By the time we got to diseases, I was at a fever pitch. It turned into a slugfest. ("I feel really bad for DiCaprio. PO-LIO.") We went all the way from the politically correct diseases into the iffier ones. It got hairy at points. Finally I couldn't think of one more. I conceded with a last pun on SIDS.

At the end of it all, the other punsters gave me the Most Viable punster award. I couldn't stop smiling. I was a punster! And I was viable! I had earned the respect of my wordy peers!

It was the first time I'd won anything in years and, clutching it in a teddy-bear-vise-grip everywhere I went, I began to realize how much I'd missed that. Real life offers sadly few opportunities to win things. There are moments that *feel* like winning—getting a job, say, or getting married. But then you have to live with another person and cannot ever again poop with the door open.

·   ·   ·

I accepted that this would be as far as it went for me. It was clearly my pun zenith. It felt like enough. I didn't want to be like Michael Phelps, going back to the Olympics every four years until he was wrinklier out of the water than in it, each time emerging from the pool with diminishing returns. I wanted to walk away when I was still viable. This year I was just going to have fun and try to make some quality puns and not care what the judges had to say.

But then the cameras came around.

Before the most recent Pun-Off, I got an e-mail from a producer at *CBS Morning News* who wanted to do a feature on the competition. He'd stumbled across a piece I'd written about it after my first year there, watched my philosopher puns, and wondered if I were still planning to compete. If so, did I mind being followed around by cameras for a bit during the run-up to the event?

Mind? I asked. You say that like this is not the dream of every child in our fame-obsessed post-Warhol era. Sometimes I drive through speed traps just to feel like someone's taken notice. You should see how I carry on when I get into the field of view of a convenience-store security camera. I start picking feuds and forming alliances within seconds. MIND? Sometimes I'll pick up a landline phone and gently whisper "Hey how about that terrorism act we were planning to commit I am the true Natalee Holloway killer" just to get that sweet feeling that someone's listening.

Soon a friendly lady with a camera showed up at my office. "Just do what you normally do," she said.

Instantly I started panicking. What do I do? I thought. What is my routine? Do I have a routine?

Sometimes I stare at the wall for a while. "The thing a writer's wife can never understand," someone once said, "is that when a writer is staring out the window, he is working."

I would have stared out a window if I had a window. Instead, I stared at the windows I had open on my computer. Frantically, I minimized most of them. Fortunately I have years of practice minimizing windows. I'm the fastest click-out'er in the West. You try reading *Lord of the Rings* fanfiction on your family computer and see how fast you get!

I opened a Word document and frowned at it.

Most of my writing process consists of typing things like "UGH SO THIS IS A THING APPARENTLY.

    UM

    SO APPARENTLY [PUT SOMETHING HERE] AND NOW
  WE HAVE TO DEAL WITH

    OKAY SO
    SO
    HI

    UGHHHHHHHHHHHHHHHH
    THIS IS IMPOSSIBLE
    I DON'T KNOW
    [PUT SOMETHING HERE]"

In movies and TV shows, people try to dramatize the process of writing, but the most dramatic it gets is sometimes I go to the vending machine and get a bag of beef jerky, and then I drop a piece on the floor immediately after getting back to my chair, and then I glance quickly over at my coworker to see if he has noticed, and then I pick it up and eat it. It's not exactly *Shakespeare in Love* territory.

Sometimes I'll leave someone an apologetic-sounding voice mail, but I don't even really do that anymore.

Frantically I tried to think what someone impressive with a totally nonembarrassing routine that was ready to be put on TV this instant would do. An Impressive Person would probably read the *Economist* and the *New Yorker* and chuckle wryly at the cartoons. "The economist," I typed. "Dot com." (This is not, it turns out, the actual Web site of the *Economist*, which is something that Alternate Universe Put-Together Me would have known.)

The other trouble with typing "The Economist" into my computer is that I haven't cleared my browser history in the Internet equivalent of hundreds of years. Autofill is like a golden retriever: very excited to bring you what it thinks you want and totally clueless that sometimes a modicum of discretion might be called for. Just a modicum. It saw me typing "E," got all excited and wanted to offer me "erotic fanart of Rick Santorum" or "erotica with Mitt Romney in it" or "erotica without Mitt Romney in it this is for research for an article I swear anyone who is monitoring my network usage hi guy who monitors the network usage."

I couldn't very well delete my browser history with the camera running, I thought. Besides, some of those sites had been hard to find!

I glanced around my desk. Maybe I could find something impressive on the desk. Maybe there was an uncompleted *New York Times* Saturday Crossword that I could fill out rapidly in pen. Maybe there were a couple of back copies of the *New Yorker* or a large set of encyclopedias that I could pick up and say, "Ah, splenetic! Just where I left off! So many twists in these pages! After sphincter, I didn't know what was coming!"

I frowned at my bookshelf. There was the Justin Bieber autobiography. There was Snooki's novel *A Shore Thing*. There was a picture and article about the World's Oldest Postal Employee. "I'm pretty healthy. I eat onion sandwiches," the pull quote read. There was a picture of the president of Haiti dressed in a diaper. There was a Venn Diagram of Things Rick Perry says. There were half a dozen books about the Civil War, several irate letters from readers, one of which began with the all-caps declarative sentence "WHAT'S THE MATTER, EVE? CAN'T TAKE A RIB?" which was, I guess, a pun, and some half-eaten food that a guy from a neighboring office had brought me in what I feared might be an effort to court me. (I tried gently explaining that bringing someone food you have already taken large bites out of was not how human courtship worked and that "you know, Carl, if I were a dog or a wren, this might be impressive and touching, but as it is it just makes me worry that you don't know what species I belong to or haven't dated human females in the past.") There was a petri dish Christmas tree ornament that someone had sent me on learning my last name. There was a tiny stuffed Chewbacca (also a gift from a reader). There was a volume of *Family Circus* cartoons, still in the original bag.

I went into tour-guide mode.

"This man," I said, pointing to the Oldest Postal Employee, "eats onion sandwiches." I scanned the pull quote. "Keeps him pretty fit, he says." I flailed around for something else to say. "Oh look, a picture of Oscar Wilde!" I added. "As someone once said, 'Oscar and George Bernard cannot be reconciled. When I'm wild about Shaw, I'm not Shaw about Wilde!'"

"What?" said the video journalist.

I sighed inwardly. "Oscar and George Bernard," I began again, somewhat limply, "cannot be reconciled. When I'm . . ."

After I had described every item on my desk, in some cases reading aloud from it, spun around in my chair a couple of times, and discovered an old laptop that I had been looking for for the past two years (it was hiding under a large pile of clothing), I gave up on any pretense of being impressive.

Very slowly. I drew the following picture of James Madison in MS Paint.

"I think that's good," the camera lady said.

So much for the edited essence of myself.

I arrived in Austin for another round of talking to a camera, this time in the company of the actual TV interviewer.

He had the whitest teeth I'd ever seen. They were so white as to be almost blue. You could hypnotize a person using teeth like that. He was just the right degree of tan and wore a fetching plaid shirt and loafers without socks. He looked like a walking advertisement for the state of California.

By the time we'd finished a half hour or so of interview, I began to feel that the pressure was on. I had thought I was going to the Pun-Off for a third time just because I loved being among fellow punsters and it would be fun and relaxed.

But now that there was all this footage of my office and my co-workers offering testimonials to my pun-making, I decided I had to put in some more effort.

I began to feel myself wanting it. Hope started forming. Hope is the most dangerous thing in Pandora's Box. It's what makes all the other things so impossible to stand.

So, apologies to:

- Kart, the friend who shared a thirteen-hour drive with me as I wavered between doing a routine on trees or presidents. Definitely presidents. No, trees. No, presidents, in order.
- My neighbors, who must have wondered why someone was repeatedly chanting the names of presidents through the wall at three o'clock in the morning
- the people on the subway who thought I was off my rocker as I murmured silently to myself while glancing periodically at my watch
- Martin Van Buren
- just everyone, really

When the day arrived, I waited on tenterhooks for my turn. I don't know what a tenterhook is, but I have spent a lot of time on them. If I had right now to give you a definition, I picture it as something like comically oversized Velcro.

The Pun-Off has the characteristic of most contests that are also communities, where you start to recognize certain people. I worried about all my competitors. I worried about Zeb, who had beaten me the previous year; the 2012 champion, who turned out not to show up; Tara, the only representative of New York's Punderdome community, whose routine on sandwiches the previous year I much admired; and Miranda, even though she said this year she was just doing it for kicks.

There were some wild cards, too: for instance, a British punster who had flown in and was wearing a chicken suit. What if he didn't lay an egg?

I hated being nervous. I wanted to win, but more than that: I wanted to be able to enjoy it.

I wanted to win while I still thought it was fun, instead of necessary. When it was like a onetime trip to a casino to play a little blackjack and the outcome didn't matter, instead of my Weekly Bus Trip To Mohegan Sun So I Can Win Big This Time and Get the House Back and Maybe My Wife Will Let Me See the Kids.

I waited. I was behind Zeb, punning on trees, and Karly, a guy who always did well in Punslingers, punning on flowers.

I gave silent thanks that I had opted not to pun about trees after all. Zeb got thirty-nine—the highest yet.

Then Karly, throwing roses to the crowd, also got thirty-nine.

I leaped up to the microphone, bypassing the steps altogether. I took a deep breath.

"Folks, I think a lady PRESIDENT'S IN ORDER," I began.

Somehow I wasn't that nervous. I knew my puns were solid. My only fear had been that someone would have the same topic. Nothing killed people's enthusiasm for your puns about kale like being the fifth kale-punner in a long line. People will laugh at any pun, *once*.

It had taken some work to come up with a theme to hang the puns on.

The routine I had devised had somehow turned into a kind of feminist rallying cry. One of the things about the Pun-Off was that the competitors were mostly male. Not overwhelmingly male. And certainly not all the good competitors. Katie Kargman had won the year before I started competing, and she was a fierce punster who was beloved by the crowd.

Still, definitely more guys than dolls. In some ways, being a girl did not hurt. You couldn't help standing out a little from the white-haired, Hawaiian-shirted crowd. But it was on you to prove that you had actual pun chops.

My first idea had been to make all the presidential puns jokes about losing control of your bladder, and that hadn't gone well.

But the lady hook seemed to bring it together. "MON, ROE v. Wade was a long time ago, and women have rights, and science," I said. "With a microscope, any JOHN QUINCY ADAMS, (John can see atoms . . . that one's rough) but any Jane can too. And if AN-DREW JACKS ON auto, he shouldn't win. If Mart pees in the van—and yes, MART, IN VAN BE URINE—that HARRISON of a gun has not earned our vote."

(You see why I apologized to Martin Van Buren?)

"If JOHN throws a TILE OR tries to POLK a TAILOR, well—we should FILLMORE offices with his female PIERCE, that's all I'm saying."

By the end—"Bad men can't fix things. HOO-EVER, FDR TRU-MAN, EISENHOWER principles, they can! KENN-EDY student win? Sure! LYNDON, JOHN'S SON, was a D student, and he was great. NIX ON dumb ideas like turning a FORD CAR TER a REA-GAN. No, when BUSH comes to shove, I see hope CLINTON on the horizon. Ladies, I DUBYA the hope of America, and I don't say, OH, BUMMER"—the crowd was going moderately nuts.

I got thirty-nine points.

And this time, I won the clap-off.

You can tell that International Pun Stardom is a worthwhile aspira-tion because the only prize you get, apart from fame (SO MUCH

FAME! ALL THE FAME!) is a trophy with a horse butt on it—the famous Quarter Horse.

I could not have been happier with my performance. I was also glad because this was what the news narrative demanded. I got to be interviewed by the man with shiny teeth, gazing rapt at my quarter horse and joking that "my punning will atrophy now that I've got a trophy."

Getting back on the plane to Washington, I darted through the boarding doors with my trophies dangling perilously out of my bag. "What's that trophy for?" one of the two gate attendants asked.

"Punning!" I said.

"Punting?" she said. "Only in Austin!"

"No," I said, "punning. You know, wordplay!"

"I know what punning is."

"Make a pun for us!" the other lady said.

"Uh," I said, somewhat lamely, "I would, but it might not be interesting, and I don't want you to be BOARD!"

"Oh," the lady said, "Well, you don't have to if you don't want to."

"No," I mumbled, starting down the Jetway, "board, like, board the plane, you know—never mind."

Ah, the real world. Just like I remembered.

Maybe puns were always the golden thread leading me forward.

"The pun is the lowest form of humor," someone wise once said. "If you didn't think of it first." Puns, according to Miranda, are "inside jokes for smart people." This made sense. The champion punster my first year competing was a Mensa member. (I found this out because he told me. That is always how you find out that someone is a member of Mensa.)

For Miranda, they were a benchmark of knowledge of a language. When I first met her, she told me she knew six languages—and could pun in three. By the third year, she could pun in six.

Punning is a dance with words. And the first rule of dancing is not caring if you look like an idiot.

John Pollack, author of *The Pun Also Rises*, told an interviewer that puns are the whole essence of life. Puns are a triumph of failure. They are built for groans. If people don't groan, you did something wrong.

The inveterate punster, that ominous fin following the conversation, knows this. He is doomed to pun and pun again and be met with bewilderment or outright rejection nearly every time.

If you can pun, you can do anything. Puns make you impervious to failure. They're the conversational equivalent of climbing to the top of the high diving board and knowing you're going to belly flop. But you do it anyway. It's a disease. It's a compulsion. It's a lifestyle.

You put yourself out there and flop, spectacularly, again and again and again. No wonder it came so naturally. And sometimes you come home with gold.

All those exercises when I was a kid paid off. Now, I'm a groan woman.

Unreconstructed

The first man I ever loved had been dead for a hundred and thirty years.

Among other problems.

First crushes are embarrassing enough when they are on people who are alive, go to your school, and did not lead the Confederate forces during the Civil War.

Yup.

Robert E. Lee was my teen idol.

I put his picture in my middle school locker. Everyone else had the Backstreet Boys and *NSYNC, proudly splayed in their Hip Jean Ensembles and big baggy shirts that made everyone in the nineties and early aughts look like they were ready to go bowling at a moment's notice. To give you a full picture of my locker, I also had a picture of Jar Jar Binks and a collage I had constructed of James Longstreet and four other Confederate generals, which I had cleverly labeled THE LONGSTREET BOYS, but in the prime position was a big glamour shot of Robert E. Lee I had printed out, resplendent in all his sepia-tinted dot-matrix-stippled glory.

They could keep their Chad Michael Murrays and their Leonardo DiCaprios, their coy Jonathan Taylor Thomases with milk mustaches ("Got milk?"). I had the one stud to rule them all.

"Sure, Leo's *okay*," I thought. "But where is his warhorse Traveller? Sure, Justin Timberlake can sing. But he would have been *helpless* at the Battle of Fredericksburg. Nick Carter? Yeah, he's cute, but would he have coped with defeat at Gettysburg by turning to his adjutant and crying out, 'Too bad! TOO bad. OH! TOO BAD'? Doubtful."

In retrospect, I see how awkward this was. Not just awkward. This was an ill-advised crush with centuries of history against it. Centuries. And justly so.

"Oh God," you're probably saying right now. "Ahhh, you are some kind of horrible racist person."

All I can do is tell you "I'm not, I'm really not, I promise," but that's never as instantly convincing as you want it to be. Starting a sentence with "I'm not a racist, but" is almost universally a poor choice. The only safe end to that sentence is to get up, walk silently away, and spend the rest of your life battling injustice.

But let me at least try to explain.

My fixation with the Civil War started in the fifth grade. We had to read historical biographies. I beelined to the L shelf a second too late to grab the Abraham Lincoln book. The Robert E. Lee biography was free, though, and I read it cover to cover. I was hooked.

I read six biographies of the man, each progressively worse, some with passages about his sex life that I demanded my history teacher explain to me. "When he wrote to a female acquaintance on her wedding night, 'How did you disport yourself, my child? Did you go off like a torpedo cracker on Christmas morning?'," I asked, "what did he mean? The biographer says the innuendo is obvious, but I have racked my brain and discovered nothing obvious about it."

"Er," Ms. Borchart said. "Er. Have your parents explain it."

The trouble with most biographies of Robert E. Lee is that they are written by unremorseful former Confederates with names like Jefferson Davis Pickett "Die Sherman Die" Jackson and they have titles like, *Robert E. Lee: God's General* and *Robert E. Lee: Like Jesus, but More Honorable*. How incredible, I thought, paging through them, that such a genuinely superior human had ever been so maligned by history. Why wasn't EVERY middle school named after him, instead of just a couple in Virginia? Where was his picture in all our textbooks?

I set out to set the record straight.

"Duty is the sublimest word in our language," I scrawled on the designated Meaningful Quote space we each were given on our desks. "Do your duty in all things. You cannot do more. You should never wish to do less. Robert E. Lee." I cut out his picture and glued it on my history textbook.

My parents tried to rescue me from an obsession they quite correctly realized would be deeply embarrassing later. For Christmas, my mother gave me a book called *Lee Considered*, which offered a critical perspective on Robert E. Lee. I refused to even skim it.

They looked on, helpless, as I carried my Lucky Stuffed Robert E. Lee figurine to my progressive middle school to bring me good fortune on my exams. Lucky Stuffed Robert had distinguished gray hair and rode a little stuffed replica of Lee's horse Traveller.

They kept trying to sit me down and explain that, while I knew that Robert E. Lee was a gentle soul who was followed around by a friendly chicken on his campaigns, and that he was clearly not a racist because of one apocryphal anecdote I had found in the third book about his postwar career, maybe other people did not know that. Maybe I could keep my voice down in this restaurant so that people did not come over and chide them for Passing Their Awful Retrograde Views on to an Innocent Child. Would I like a book about General Grant? How about a nice book about General Grant? General

Grant was really cool. He smoked cigars! Once he got arrested for speeding . . . with a horse! Didn't I want to get into General Grant?

No, I said. I was adamant. What Robert and I had was real, and I knew it.

Every conversation was a land mine. Scratch any subject and I could find a Robert E. Lee connection.

My high school put on *Les Misérables*. "*Les Misérables!*" I said. "That reminds me of a great joke from the Civil War era, when someone asked an old Southern lady, 'Hey, have you heard of *Les Misérables*' and she said, 'Well, they're a darn sight better than Grant's Misérables!' "

There was a silence.

"That was the punch line," I added.

At home, our cat jumped on the dinner table. "Get that cat off the table," my dad said.

"Robert E. Lee's cats used to sit on the dinner table," I volunteered, cheerily. "I found it in his wartime letters."

The cat looked menacingly at us. She got vicious if you tried to remove her from a surface, hissing and lashing out at everyone around her, like General McClellan if you tried to get him to move his army before he was ready.

"See?" my mother said. "There's precedent."

"Well," my father said, looking a little pained, "if it was good enough for Robert E. *Lee* . . ."

Back at school, we studied sexually transmitted diseases. "Gonorrhea!" I exclaimed. "Robert E. Lee's corps commander A. P. Hill had that!"

"How do you know these things?"

I shrugged modestly. "You read a few biographies, you pick these things up."

.   .   .

Online it was worse, if that were possible. My screen name was RELee[string of numbers I should probably not divulge]. (Embarrassing old screen names are the lower-back tattoos of the Internet age.) I spent hours in AOL Reference chat rooms pretending that I actually was Robert E. Lee, because I was unclear on the concept of how screen names worked.

The conversation usually went something like this:

ScreenName2: A/S/L?

ScreenName3: 42 M Texas.

RELee: 61, but vigorous/M/The Maryland countryside, astride my loyal horse Traveller

ScreenName1: whut

RELee: Good evening to all.

XXXlubeee7: want 2 see sexxxy vids of Britney & Xtina mud wrestling?

RELee: I am content in my marriage to Mary Custis Lee, thank you. What think you of the present time of trial?

ScreenName3: haha HI Robert

RELee: Good evening to you, sir. Have you news of General Stuart? I fear that he is riding around the Union army again, in defiance of my orders.

(XXXlubeee7 has left the chat)

(ScreenName2 has left the chat)

RELee: Ah, I see Mary is calling. I must leave you, gentlemen. Remember, duty is the sublimest word in our language.

Finally I became discouraged and stopped going in. What was the point? If they were just going to talk about sexy mud wrestling, I had nothing to contribute.

My love life was rather quiet. I knew sex had something to do with torpedo crackers and Christmas and that if you had it you might get gonorrhea like A. P. Hill. But if you wanted a hobby that would introduce you to large crops of good-looking men, sitting alone with a mound of Civil War books was not really the best choice.

In the books themselves it was hard to find good-looking men who were not lying in the middle of a ditch with a bayonet protruding from their vital regions. Of course, Robert E. Lee stood head and shoulders over most men in these books—literally. He was five foot eleven. His West Point classmates called him "the Marble Model." Yeah they did, I thought, gazing rapt at the picture of him in my locker. He also had size four and a half shoes, which worried me a little, but I had heard that this correlation was an urban legend anyway. Besides, it was unlikely that we were ever going to consummate this union. I wasn't going to be a *home wrecker*.

I mean, it was all very well, in theory, to feel a deep passion for a guy like Robert with nice wavy hair, good posture, and a keen grasp of nineteenth-century military strategy. But this was a married man! He had six lovely children: Custis, Fitzhugh, Rooney, Robbie, Anne, and Agnes, who was afflicted with neuralgia. And his wife, Mary Custis Lee, had been a real trouper. According to the guide at Arlington House, she was a big believer in hygiene, back in an era when everyone else still thought the best way to keep you disinfected was to pack your wounds with salt and mutter runes at you. This was why all her children had been born so healthy. Did I really want to ask Robert E. Lee to betray his values by cheating on his wife? Who did I think I was?

I can attest that Not Being a Historical Homewrecker was a sincere concern because I recently found a scene I wrote at a sleepover in sixth or seventh grade when my friends asked me to describe my crush. It ran as follows:

> *Lee leaned against the door panel, waiting, waiting. He was waiting for her, his visitor from the future. He had staked much on this, her theory of time, that nothing they did would affect him, but was still nervous.*
>
> *A knock —she was there.*
>
> *"Alexandra!" he exclaimed. She ran to him, entered his arms, and she felt his strength. She pulled back.*
>
> *"Let's go in," she said. They turned to enter, but Lee stopped her gently and leaned toward her, his arms weaving around her slight waist. "I love you," he murmured, and they kissed on the lips, a long slow kiss that was just long enough for him to use his hands.*

This was the first, if not the most embarrassing, of my Civil War writings. I heard Faulkner wrote about the Civil War, so I slogged through *Absalom, Absalom!* and *The Sound and the Fury*. Afterward, everything I wrote consisted of thick clusters of overwrought adjectives and slightly dazed nouns huddled together without commas and erratically italicized, with the occasional pronoun wandering the lines between them trying to figure out whom it belonged to. This influence culminated in a hideous four-hundred-page tangle of a novel that I called *The Sisters of Mountingbrook*, about two neighbor families in the Old South, one of which had a plucky pair of daughters who attended all-girls' schools and learned self-sufficiency, the other of which had two sons, one of whom was deeply insecure about his masculinity because he had fallen in love with his college roommate while they gazed out the window discussing states' rights. Once, I forced it on a houseguest. "Wow," she said. "This had so many more words than I was expecting."

But it wasn't like I could actually make my way back to the Civil War era and do anything about all these feelings, could I?

Then I learned about reenactment.

When I first got invited to go reenacting, I was ecstatic. It was like I had gotten a golden ticket, except instead of going to a giant, sprawling chocolate factory full of every wonder a child's imagination could conjure, I got to go to a gross muddy field full of bearded men with bayonets who wanted a do-over for the Civil War.

In general, the people who show up in droves with bayonets and rifles and authentic canteens in hand are not the people who think the war went right the first time. Which is why someone at every Civil War reenactment looks out over the field and jokes, "How on earth did the Union win when they were so hopelessly outnumbered?"

In fact, the most satisfying reenactment I ever attended was at a little town that did the battle twice, once as a Union victory and once as a Confederate, so that everyone would leave happy. If only the people running the real war had been so considerate.

The man who had extended the invitation was Mr. D, the history teacher at the all-boys' school across the way. He had a beard and was part of a historical Southern rock band called Johnny Reb and the Lost Cause. We listened to their CD, *Sabers and Roses*, as we bumped along toward the reenactment in Mr. D's large white van full of authentic Confederate gear and camping equipment.

Johnny Reb and the Lost Cause played historical, guitar-driven rock whose target audience was Confederate cavalry generals. On their Web site the slogan reads, "It ain't over—it's just the longest cease-fire in history."

Mr. D's major contribution to the CD was an impassioned vocal on "Maryland, My Maryland," not just the first verse, but all the grimy old verses about how Maryland hoped to join the Confederacy and how it violently hated Abraham Lincoln. "The despot's heel is on thy shore," he sang. "Maryland, my Maryland. His torch is at thy temple door. Maryland, my Maryland. Avenge the patriotic gore that flecked the streets of Baltimore and be the battle queen of yore, Maryland my Maryland."

They also covered "Brown Sugar."

Mr. D's whole family came along on the trip—his son as a drummer boy, his daughter as a camp follower. She walked around barefoot and cooked us breakfast over the campfire.

And—wonder of wonders—there was a boy my age.

His name was Winfield. He was shorter than I was, with blond hair. Dressed as a Union messenger boy, he was striking, and we took to each other at once.

He wasn't dead or from 1830, but I was willing to overlook these deficiencies because he looked like Haley Joel Osment. He had almond eyes, which is something I have always wanted to be able to write in a sentence describing a real human being. Now I just need to meet someone with "bedroom eyes" or "roseleaf lips" and I will be all set to go.

We were sitting by the campfire one night under the pines, watching the flames die, poking with a stick at the glass bottle someone had allowed to fall in among the piled logs. Over at the bandstand, music started up. There was a dance. Fiddle tunes wafted over to us as the light leached slowly out of the sky and the fireflies sparked to life in the pine trees.

I smiled at Winfield in what I thought was a winning manner and flexed my personality sensually. Given that I was wearing a man's full Civil War uniform, white shirt tucked into giant baggy pants with suspenders and a cap covering my hair, I had to rely a lot more on my personality and a lot less on my raw physical magnetism than usual. I fidgeted with my suspenders. The pants were much too large for me. They hung baggily off my hips. Even under the hat you could tell I was a girl. My growth spurt had showed up early and decisively, like Buford's cavalry at Gettysburg. I was wearing a training bra by fifth grade, and I got to stand at the back of all the class photos. By middle school we had begun to sort our heights out, unlike the boys who were just getting the uneven growth spurts that made them look like they came from different breeds— clumps of dachshunds standing between gangly greyhounds and the occasional malamute, yet all technically classed under the heading "dog."

But I wasn't thinking about that. I was lost in Winfield's eyes, like certain parts of the Army of Northern Virginia had been lost during critical portions of the Battle of the Wilderness.

"Let's go check out the dance," Winfield suggested.

I acquiesced.

I began to feel the kind of nervous, electric excitement that people liken to butterflies taking off and landing and beating around your stomach. I felt the way cannons surely felt when you had packed them with powder and canister according to specifications and a man was standing next to them holding the string that would ignite the fuse.

I felt the way Atlanta felt after Sherman got through with it, by which I mean "my entire body was on fire," not "deeply resentful of all Northerners now and forever and hey whoops there go all my landmarks."

I felt the way a torpedo cracker probably felt right before Christmas morning, if you had to put a fine point on it.

We neared the bandstand, talking of this and that. The moon was up. Damn, I thought, glancing up at it. I began to see what all those poets had been getting at.

Maybe we would dance.

No, that was stupid. Dancing was stupid. At dances, I was always the person who stood flush against the clammy auditorium wall shouting what I took to be insightful remarks over the blasts of *NSYNC. ("GETTYSBURG WAS LONGSTREET'S FAULT!" "Who?" "LONGSTREET!") I couldn't dance. I especially couldn't Virginia Reel. It looked intricate and impossible, like knitting but with humans.

"You don't want to *dance*, do you?" Winfield said. He said the word like it was something unpleasant you had to pick up with tweezers.

"No!" I said. "No, sir. No, thank you."

The music continued to waft up from the bandstand. The dancers completed their reel and began to drift to and fro in the moonlight, couples dotting the grass, their shadows mingling. A firefly flickered on and off.

We stopped under a tree, and as we talked I became aware that we were gradually moving closer, like the Union and Confederate armies converging on Gettysburg in June of 1863, clumsily and without the usual cavalry reconnaissance.

"Alexandra," Winfield said. He leaned toward me.

"Yes?" I leaned in as well, making certain that my feet were pointing toward him. I had read that pointing your feet toward someone was a sign of interest. The moonlight caught on his upturned face. This is how it's going to go, I thought. This is how it's going to go! Was this, I wondered, how General Pickett felt at the start of his fateful two-mile walk? A little nervous, sure, but at least confident that his hair looked good.*

He leaned closer. I leaned closer.

"What do you think about world politics?" he asked.

"Ahmrrgh," I managed, swallowing. I began the long lean backward. No, *that* was how General Pickett felt.

The battle itself was uneventful. Marching and more marching through buggy dry grass with an authentic nineteenth-century fabric-covered canteen clanking against your thigh. Plenty of time to ponder exactly what had gone wrong.

For me the essence of reenacting is those moments when things could have gone differently. If the troops had just swept over the crest of the hill. If. If. If only Ewell had moved. If only I had moved. If only someone had moved.

But no one did, and that was just the way it went.

The funny thing about this embarrassing piece of my past is that it coincides with an embarrassing piece of *America's* past—that ill-advised fixation with the Lost Cause, the One That Got Away, historically speaking, the abusive ex who suddenly became the sum of his politest moments and most dashing cavalry maneuvers because you didn't actually have to live with him.

Winfield was just the first in what would be a long series of romantic anticlimaxes; I'd reach what George W. Bush in his memoir calls a Decision Point, and—nothing.

"You're intimidating," my mother reassured me. "I think guys find you intimidating." She made me sound like a heavily fortified

---

* His hair never looked that good, to be completely honest. You know who had good hair? Custer.

position with lots of Napoleon cannons peering over my battlements. Like Vicksburg, I thought. Of course even Vicksburg had fallen eventually. I just needed to wait for Union troops to blockade my harbor as part of the Anaconda Plan.

Anaconda Plan. That sounded like it could be a way in. "Hey," you could say to a guy, "is that your Anaconda plan or are you just happy to see me?" This was a lot better than the other Civil War–related pickup lines I had come up with. ("Hey, are you the fire that killed General Stonewall Jackson? Because you seem friendly!" "He's a total John Brown—crazy, bearded, but definitely hung.")

With time, the passion faded. Every so often a trapping of my former life would flare up unexpectedly, like an appendix.

"Don't send your college application from THAT e-mail address," my mother said, as I fired up RELee.

"Why not?" I asked.

She gave me a look. "They'll think you're some kind of horrible racist."

"I'm not!" I said. "And Robert E. Lee wasn—"

She gave me another look.

"Oh my God," I said. "You're right."

I got a new e-mail address. Robert E. Lee faded back into the past, in my life if not in our nation's history.

I went to college, made new friends. We were all grown-up, we assured one another. Not like then.

"I had *such* embarrassing celebrity crushes in middle school," my new friends said.

"Oh yeah," I said. "We've all been there."

God, that first infatuation is embarrassing. Even the ones that *aren't* doomed from the start.

It's all so much worse now, with the Internet there. The Internet is like having an elephant for a drinking buddy. It knows all your most mortifying secrets—and it *never forgets*. You know that somewhere out there, always, lumbering along the savanna, is a record of every embarrassing thing you have ever done or thought, unless you've had the presence of mind to mortify yourself exclusively in longhand.

But you never think like that at the time. This is your first love. You *have* to carve it into your screen names and tattoo it on your Tumblr. You don't even care how it looks.

When you love it, you love it so much that all you can see are the bright spots. You love it so much because you have filled it up with little pieces of yourself, all the brightest bits, because that is what love means, that first, that most shocking, that most unrequited love—when you first find yourself in someone else, or think you do.

This is the thing that comes burning out of you, this is the thing you have to talk about again and again and again, it is the song you never tire of playing, the count creeping up into the thousands of thousands, the page you keep turning back to read over again.

But anything you loved, however intensely, becomes mortifying the moment you cease to love it. That is love's curse and power— you miss all the parts that drive everyone else bonkers. Then one day it's over and you notice: He gurgles when he talks. She's not as funny as you thought. He's a Confederate general.

For example.

Trivial Pursuit

One of these days, I'm going to kill Alex Trebek.

I mean it.

Jeopardy! has a rule that prevents you from returning as a contestant so long as Trebek remains the host.

I don't know exactly how I'm going to do it. But one morning he's going to wake up and there I'll be, perched over him. Looming. Ominous. "This is FINAL Jeopardy!" I will say.

"Put the knife down," he'll say.

"No!" I'll bellow. "In the form of a question!"

"Would you kindly put the knife down?"

"Less supercilious," I will hiss.

This will go on for some time. I want to make him suffer.

It's not that I'm bitter. Not exactly.

But let me start at the beginning.

Once, I was on *Jeopardy!*

The process for getting on *Jeopardy!* is simple but heavy on the nail-biting. First, you take an online test. Then you wait. Then, if you pass, and you're lucky, you get invited to audition.

I was lucky. The e-mail told me to show up at the St. Regis hotel, a swank-ish spot in downtown DC. The auditions took place inside a conference room deep in the windowless bowels of the hotel. (If I have learned one thing in my comparatively brief time on Earth it is that every conference room in every hotel in the world looks completely identical. The hotels can be on opposite ends of the earth, but the second you walk through the conference room doors, you are at the same folding table (circular or rectangular) on the same carpet under the same lights on the same metal chairs staring at the same PowerPoint, and someone is offering you the same ice water in the same squat goblet that looks like a wineglass that let itself go.) In this particular conference room, the tables were rectangular and arranged in rows so we could take a test at them.

Everyone else there was an actual adult and looked much more nervous than I felt. I had the total unshakable confidence of someone with absolutely no idea of what she was getting into. (There is a microscopically thin line between being unintimidated by anything you encounter and not having stopped to Google it first.)

The audition consists of another written test and a live practice round of play, during which they determine if you have enough personality to be on television. I didn't know exactly how much personality they wanted. Given that you frequently see people on air with all the vigor and charm of cakes that have been left out in the rain, I wondered what the bar was.

They asked each of us the same two questions: What are your hobbies, and what would you do with the prize money.

The man ahead of me was middle-aged, with receding hair.

"What are your hobbies?" they asked.

"I collect kidney stones," he informed them.

"Ah," they said. "And, uh, what—what would you do with the prize money?"

"If I won, I would use the money to pay for a lysterectomy on my ninth kidney stone, which I postponed to come here to audition."

Compared to him, I seemed completely ready for television.

"I am a *Star Wars* buff," I told them. "And I play the accordion and I do stand-up, and if I won I would probably waste the money on one of those life-size breathing statues of Darth Vader."

This was true. I had seen it at the Sharper Image in the mall, and I had fallen for it instantly. It was far out of my price range, but that didn't stop me from salivating in its general direction as I waited for them to kick me off the free massage chairs.

"Or college," I added, a bit lamely.

It didn't matter. They called me a few months later and informed me that I was on.

I would like to say that I spent the months between getting the call and my taping date intensely preparing.

But why study? As a trivia buff, my *entire life* was preparation for my appearance on *Jeopardy!*

A love of trivia is not something you decide to pursue. Miscellanea simply cling to you like burrs. You find them in your socks after long walks. You wander into bookstores and come out hours later with stray facts clutching at your elbow.

My mind is a disaster zone full of a great mess of facts. I know when Oscar Wilde was born (October 16, 1854) and when he died (November 30, 1900) and what he allegedly had to say about it ("Either the wallpaper goes, or I do.") I know that the working title of *Gone With The Wind* was *Tote the Weary Load*. I know that Ernest Hemingway's penis was larger than F. Scott Fitzgerald's, at least according to Ernest Hemingway. I know that the painter James Whistler failed out of West Point because he began his final examination with the words "Silicon is a gas." I can tell you that there was a guy named Colonel Jasper who distinguished himself in the defense of Fort Moultrie on June 28, 1776, at the Battle of Sullivan's Island, although I mistrust this fact because I heard it from a place mat.

A better way of putting this might be that I'm a fact-hoarder. If there were some sort of physical external manifestation of all the stray quotations and bizarre bits of trivia that go banging around my memory, my family would be staging an intervention. They would come to the house with a big bin and several specialists from cable.

"You don't really need to know anything about Rutherford B. Hayes' wife," they would say reasonably, loading that fact into a garbage bag.

"They called her Lemonade Lucy!" I would yell, clinging to it. "She was a teetotaler who served nonalcoholic drinks at White House functions!"

To love trivia is to be a hoarder. "You never know when this might come in handy," we insist, holding up the factual equivalent of a dead cat impaled on a plastic fork. "See? Fuliginous. It's a word meaning 'sooty.'"

Maybe our quality of life would be higher if we didn't have to step around these facts on our way out in the evenings. But in the meantime, we can go on *Jeopardy!* That's the golden carrot shining at the end of the tunnel, to mix some metaphors into a nice fine hash.

Some people say you can't study for *Jeopardy!* If you don't already know a given piece of information, there is absolutely no way you will know it on the instinctual level that's required in order to succeed on the show. Your brain will clank around trying to remember Edgar Allan Poe's minor works and eventually produce a few names that turn out to be Lifetime movies, and meanwhile everyone else will have buzzed in.

Other people say that you should, in fact, study. I split the difference by not studying and feeling vaguely guilty about it.

I tried, a couple of times, to restore my instinctual familiarity with broad general topics. I went to the grocery store and wandered through the produce aisle, carefully reading the names of all the brands of apple. But I knew what my true blind spot was. Sports.

Sports were my Achilles' heel. I was the captain of my school's trivia team and every time we showed up at a tournament and the category turned to sports, we sighed and sagged into our seats. The only thing I knew about sports was that something existed called the Dick Butkus Award. I was not sure what it was for. "For most unintentionally homoerotic sports moment of the year?" I suggested. "For being the tightest end?"

After the sixth or seventh repetition this remark ceased to amuse.

It's not that I don't know sports because I'm a girl. I don't know sports AND I'm a girl. I know about plenty of Historically Male subjects. Give me a napkin and a pencil and I can reconstruct the Battle of Gettysburg for you, with fishhooks of troop placements and side cavalry movements and everything. Sports just never sang to me, except for one time when I saw a musical about baseball. But none of the information in *Damn Yankees!* was current. The Senators no longer existed, and "sell your soul to Satan in song and then sort of stand there during a big dance sequence" is not actually how you get to the World Series.

It wasn't that I had no sports experience. I'd played volleyball. Well, "played" was strong. I'd provided some very strong support from the bench. "Spike!" I would yell. "Did we just complete the Transcontinental Railroad? Because that was a GOLDEN SPIKE!"

"Stop," our coach said.

"That serve must be World War I pilot Manfred von Richthofen! Because it was an ACE!"

"Please stop."

But they never asked about volleyball, anyway.

Sports, as far as I could tell, were just a way to feel really manly while wearing colorful socks.

Even after studying several books with names like Mad Dog Lists the Most Athletic Sport Truths, the most I could say about baseball was that you could get up during a game to go get snacks and then run into someone you hadn't seen in a long time, talk to him, hit it off, share your hopes and dreams, decide to start a life together, walk down the aisle after a reasonable courtship, give birth to a son, watch that son grow into a man you could be proud of, and then go back to your seat and nothing would have changed. Possibly someone would have one or two more balls. Football I had no grip on at all. You could tell me almost anything about it and I would believe you. "That's a first down," you could say, "and he got that because of nepotism." "Sure," I would say.

Soccer was like that, but the people who got angry about it were thinner.

That was as far as my studies went.

The same "They" who said that you could not study for *Jeopardy!* also said that it all came down to buzzer technique. Corner a disgruntled *Jeopardy!* loser in a bar and he will maintain that he knew all the answers, he just couldn't get the dang buzzer to work the way Ken Jennings did. *Jeopardy!* contestants have penned numerous books on this subject, with titles like *Buzzer Zen* and *You Know the Buzzer, but Does the Buzzer Know You?* and *What Ken Knew.* For the next few months, I stood in front of the television watching *Jeopardy!* and practicing with a retractable pen. Click-click. Click-click-click-click-click. It was like having an angry cricket in the room.

The trick was that Trebek's contract mandated that he got to finish reading the question before anyone buzzed in. If you buzzed in before he stopped talking, your buzzer locked for several critical fractions of a second. *Buzzer Zen* said you needed those seconds.

I knew this would be a problem. I'd been on a local quiz show called *It's Academic* where my strategy was to buzz in as early as I possibly could, as soon as I had a vague inkling of what the question might be. Sometimes this worked. More often, it did not. But it was my only weapon.

I had appeared on the show yearly ever since I was a freshman, but the teetering elderly host, Mac McGarry, who looked like an amiable rectangle, still had difficulty pronouncing my name. "Pea-try," I reminded him. "Like a vegetable that's making an effort."

"Ah," he said.

I wondered how Trebek would like that mnemonic.

My biggest fear was that I would show up at the studio in California and the Kidney Stone guy from auditions would be there too, with a little jar. "I brought my lucky one," he would whisper.

But when I got there, there was no one carrying a kidney stone. Openly, anyway.

All the contestants for the week are directed to the same hotel in Culver City. It was like summer camp, if your summer camp was full of people who muttered threatening facts at you in the elevator. ("Henry VIII beheaded both his second and fifth wives.")

The actual day of the taping dawned bright and clear. All the *Jeopardy!* contestants boarded a very tense shuttle to ride to the taping and back. It was like being in one of those tumbrels that carted people to the guillotine during the French Revolution, except you had to ride back with them afterward.

On the shuttle with me and my mother (who had come along for the ride) was a one-armed man who had booked an entire week's stay in LA on the assumption that he would win. "I don't want to have the hassle of travel," he explained.

My mother, on the safer assumption that I would not win—or, at least, that I certainly would win no more games than could be taped in a day—had bought us flights back for that same weekend.

The ride to the taping offered the nerdiest one-upmanship I had ever heard in my life. Obviously I don't remember any of the dialogue exactly (even Thucydides said that the best you could do was come up with words that seemed appropriate to the occasion) but here is my general sense of how it went.

Person A: I've been studying types of trees.

Person B: Sure, types of trees. Larch. Poplar. Chestnut.

Person A: Maple.

Person B: Willow.

Person A: *Sophora japonica.*

Person B: Of course. That's basic. Mistletoe.

Person C: (who has been waiting for this chance) Isn't that more of an EPIPHYTE?

Person D: (hastily) Frankly I think we're better served by not studying. I've been focusing on my buzzer Zen.

Person E: Absolutely.

Person D: (unable to stop himself) Although I did look over all the flags of all the countries past and present and fictional and dreamed-of and certain insignias floated but not approved by the UN.

Person F: And don't forget ESPERANTO!

Person C: (says something in Esperanto, a nonexistent language that some guy made up in the 1880s)

Person F: (says something obscene and hurtful in Esperanto, to which Person C has no idea how to respond)

Person G, who has said nothing up to this point and is desperate to make his mark: (starts speaking Elvish)

(Everyone turns to glower at him.)

Person A: That's not Esperanto.

Person B: That's *Elvish*.

Person C: This isn't *Who Wants to Be a Millionaire!*

(Dismissive laughter)

Person G: (recedes from the conversation in shame, pretending to be suddenly very interested in something that is going on outside the window)

Me: So how about this LA weather, huh?

Person A: I was on *Who Wants to Be a Millionaire*, but I thought the caliber of question was frankly beneath me.

Person B: Oh, absolutely.

Person C: I can't wait to meet Trebek.

Person D: I miss the mustache.

Person C: Me too.

Person E: I wonder if he'll sign my picture.

Person F: (hushed, reverent) I hear he hates autographs.

Person A: (fervently) I hear he takes all the contestant quizzes and the year he doesn't pass it he's going to quit.

Person B: I hear he sleeps in a golden box like a pharaoh and is made of magic.

Person D: When I was married we walked down the aisle to the *Jeopardy!* theme song and we named all our pets after Potent Potables and my son's name is Portmanteau and sometimes Trebek comes to me in dreams and reads me facts from the future.

Person G: (grimly, with some satisfaction) I know everything there is to know about *sports!*

(Awkward hush)

The shuttle finally arrived at the studios. We showed our IDs to the guard and walked inside, to makeup and the waiting room.

There, we ate fruit from a tray, marshaling our favorite facts around us for comfort ("The World War I poet Wilfred Owen loved pineapple chunks," I murmured to myself, as I loaded my plate with them) and listening to the instructions from Maggie, a hoarse-voiced, good-humored lady who was tasked with herding us from place to place.

In that room was the kind of frenzied camaraderie that I assume gladiators felt before rushing out to the arena. In a moment, we would be at one another's metaphorical throats. But right now, we were all brothers in useless trivia. Overcome by nerd relief at being in a roomful of others of our kind for once, we thought it might be a good idea if we sang together, though I can't remember what the song was. I want to say it was "The Elements" song by Tom Lehrer ("antimony, arsenic, aluminum, selenium"). But it might just have been "One of These Things (Is Not Like the Others)." Maggie seemed used to the response. It was like if you were to go out into the wild and round up a strange beast that had believed all its kin extinct. "Oh my God!" we exclaimed. "You mean other people like me exist, out there, in the world?" "Yup," they said. "And now, you must destroy one another, on television." "Okay."

They let us practice with the buzzer, but not for long. Then we sat down in the audience to watch to see if our names would be called to compete. The studio was freezing. Well, not quite freezing. It was like sitting in a meat locker. If I were a beer, I would have been very comfortable. Alex Trebek regaled the audience with corny jokes and the audience laughed hysterically just so they could move and warm themselves. "I went into the closet to get a suit," he said, "and then I came out, out of the closet. Ha-HA!"

"Wahaahahaha," we all laughed, nervously.

Then ensued several hours of waiting as they taped episodes with players who were not me, otherwise known as The Part of the Day Where Every Fact You Have Ever Learned Slowly Seeps out of Your Body. As I sat in the audience, I was suddenly struck by the realization that I knew nothing. "The beginning of wisdom is the knowledge of your own ignorance," I muttered reassuringly. "As— what's his name said." I began panicking.

Finally my turn came, after a round hinging on English Castles, during which I realized that "English Castles" was one of the numerous areas of knowledge that had slowly melted out of my brain. I was beginning to have sincere doubts about my own name by the time they called it.

Breathing a sigh of relief that at least I had been spared the castles category, I stepped onto the stage. The stage of *Jeopardy!* looks like a spaceship designed in the 1980s.

Most people who compete on *Jeopardy!* are, if not in the prime of life, at least in the twenties or thirties of life. They have been informed that the studio is cold, and they are dressed accordingly in sensible dark suits.

I was none of those things. I was eighteen, wearing a pink sweater set that my mother had selected. My mother had the awkward habit of picking clothes and giving advice that was several years ahead of my stage in life. At fourteen, I already owned numerous Talbots pantsuits, and she was always advising me not to sign prenups.

Things got off to an optimistic start. The first category that greeted my eye was something called "Math Jokes." It is no exaggeration to say that I had been preparing my entire life for this.

"What is the circumference of a pumpkin divided by its diameter?" "Pi," I shouted. "Pumpkin Pi," Trebek corrected. "That's the joke."

We tore through logarithms (why are lumberjacks such good dancers?) and what the chicken crossed to get to the same side (a Mobius strip) and the square root of 4 b squared (2 B, or Not (negative) 2 B).

I was ahead at the commercial break.

But then the dark times came.

One of the categories was "Cars." I had no idea how many car companies there were. For the better part of my childhood, my family drove a 1979 Chevy Zephyr with no air-conditioning and a broken speedometer, and I thought that this state of things was typical. One day, we got pulled over. "How fast were you going?" the cop asked. My father looked gravely at the broken speedometer. "Zero miles per hour," he said. The cop glanced at the car. "If that's all you're making," he said, "I'll let you off with a warning." Although this was a vivid and cherished memory of my youth, it offered no clues for this category.

"The first logo of this sporty Italian car maker included the Visconti serpent, a Milanese symbol," Trebek read. I had no idea. (It's Alfa Romeo.)

"'The relentless pursuit of perfection' is the goal of this luxury automaker," he tried.

"What is a Jaguar?" I suggested. The jaguar seemed like he was pursuing something or other with ruthlessness. (Nope, Lexus.)

I was still leading when we finished the Jeopardy! round, but only by a hair. And not a big hair.

There was a brief lull, during which Trebek asked us questions intended to draw out our personalities. I have no idea what I said. I remember opening my mouth. I remember closing it again after nearly a minute had passed. What emerged in the interim is an utter blank to me, as it was at the time. I think I said something about squirrels and camaraderie.

The Double Jeopardy! round offered such arcana as "Produce" and "Famous Duets."

I remembered my time in the produce aisle. I tried to rifle through my recollections. There had been—apples there. And—also—potatoes. Or maybe those had been more apples. I fumbled blindly through the aisles of memory, overturning things.

My competition—Sara, a veterinary assistant from Connecticut, and Nick, a paralegal—were perking right up.

Paralegal Nick was all over the vegetables. He apparently had spent the better part of his life surrounded by loving, supportive produce. He knew all the varieties of apple. He identified lettuce correctly. When he found a Daily Double in the produce lane, he added two thousand dollars with ease. Sara, who had won the previous two games, chimed in with the French for green beans.

When Double Jeopardy! concluded I was several ells behind.

The other two were tied.

This is the point when the people who post often in *Jeopardy!* on-line forums determined that I made the Worst Final Jeopardy! wager of all time.

In retrospect, it's obvious. When the players ahead of you are tied, you know that they are forced to bet everything they have, and you should just sit back and bid nothing and hope they get it wrong.

A man on the forum was so angered by my wager, in fact, that he Googled me and my entire family and posted lengthy, erratically capitalized screeds about what fools we were and how we had polluted the Great Game. ("THESE PEOPLE ARE RUINING THE COUNTRY WITH THEIR IDIOICY AND I AM SICK OF IT.") Shortly thereafter, he suffered a bicycle accident. He attributed it to karma and posted an apology. This was the first and last time that a stranger has apologized to me on the Internet, and in some ways it is more miraculous than my appearing on *Jeopardy!* in the first place.

He was right about the wager, though.

They say that in high-stress situations like war and skydiving and landing planes in blinding snowstorms, there comes a point when your training just kicks in. "Ah," you say, "just like training," and you activate the chute, or start artificially respirating your companion under the foil blanket, or throw the plane into a splendid barrel roll. If only I'd been in a profession, "my training" might have "kicked in" at this critical juncture.

Instead, what kicked in was the sense that "In The News 2006" was a Final Jeopardy! category at which I was bound to excel. "I'm not betting on them," I thought, with some totally misplaced satisfaction. "I'm betting on me!"

I am glad I have never tried skydiving.

To this day, I maintain that my answer was right, if not specific enough.

"Justice Peter Smith embedded a secret code into a 2006 ruling that said this author hadn't violated a copyright," Trebek read.

I blanked. I had just read an article on this very subject. I could visualize the article. I could see those tormenting black words on the page. I could see everything except who the article was about.

"Who is Dan Brown?" wrote my competitors.

"Who is that dude?" I wrote. This is technically correct, if lacking in detail.

You may know that during Final Jeopardy!, after that insanely catchy "thinking music" plays, the camera pans over you to show how satisfied you feel with your answer. Sarah and Nick exuded calm and confidence. I made the kind of face that you generally make when you accidentally walk in on your grandparents having adventurous sex.

In the end, I wound up with two thousand dollars, which just about covered the plane and the hotel.

My mother and I slunk away soon afterward.

Now what do I do with the rest of my life?

When you are a tall kid, they tell you to play basketball. When you hit a certain weight, people suggest that you look into sumo wrestling. When you hit a certain level of saturation in facts—well, why don't you go on *Jeopardy!*?

Now that door's closed.

Everyone else from that tumbrel is struggling alike. Sure, we make do. Bars have trivia nights. We can live off sliders and wings for the rest of our days. But there is more to life than sliders and wings, surely! What about glory? What about usefulness?

Ever since the advent of Google, our prowess has been on the wane.

I interviewed Ken Jennings for a story after he competed with the IBM supercomputer Watson and he was sympathetic. "Trivia geeks are not the public resource they used to be," he admitted.

We drift listlessly around the watercoolers and dinner tables where we once held sway. Once, if you needed to know who Tom Hanks' costars were in *A League of Their Own*, you called us. Now—any fool with IMDb and an iPhone can beat us to the punch.

Woody Allen summed up our predicament nicely. "My father worked for the same firm for twelve years. They fired him and replaced him with a tiny gadget that does everything my father does, only much better. The depressing thing is my mother ran out and bought one."

Even as I type this, my iPhone hums in my pocket, capable of Googling almost anything just as fast as I can remember it.

The world is increasingly hostile to trivia. We require artificial environments to practice our skill: tournaments in pubs where everyone has to turn off his phone, game shows. The regular air does not support us. You know your skill is really valuable if, in order to practice it, everyone has to pretend that you are living in a different year without full use of modern technology. It's like sewing clothes from scratch or healing people by letting out their bad humors. Maybe it works, but there's a more efficient way.

I can't help feeling a little like an appendix—both in the sense of that chunk at the end of a book that is full of unwanted information, and the useless body part that sometimes flares up and kills a person for no reason. Probably frustration.

It's not just that my friends don't need me and that Watson can take me on. I don't need myself either. "Memory, my dear," says a character in *The Importance of Being Earnest*, "is the diary we all carry about with us." (I think that's what she says. I'll have to Google it, to be sure.) If I want to know where I have been, doing what, with whom, my data can tell me. "Where were you last night?" an officer will ask. "Wait," I'll say. "Let me check my GChat logs."

We store things on the outside that we used to store on the inside. Not just facts, but moments, memories.

As I write this, I'm struck by how little attention I have paid to my own life. I remember fewer of the details of this excursion than names of fifteenth-century explorers.

There is a point in the Sherlock Holmes books when Sherlock asks Watson (human Watson, not IBM Watson) how many stairs are in their apartment and Watson has to confess he has never counted. Upon reading that I went home and counted the stairs. There were nineteen. This piece of knowledge has never come in handy. But I know how Watson felt.

It's not that I don't notice things. I notice all kinds of things. I have an uncanny and frankly irritating memory for any actor who has ever appeared in anything ever, particularly if I have not seen the film in question. But the things I want most to remember—the isolated moments you know are Important—go sliding away. Graduations and weddings and funerals blur.

Memories committed to paper perish like insects pinned to cards. The moment writhes a little on the pen and that is it. I wish I could tell you what we sang before the game and what I said to Alex, and what-all happened, with precision, but I've given you all the shreds I have. Instead I can tell you about Ethelred the Unready and list all the characters in *Othello*.

I suppose the strange selectivity of memory is half its charm. Our lives are burning houses, and we come running out with whatever we can carry.

Sometimes I think the reason I don't remember more about my *Jeopardy!* experience is that I know I could find it if I had to. There's a tape somewhere. There's an online archive of all games and players.

If I want to know exactly what questions were asked, I have only to Google it. It's not like Ancient Greece, where if you wanted to know what happened to Achilles at the end of the Trojan War, your bard had to dredge it up from memory.

Most of my memories these days are like that—stashed on the outside, strewn carelessly in texts and GChats. "I can always search the archive," I murmur. "It's out there if I ever care to look for it." But you know what happens the moment you say "I'm going to put this somewhere special, where I'll remember it." You might as well say, "I'm never going to see this again."

But when you can take everything with you, you're no longer forced to choose the things you cannot leave behind. You no longer have to carry anything with you, at all.

In theory this was the point of all this wonderful new technology: to store everything externally and free our minds to think great thoughts. Throw a stone in a high school or university and you hit someone who is pleased to say that We Have Moved Away from Rote Memorization of Facts Toward Frolicking Freely in the Fields of Pure Thought. You don't have to learn what to think. You just have to learn How to Think. Then you will be prepared in the unlikely event that you ever run across a fact.

Maybe it's time to let go, embrace the free mental space.

Been on *Jeopardy!* Done that. Better clean house and approach the future with an open mind. Maybe trivia is over and I need to accept it.

But that's the trouble with trivia. You can't get rid of it. It chooses you, not the other way around. You think I really want to know the names of all these *Law & Order* guest stars? I'd much rather remember the song we sang, or any of a myriad of moments that count.

Instead, I get these odds and ends. I can't choose to remember the hundreds of ordinary wonderful days when nothing much happened, the faces that I saw every day that didn't change—it is only the moments that are out of the ordinary that stick their claws in, the nights spent in unfamiliar rooms, the jolt of a phone call with bad news that pulls you up gasping like a hook yanking you to the surface. Instead of saving the good parts, the ordinary warmth of days, I remember trivia. I have to go through my life constantly aware that starfish eat things with their anuses.

It seems unfair.

But maybe there's a point, after all.

Ken Jennings thinks there is. "Even when machines are doing more of our thinking and remembering for us, it'll be more useful to have the wealth of information," he said. "To make informed decisions about anything in life, you need to have knowledge. If you need a Google search, you're still at a disadvantage."

The trouble with only learning how to think is that without the necessary roughage of fact you wind up backing into your opinions. You don't start out with a healthy ballast of information and so you can assume that there is something optional about facts, that they can be produced or dredged up at a moment's notice and made to agree with you. You go hunting for facts that support your case. "Why is this good?" you Google. "Why is this bad?" You induce instead of deducing. Facts become a kind of parsley garnish to your premade opinion.

Life with them is a pain. But life without them? Unthinkable.

At least, that's what I tell myself.

You have to tell yourself something.

Once *Jeopardy!* is closed to you, a big life full of trivia night sliders and wings and nothing to do with your facts stretches out ahead. Losers can't appear on it again until the host is gone.

So these are my alternatives. Accept my increasing irrelevance in a world where trivia is something you entrust to IBM's Watson or your phone, where even the highest-level human beings can't hope to compete.

Or try to find a way back in.

And as long as the host lives, what can I hope to do?

That's why one of us has to go, Trebek.

It's nothing personal.

Grab Life by the Debutante Balls

"It's not really a debutante ball."

That was the first thing my grandmother said when she announced that I was going to have a debutante ball.

"Your mother had one. She knows. It's more of a nice family party, a sort of coming out into society."

"Okay" I said as I looked up from my Ancient Greek textbook. "I've always wanted to come out."

My mother and grandmother exchanged a nervous look. This, the look said, was what came of sending me to an all-girls' school. Our school motto was "Hey, a Few Years of Wondering Whether You Might Be Attracted to People of the Same Sex Is a Small Price to Pay for Confidence in Your Math Skills." (I am pretty confident in my math skills.)

"You'll need two male escorts," my grandmother said, moving on quickly. "They're going to need red sashes, and you'll have to wear a floor-length white gown for the Presentation of the Daughters. Or your aunt can arrange escorts for you. I've got her on the lookout for smart young men."

"Oh, good," I said. "That doesn't sound like a debutante ball at all."

"And gloves," my grandmother said. "You're going to need long white gloves."

I frowned back down at the Greek textbook. Truth be told, I had been waiting for this moment my whole life.

Everyone has one erroneous belief that gets him through the chilly February mornings of the soul. Some people think the Rapture's bound to strike at any moment. Then your neighbors who wouldn't hang out with you because you kept speaking in tongues will finally get what's coming to them! Then all your hours chanting psalms and waving palms and avoiding shellfish and sex and sexy shellfish will let you blend straight in with the heavenly throng. Other people get really into Survivalism, operating under the assumption that civilization is hanging by a fragile thread that is liable to snap at any moment, and that when it does, only the people who have spent hours camping in the dank woods and learning how to identify poisonous mushrooms and dress a deer carcass while fighting zombies with one arm tied behind their back will make it out alive.

I have no delusions about my ability to make it through a Rapture or apocalypse of any kind. In disaster movies, I am the person getting mowed down by killer hornets in the very first frame. Survive in the wild? I can barely survive in the grocery store. Until this week, I thought that dressing a deer carcass meant putting it in a little outfit. The only way I can tell if a mushroom is edible or not is: If it is in the woods, it will kill you, and if it is in a Trader Joe's in a little cardboard tub covered in plastic wrap, it is probably safe to eat. (This system would not hold up very well in a postapocalyptic wasteland.)

I know all this. My belief had nothing to do with that.

My sustaining conviction was that if I ever traveled back in time, I'd be cool.

I certainly wasn't cool in the present. I was sitting in my grand-parents' kitchen, teaching myself Ancient Greek over the Christmas break. At social gatherings with people my own age, I stuck out like a sore thumb in a gathering of cool fingers with an unlimited com-mand of pop culture. Crouched over a copy of *Jane Eyre*, I had missed all the basic cable moments that defined everyone else's childhoods. Clarissa had explained nothing to me. Why was it always Degrassi that they wanted to talk about, and never Admiral de Grasse, the French fleet commander around the Battle of Yorktown? While peo-ple around me started debating the plot twists on *The O.C.*, I left lunch early to sit by myself reading *Moby-Dick* in the vestibule.

The past was my consolation. I knew with every fiber of my be-ing that if I was ever seated at a dinner table next to Oscar Wilde, I'd be able to engage him in conversation for the whole evening. Or, heck, Dorothy Parker. I wasn't picky.

I just had to make it back there. My vision of this heaven looked something like the wall pattern in the café at Barnes & Noble, where D. H. Lawrence is saying something to Thomas Hardy while James Joyce knocks knees with Virginia Woolf. Depending on time pe-riod, the exact combination varied. 1865 would give me Victor Hugo and Lewis Carroll and Charles Dickens and Hans Christian Ander-sen, who'd once stayed at Dickens' house for a few weeks ("which seemed to the family ages," Dickens complained). Go back further, and I could grab a couch next to Plato and Alcibiades at the Sympo-sium. My Greek wasn't quite ready, but I bet I could pick up most of it from body language. Wherever it was, I'd sit down and, for once, be right at home.

Well, maybe not quite. The trouble with all my time travel dreams was that I was, well, female. Louis CK does a great bit about how impossible time traveling is if you're anything but a white man. He has a point. Land pre-1900, and you're bound to have a very tough time of it, losing your rights to land and property and the vote and even pants.

But—wasn't that a small price to pay for finally being with people who shared my base of reference?

So I became a time travel survivalist, prepping constantly for the moment when some benign anachronist would realize my distress and come spirit me away. After the house was dark, I lay awake under the covers reading my way through the collected works of Aristophanes, boning up on the Athenian politicians who had been the butts of fifth century BC jokes. (Get it together, Cleisthenes!) It wasn't homework, in the traditional sense. But I knew I had to do it anyway. I had to be ready.

Outside, on my grandmother's patio, my cousins were texting their girlfriends. How they had girlfriends already, I had no idea. We were barely into ninth grade. The ball was years away—not scheduled until college—and we clearly didn't need to find dates yet. What were they doing? Evidently their middle school experiences had been vastly different from mine.

I was still recovering from middle school. My reading had offered few insights on how to navigate it. Captain Ahab, for instance, went to zero middle school dances. I supposed I could share a few of the numerous fun facts that I had learned about whale sperm in chapter ninety-four, "A Squeeze of the Hand," but it was difficult to yell over 98 Degrees. Rudderless, I spent many a freighted hour in my bedroom pondering what I was going to wear. I didn't own a pair of jeans, and I knew you could get impregnated up a skirt by mistake if you danced too close (or something). Fortunately, I had a lot of loose-fitting khakis that had been treated with Scotchgard, so the building blocks of a winning outfit were there. What revealing tank top or halter top, I pondered, would I wear over my khakis?

The blue one with stripes? The red one with flowers on it? Should I wear a pencil behind my ear, as was my custom on school days, or omit it?

Finally I decided on something (usually a long-sleeved tie-dyed shirt) and pulled on my brown Merrell loafers, which added an extra inch to my height just in case any middle school boys were having doubts about not approaching me.

People tell you to "Leave room for Jesus" at these dances. To be safe, I gave Jesus the whole dance floor to himself, lurking in the corner as far away from the pounding strains of "Bye Bye Bye" as possible. If anyone was hardy enough to ask me to dance, I had prepared a series of talking points. "Gee, how 'bout this lighting! It's like a reptile tank in here!" "Sorry, whenever I attend a dance it is as though someone flips a switch in my head to 'boring'!" (I literally wrote this down in my diary at the time as a possible thing to say.)

Everyone else, it seemed, was going to a party afterward with People They Knew. There might be Alcohol there. Someone had even gotten a hotel room and it was going to be Crazy.

I got into the car with my mother and headed home to my books.

Let me pause and note that middle school is terrible. Middle school is when your friends on the softball team mysteriously decide to become your cold, distant acquaintances on the softball team and you spend your time squatting in left field feeling lonely and cold and wondering what you did wrong and tying the grass together into little grass knots. Middle school, in our case, was when we went from "An All-Girls' School with Uniforms So Everyone Looks the Same Even if You Suspect That Danielle Has Slightly Cooler Shoes" to "An All-Girls' School Without a Uniform Thereby Exposing the Fact That You Were Wearing Those Brown Men's Docksides Not by Obligation but Because You Genuinely Thought They Were a Quality Fashion Choice, and, If Given the Chance You Would Combine Them with Cargo Khakis. Also Sometimes You Wear Vests for No Reason, and Clearly the Abercrombie Crowd Was Correct in Excluding You."

If I could grab middle schoolers by the ear (hey, you, reading this book—are you anywhere near a middle schooler? If so, grab him or her by the ear for me! Though I take no legal responsibility!), I would tell them this. No one who enjoys middle school is a good person.

Hope for a better experience somewhere else in time was what kept me going. I consoled myself with the thought that, hey, if this were not 2002 but 1902, my dance card would have been bursting at the seams. The past was my equivalent of Hogwarts. It was the fantasy world where all my dreams came true, all my jokes landed, and I could wear a festive tie.

Such visions are always the solace of the uncool. The best way of getting excited about Paradise is to have the worst existence possible. This also means that your idea of Eternal Bliss can be something vague involving harp-playing and chanting in a robe, two activities that seem somewhat lacking after the invention of AC and cable. But if you're a medieval peasant whose life consists of carrying plague-infested rats from one dung heap to another, almost anything else sounds good!

And compared to middle school, carrying plague-infested rats from one dung heap to another sounded almost appealing. I knew smallpox was no picnic, garderobes would be gross, and I might die in childbirth, but if given the choice between middle school and the Middle Ages, I'd really have had to think it over.

In the meantime, I just had to prepare myself for all possible time jumps as best I could. That was why I was learning Greek.

I'd made some progress. My Ancient Greek was at the precise level where if someone dropped me back in time I would be able to converse for a few seconds, and then it would just be embarrassing. The only phrase I knew off the top of my head was "Go to Hell, a single, specific time!" so I doubted I could form many lasting friendships.

I frowned down at the exercise. The textbook's protagonist was an Athenian farmer named Dicaeopolis and he was sitting there on the receiving end of a strange verb.

I knew from studying French that the earliest chapters of a language textbook tended to have the most excitement. People in textbooks start off performing bold, dramatic actions and being very candid about their feelings and possessions. ("I am the king! I am strong!" "I am the queen! I am beautiful!" "You are happy!" "Yes, I am happy!" "We buy an ice cream in the park!" "Give me the big green book!")

Confrontations are rather elliptical because of everyone's limited vocabulary. Instead of telling Jean the Gardener that he is getting too close to the princess and he needs to back off, the villainous Corvax has to stride over menacingly and force him to count things.

Corvax: Jean!

Jean: Yes?

Corvax: Forks.

Jean: Forks?

Corvax: How many forks are there? Count them!

Jean: One, two, three, four, five.

Corvax: Plates. How many plates? Count them.

Jean: Two. Four. Six. Eight. Ten. Ten plates.

Corvax: How many cars are there?

Jean: Two. Four. Six. Eight. Eight cars.

Corvax: Nine.

Jean: Nine?

Corvax: You are in error. There are nine cars here. One. Two. Three. Four. Five. Six. Seven. Eight. Nine. Nine cars.

Love scenes, on the other hand, ran something like this:

Sylvie: I would like a grapefruit. I like grapefruits! Could you give me a grapefruit, please?

Jean: Here is your grapefruit. I love you.

Sylvie: Look what I have! I have a train ticket, a Walkman, a grapefruit, and a skeleton!

Jean: And me, I have a motorcar! I love you.

Sylvie: I also love you.

The more phrases you learn, the less exciting these people's lives seem to get. Princesses fall out of the picture altogether and in their place (at least in my case, since our textbook had not been updated in a while), all you have are people dressed in eighties fashions who are having very specific problems with their magnetoscopes, a word I think means "Betamax player." In the accompanying videos, everyone goes into slow, clearly enunciated hysterics over routine daily problems. "ARE WE GOING TO BREAK DOWN WITH RESPECT TO THE PEUGEOT CAR?" they ask. "UNFORTUNATELY, I BELIEVE THAT YES." "I WAS SITTING PROGRESSIVELY IN THE BATH WHEN THE TELEPHONE RANG. MICHAEL, WHEN

WILL WE GO TO THE DISCOTHEQUE FOR THE SURPRISE PARTY?"

Dicaeopolis in my Ancient Greek textbook never got invited to any discotheques, but he still had his share of adventures. His oxen broke down. He acquired a mule. He farmed. He went into, out of, and around places. Sometimes he went toward them. It was not the most riveting thing that had ever happened, but it was still better than the Latin textbooks, where my friends informed me that the protagonists had been sitting under, near, and around the same clump of trees for the past six months. "For a while," my friend Marissa confided, "we thought we had gotten them out, but the next chapter they were right back where they started." It was like *Groundhog Day* with verb forms.

Now I gritted my teeth and stared down at Dicaeopolis. I would learn these verbs, so help me. And when the call came, I'd be ready.

My debutante ball was scheduled for when I was a college sophomore. For years I could see it approaching slowly from a great distance, like one of those ominous lights at the end of long tunnels that they tell you not to walk toward.

I know why I thought it was a good idea: It was bound to be a strange, out-of-time experience that would be good fodder for tales.

I don't know why my family thought it was a good idea. It was 2008 and having a debutante ball was a horrible way to meet anyone, unless the person in question was a visitor from 1830 who had yet to assimilate. Then again, we had strange hobbies. My mother was a big history buff who had the house set up so that if George Washington ever happened to drop by he would feel perfectly at home, if a little creeped out by all the pictures of him everywhere. She had chairs like he would have sat on and green felt tablecloths like he would have seen at Colonial Williamsburg (I guess to him it was just "Williamsburg") and decanters of whiskey that had been made at a replica of the distillery where he used to make whiskey himself. She also had bought me a complete set of Colonial attire so that I could spend weekends at a historic farm pretending to be an eighteenth-century farmer's daughter. We tried to get this to count toward my high school's community service requirement, but the effort fell through pretty quickly.

"What is it that your volunteer work consists of?" Ms. Deaver asked.

"Um," I said, "well, I go to the Colonial Farm and I get into colonial garb and I spend three to nine hours there doing farm chores, you know, hoeing and also making the root vegetables comfortable and such, so if anyone visits the farm that day, they can see somebody hoeing like they would have hoed back a few centuries ago."

"I don't understand," Ms. Deaver said. "How is this helping people?"

"Well, nothing helps someone as much as seeing how people lived in the eighteenth century," I ventured. "As they say."

She fixed me with a flat stare. "What about making sandwiches?"

"I'm not feeding the body!" I said. "I'm feeding the soul! Nothing feeds the soul like people in sweaty linen outfits and bonnets pretending not to know what airplanes are."

"Yeah, no," Ms. Deaver said. "I think you'd better find something else."

Sometimes we got into heated family discussions in which my mother and my grandmother loudly agreed that arranged marriages weren't so bad while my father and I maintained aggressive silences. ("It worked for centuries! Why mess with it? And I think it's good that the family's involved in the choice. The family SHOULD be involved. Hey, Alexandra, you know who you should consider? That nice Pederson boy!")

So maybe the ball was no surprise.

Having a debutante ball in spite of yourself was a long tradition on my mother's side of the family. "I was really into feminism," my mother said, wistfully. "But your grandmother insisted."

My grandmother seldom insisted on anything. She and my grandfather were the fun side of the family. They liked to crack jokes, wrote funny toasts for their friends' birthdays, and referred to lunch as "Beer and Wine Time."

They had been retired long enough that they found going to the grocery store almost painfully exciting, deserving the kind of excruciatingly detailed attention other people reserve for attempts to scale Mount Everest.

They spent most of their TV viewing time alternating between FOX News and The Weather Channel, which put them in an almost constant state of panic, either about Something Ominous and Red That Is Sweeping into the Country to Devour Your Cattle in a Funnel of Wind, or Something Ominous and Blue That Is Sweeping into the Country to Make Your Children Dependent on Government Handouts.

Like my mother, they were proud Hoosiers. Of course, if I were to come out into any society, it would be *Indiana* society. Thanks to their years of lavish praise, I had come to view Indiana as a place almost as magical as the past—a state with no equal in the world.

Whenever we drove across the Indiana border, my mother insisted that we roll the window down so she could inhale deep lungfuls of Indiana air.

"Mm," she would shout over the rushing wind. "Doesn't the air just smell sweeter here?"

It smelled okay. It smelled like air. If I had to describe it at an air tasting I would probably say "distinguished, yet approachable" or "like air" or sneeze uncontrollably so that you would skip me.

My mother's family has always believed that all good things come from Indiana. Indiana people are superior to other people. Indiana corn is the best corn. Indiana dogs are better behaved than dogs from other places. Indiana writers are the best writers. Hoosiers play the best basketball. Films about Hoosiers are more stirring than films about other people from other places. Hoosiers, Hoosiers, now and forever!

My father was from Wisconsin. But who did Wisconsin have? Jeffrey Dahmer, Ed Gein, Joseph McCarthy, and Liberace. That, my mother said, was Wisconsin in a nutshell. Indiana had Benjamin Harrison. James Whitcombe Riley. Kurt Vonnegut. (I knew from reading *Cat's Cradle* that Kurt Vonnegut considered the group of people bound by the simple fact of being from Indiana a "granfalloon"—that is to say, a superficial grouping that signified nothing. "If you wish to study a granfalloon," Vonnegut had written, "just remove the skin of a toy balloon." Somehow this never came up in conversation.)

I thought Indiana was cool, but only because Indiana had produced my two male cousins. I idolized them. They were by far the cool half of the family. In middle school they wore hemp necklaces, and followed sports as avidly as I didn't. They addressed me as "Z" and used terms like "dece." "That's dece, Z," they would tell me.

For several years after they let the word drop casually at a family get-together, I worked hard to incorporate it into my conversation. ("Yes, seeing *Lord of the Rings* sounds like it will be totes dece, yo!" "*Macbeth* is my favorite Shakespeare play, but *Hamlet* is also pretty dece.")

While I sat at my grandparents' kitchen counter dragging Dicaeopolis through his paces, they read books with titles like *K-Dawg: Rize from the Streets* and *365 Days of Andy Roddick*. My aunt thought it was good that they were reading something. But I knew better. They were as cool in the present as I was going to be as soon as someone came along to whisk me back to 1919. What did they need to escape into books for?

Drew was my age and Scott was three years younger, which, when you're little, is a lot. To a seven-year-old, a four-year-old might as well be a side table. As a consequence of this mismatch, whenever we put on family skits, I forced Scott to play inanimate objects like Turkey and Barrel.

It never ceased to amaze me as a child that people would simply clump you together willy-nilly with anyone else who fell under the heading "child"—as though you had anything in common with someone who still believed in the tooth fairy and had yet to arrive at any awareness of death. This is hard to explain to grown-ups, as they have lost all sense of how rude and arbitrary it is to be expected to make hours of conversation with people you have nothing in common with but age. "How would you like it if I said to you: Mr. Miller is also over forty, and even though you have never seen one another before and have nothing in common but your age, I expect you to spend two hours together without throwing mashed potatoes at one another or stomping on Mr. Miller's toy truck?" you say. "That's how I spend most of my evenings," your parents respond.

The other thing my cousins excelled at, apart from sports and life, was chess, which left me utterly flummoxed. It seemed wildly unjust that people who could actually have a good time at a middle school dance without taking any breaks to curl up and read Faulkner in the bathroom should also be lords of the ultimate nerd's game. I spent a summer as the only girl at chess camp desperately trying to rectify the situation, but got nowhere. I won zero games. If you didn't win many games, they had a prize for most improved, but I couldn't win that because I hadn't improved. There was no prize for Most Stagnant. I couldn't even get a trophy for best sportsmanship because my sportsmanship was terrible.

Even though they were the only people I knew, we thought it might be a little too Osmond-y for my cousins to double as my escorts at the ball. Besides, Drew was already escorting someone else.

I pitched the idea to my college friends but got no bites. I think they thought I was joking. "Hey," I told them, "want to come to a debutante ball? I need two of you."

"What?" they said. "Where?"

"INDIANA!"

"Are you even from there?"

"NOPE!"

"Isn't that a little retro?"

"A LITTLE? It's literally feminist hell! For the afterparty, I bet we burn Betty Friedan in effigy. I assume there's a big ice sculpture of a glass ceiling."

"And you're going?"

"Duh I'm going! ANYTHING CAN HAPPEN AT A DEBUTANTE BALL! It's like an all-expenses-paid vacation to 1876! DEBUTANTE BALLS TO THE WALLS! Maybe they'll marry me off to a TOTAL STRANGER from a NEIGHBORING COUNTY!"

"Why are you speaking in all caps?"

"BECAUSE I'VE BECOME HYSTERICAL! I'M PRACTICING MY HYSTERICS!"

Instead, we had to fall back on my aunt. But she delivered. "Don't worry," she told my parents. "She'll like them. They're intellectual."

The debutante ball was organized by something called the Indianapolis Performance Society. Once or twice a year, they got together and put on an amateur production of something that had gotten big laughs in 1890. One year my aunt played someone who was bitten by a penguin, which allowed her to display a lot of range.

The party fell right around Christmas. I flew to Indiana from college, my excitement mounting. This was it. My big, time-traveling break.

That was where all my skill sets lay. I'd been studying hard and reading up. I could curtsy. I had passable skill on the pianoforte. I couldn't swoon, but I did occasionally get light-headed if I locked my knees by accident. My Greek was in line. I had all my drawing room quips locked and loaded. "To lose one parent may be regarded as a misfortune. To lose both looks like carelessness." I could even dance, although not well enough to attract a Gentleman with Tracts of Land. At least, not very much land.

My time machine was set to 1890, my dance card was open, and my giant white dress and gloves were on their way in the car with my parents. I was good to go.

The place where we went to rehearse for the ball was located at the top of a large warehouselike building that was full of vintage cars. The whole top floor was packed with shiny chrome and big fins and front seats that went all the way across and those pointy hood ornaments that you could use to impale unsuspecting pedestrians in crosswalks. It seemed like an appropriate place to begin your voyage back in time.

We waited among the vintage cars to receive etiquette and basic dance instruction from a woman in a dress large enough to slipcover New Jersey. She told us to keep good posture, make eye contact, and not disgrace our families. Then we went slowly through the motions of learning how to waltz.

Immediately on arrival I was introduced to my two escorts. I could see right away what my aunt meant. Russell was attending Stanford. Nick had just gotten back from a mission to South America and had a lot of feelings about it. In order to demonstrate that my aunt had been correct in selecting him, Russell spent the whole evening talking earnestly to me about eigenvectors. I kept leaving the conversation and crossing the room and returning and he was still there, a little bit farther along, like an instructional video through which you could not fast-forward.

Next there was a luncheon for honored grandmothers, because of course there was. I don't know where they sent the dishonored grandmothers. Maybe they had a separate buffet.

As I walked to my table, I overheard someone's mother speaking to an Honored Grandmother in an urgent tone.

"Her father would be escorting her but he recently died of a brain tumor so my brother is," she said, sounding apologetic. Yes, I thought. How DARE he? You SHOULD apologize. He must have done it deliberately, to spite everyone and sour his daughter's prospects. What a whimsical, self-centered act, to die of a brain tumor, when you were wanted at a debutante ball!

I sat down at the table full of debutantes. They were all skinny and had lovely glossy hair, the one trait that most intimidates me in women, apart from an ability to walk confidently in heels. They looked like they'd been poured into their dresses and said "when" way, way too early. Not that I blamed them. One of my fellow debutantes was still smarting after trying on a dress in front of her Honored Grandmother.

There had been a long pause. "Well, clearly you're not anorexic anymore," her grandmother said.

"Who's doing your hair?" one of them asked.

"Me?" I said. I tried to pronounce it in such a way that if you didn't know, you might think that Miiiii? with a rising intonation was the name of a sought-after hairstylist.

"Who's doing your makeup?"

"Evian Plump is doing *my* makeup," someone else said. (I do not actually remember the name of this person, but I remember that it started off sounding somewhat exotic and wound up with a good Hoosier surname.)

I thought it might sound suspicious for Miiii to be doing all my beauty maintenance, so I maintained a respectful silence. My makeup regimen at the time consisted of seeing if I found a tube of CVS mascara in one of my coat pockets and, if I did, applying a painstaking single coat to my lashes, getting just a little bit on my nose in the process. I looked like a Dalmatian who was bad at applying eye makeup. If this were the eighteenth century I could probably have passed it off as a beauty spot, but even then it would be a bit suspect.

Glancing around the table, I began to worry a little bit about my concept of how the evening was supposed to go. These girls didn't seem to know that we were in the past. My watch was all set to the Gilded Age but . . . they were talking about pedicures. This felt suspiciously like middle school.

Come now! Bring up the dance cards!

I already felt like a sore thumb—in flats, in a dress I'd purchased online from a disgruntled bride and had already worn to my high school graduation, no hairstyle, less makeup, and no friends in the crowd. And the night hadn't even started.

The actual venue was a place called the Indiana Roof. It looked like a theater set of a Spanish village. You kept expecting a bullfight in the middle of the dance floor. There was a stage at one end, lit up with red and green floodlights and little strings of white Christmas lights. That was where we were going to stand for the big presentation.

We debutantes and our escorts ate dinner in an upstairs area overlooking the dance floor while our parents, friends, and acquaintances drank at the bar downstairs. Periodically, a wave of laughter from below crested, broke, and washed over us as we sat picking at our tepid salad.

I tried not to spill spinach down my bodice. Class and taste, I told myself. Fine, this wasn't quite what I'd been expecting. Fine, what I'd been expecting was that I would get out of the car and walk into the room and everyone else would be sepia-tinted. So far nobody was. If young F. Scott Fitzgerald was here, he was crouching behind the bar, mainlining gin and attempting to avoid notice.

The trouble with all the things that People Don't Do Anymore is that some people still do them.

Sing barbershop quartets in coordinated sweaters? Hold doors for women? Wear hats? Attend Regency balls? Carry on as though the outcome of the Civil War is still undetermined? Sure. Chivalry's not dead. Chivalry's active on Reddit. Chivalry wears a fedora and expects you to put out. People keep telling Chivalry the hat looks dumb, but Chivalry won't listen.

It's all going on somewhere.

People still do all the things that people don't do anymore. But they do it *now*, and that makes all the difference. It's like you relocated your family to 1838 to build a new life with peace, quiet, and smallpox germs, and discovered that your entire high school had moved in next door. You can go to a debutante ball or a medieval weekend and there's never a there, there. You can never get inside. It's a gathering of everyone else who couldn't make it under the velvet rope, dressed in scratchy, uncomfortable outfits, consoling one another. These weren't historical strangers I could charm with my knowledge of the clavichord. They were people my own age. This was exactly what I'd come to 1890 to avoid, and it spelled disaster.

The thing that I hate most on this green-blue Earth is when you are stuck by yourself in a group of people who all know one another and don't know you. That, and the opposite—because really, it's terrible no matter which end you're on.

There is never a moment when you sound more like a jerkturd than when you are talking to people whom you have known for years and there is a stranger, lurking somewhere in your midst, like the Ringwraith at the party. "Did you hear Christine broke three ribs?" someone asks.

"Yes!" you say. "FINALLY!"

"I'm so glad she's not volunteering with those orphans any longer."

"I hate her so much."

"Everyone hated her."

"She was just using those orphans to get into business school."

"I KNOW! I was so worried she had *changed*."

"She would never change."

"I'm glad she's not paralyzed."

"If she were paralyzed she would post the WORST Facebook updates."

"I bet she'd do marathons."

"UGH SHE WOULD."

"And untag herself."

"OH GOD, I'M BOILING OVER WITH VITRIOL."

The person listening timidly interjects that "Christine doesn't sound so bad."

At this point you have to scrounge for anecdotes that explain why Christine was so terrible. Usually it turns out that you really had to be there. "She was always asking about the point value of our math assignments," you say.

"OH GOD," your friends chime in. "Always."

"And she went to prom with Jim Billington."

"THE Jim Billington."

"I don't know these people," the intruder says.

"Jim was the worst."

"He used to ice-skate."

"This doesn't sound bad."

"They always used to say, it's okay to HAVE hooked up with Christine, but it's not okay to BE hooking up with Christine."

Your listener gets a pained expression. "Your high school was the basis of *Mean Girls*, right?"

"YES, BUT THAT HAS NO BEARING ON THIS!" you shout. "TRUST ME! I WORE KHAKIS EVERY DAY."

And if you're the listener—well, the same applies. Once the conversation gets away, it is gone. Your only hope is to hold it aloft as long as possible and strangle it before it can touch earth and gain strength from its native soil.

This was always harder if you were me. "Did you ever hear the story of the ancient wrestler Antaeus?" I would ask. "Hercules had to hold him aloft so he wouldn't gain strength from his native soil."

"Huh."

"Gotta watch out for that soil."

"Speaking of watching out for, guess who I just saw? Davy! Crazy Eyes Davy! From sophomore year!"

"NOT DAVY!"

"Oh," I would say, mostly to myself, "Davy! Sure!"

"You know him?"

"Davy from sophomore year! With the crazy eyes!"

Understanding then breaks slowly over everyone's faces. "Oh, ha-ha, very funny."

After that, the conversation is gone and you can't get it back ever. That was what was happening now. As I forked down ruminative mouthfuls of salad, I felt myself slowly evaporating from the room.

It wasn't the past after all. Not the real past. Not the past I'd prepared for and expected. It was just middle school all over again, in a big fancy venue that looked like a luminous doughnut.

The way the debutante ball worked, as the instructress had drummed it into us, was that you lined up in the hallway and then proceeded out onto the dance floor in a stately manner, escorted by your father and followed by your two escorts, both in red sashes. As you walked, someone intoned your name and where you and your escorts were going to college. Then you curtsied to the hosts of the evening and took your place in the lineup next to the other debutantes. You just had to avoid falling over. I could do that, I thought. I'd spent most of my life not falling over.

"Now, wait a second," you are probably saying. "So you just stood there and took it? You were being handed off from your father like a piece of property. What do you have to say for yourself? Susan B. Anthony didn't die fighting in the snows of Mount Rushmore so you could get presented to society like a piece of vintage meat. Think of the patriarchy!"

What can I possibly say? Er. "Does it count as patriarchy if it was your grandmother's idea?"

Yes? Okay. Fair. Shhhhh.

Which was why my grandmother was so eager to deny that this was a debutante ball. She was a feminist, herself. "That was not a deb ball," she repeated, when she heard I was writing this. "It was a nice family party."

"Yes," I thought. "A nice family party, like all nice family parties, where I have to wear a long white dress, curtsy, and get introduced into Indiana society along with my two escorts. Typical Tuesday, really."

But it wasn't a debutante ball like I'd pictured, either. Debutante balls were supposed to be packed with high drama. Midway through the evening one of the debutantes would reveal that she had an impoverished fiancé and he would come bursting through the door dressed in his humble gamekeeper's suit, and then he and her father would fight, and one of them would be flung onto the buffet table and send all the silver dishes crashing to the ground. At least that's what happened on one episode of *The O.C.* I'd heard. I hadn't actually had time to see it. Too busy time-travel prepping.

After the handoff came pictures. Then the dance with the father, dance with Escort One, dance with Escort Two. Between the venue, the white dress and the father-daughter dance, it was like the world's most efficient wedding. Once we had finished dancing with our escorts, the people who actually had been drinking came flooding onto the dance floor like a drunk dam breaking. I perked up immediately. In the vanguard was a man with a neat white beard, dressed as a ship's captain, who insisted on being called the Admiral. He shoved jauntily through the throng toward his daughter. She looked completely mortified.

"Don't worry, Sweet Potato," he bellowed. "I've got you covered."

The Admiral winked. His nautical livery was quite something. I have no idea where you would purchase it. "I would like formal wear that makes me look like a drunk sea captain," he must have said to someone. "Think Popeye, but maybe—and I'm just spitballing here—maybe a kilt, to go with?" Whoever he said this to had delivered in spades. The Admiral was holding up his end by appearing as drunk as possible, lurching around trying to help the debutantes obtain alcohol.

Sweet Potato rolled her eyes.

It didn't take long for mayhem to break loose. The live band sang some covers of popular songs and pretty soon my cousins' dad was out on the dance floor doing a great impression of what looked like a spider about to vanish down a drain. I did what I always did at dances (how had I expected anything different? Who are these people who go to summer camp and suddenly become other people?) and stood in the corner yelling about the music and trying to work my talking points into the conversation. ("This place is like a reptile tank!" "WHEN WILL WE GO TO THE DISCOTHEQUE FOR THE SURPRISE PARTY?")

My grandmother smiled at me.

"Isn't this all silly?" she said. "I think it's a bit silly."

I looked around for someone to make eye contact with.

Grandma, I wanted to say, this was YOUR idea. If you think it's silly, why are we doing it? Did we Gift-of-the-Magi ourselves by mistake, where we all thought we were doing what somebody else wanted? Because that can only end in unflattering haircuts and tears.

This was right about when someone should have come dashing in dressed as a stable boy, overturned a table, and shouted, "NO, OLLIE HAMLISH! YOU MAY NOT HAVE HER!"

Nothing, of course. The dancers continued to dance.

"You look lovely," my grandmother added.

And another horrible thought struck me.

It was always like this.

Yes, the black-and-white debutantes of yore looked prim and proper and decorous and calm—like a row of carnations in white silk.

But so did we, in our picture.

In actual life there are no sepia tones.

Call it the Unified Tastelessness Theory of History. In historic homes, people are always uncovering hidden layers of really hideous paint; James Madison's bedroom was a wince-making teal. That statue was not the tasteful white you see; it used to look like Liberace on a bad day. There was a time when no yard in Ancient Athens was considered complete without a cheery stone phallus; they were like rude garden gnomes.

Why would it have been any different in the ballrooms of a century ago? No one notices she's living in a golden age. Probably if I'd been around then, I'd have spent most of my time lurking in the powder room, admiring the fractal patterns in the woodwork, catching up on my reading. If I were stuck at a dinner table next to Oscar Wilde, I would have sighed and wished myself back in time, next to Samuel Johnson. And so on, back and back and back until I ran into Dicaeopolis.

In a strange way, that was comforting.

The dance floor slowly emptied.

Afterward, Drew said, everyone was going to a party with People They Knew. There was going to be Alcohol there. Someone had even gotten a hotel room and it was going to be Crazy.

I got into the car with my mother and headed home to my books.

That was where I did most of my best time traveling, anyway: between the covers of a book. That was where I found the people whose jokes convulsed me with laughter, whose lives enveloped and extended outward from mine, who welcomed me instantly into their worlds without question. And I didn't even need gloves.

Time Traveler's Yelp

Given my luck traveling in space, it is probably naive of me to think that traveling in time would be any less awkward. But what can I say? We all have our fantasies.

With space, the stakes are fairly low. You might wind up at a bad restaurant. But traveling in time poses infinitely more risks. You might wind up on the menu. Talk about awkward!

So as an aspiring time traveler, I found these Yelp reviews super helpful.

That's right, the same guide that tells you to avoid restaurants where they were rude to User Karen (Average Rating, 4.3 Stars) is now urging you to steer clear of 1830 altogether. Among other eras.

PALEOLITHIC

User: John
5 Stars

> Fun! Great diet! Killed a mammoth with my bare hands! Great if you like camping and the outdoors—lots of fresh food and water, great vistas.

User: Kate

1 Star

> Hate it hate it hate it hate it
>
> Guys went out clubbing and dragged a bunch of women back to cave. Nobody is really sure about what's edible. Nobody in this era can draw. Lots of peer pressure to wear fur, which I didn't appreciate.
>
> Still not worse than 1812 though.

User: Ann

0 Stars

> Guy asked me, using hand signals, to come back to his cave to see his etchings. He offered to etch me like one of his French mammoths. It looked nothing like me. Then he made me stay in the cave and cook his meat and tend his fire.

ANCIENT EGYPT

User: Jim

3 Stars

> Fun, but not what I was expecting. Pyramids, which I thought would be a big attraction, weren't finished yet. Egyptians just walked like regular people. Most information we have about this time is not correct.

User: Sarah

2 Stars

> Ancient Egypt was okay. Drinks menu was limited. Not the best place to meet people. Reminded me a lot of the Internet in the sense that it was full of pictures of cats and people seemed pretty excited about them. Also lots of fun emoji. Still not sure what "Feather Squiggly Line Bird" means.

ANCIENT ATHENS

User: Sarah
3 Stars

> I'd heard a lot about Socrates and the Socratic method but he
> wouldn't really engage with me because I was a woman. Would
> not recommend bringing your kids here because everyone seems
> a little iffy on the age of consent.

User: Aaron
5 Stars

> Love it. Love it. Great comedy. The chorus got old quickly, but
> the dude dressed as a giant penis totally stole the show. A+ would
> go again. Not recommended for the agoraphobic because lots of
> the most fun stuff happens literally inside an agora.
> Everyone seemed to belong to some kind of fraternity.

BIBLICAL TIMES

User: John
1 Star

> Like Medieval Times but so so so much worse. My wife got stoned
> to death. Even if you think you like the Bible this is not your scene.

ANCIENT ROME

User: John
3.5 Stars

> Everyone talks a lot about how great the Roman aqueducts were
> and how wonderful their sewer system was, but it wasn't all that
> entertaining. Good if you're into nonstop toga parties. Colos-
> seum was cool. Very realistic violence.
> Also, Latin is not pronounced how we think it is pronounced.

MEDIEVAL TIMES

User: Amy
1 Star

I thought "Serf Experience" was misspelled. It wasn't.

Total downer. Would not recommend. Music is awful (unless you're really into plainsong chanting). Everyone gets divided into four types based on the balance of humors in their body. It's like being assigned Samantha, Miranda, Carrie, or Charlotte except it determines your medical care.

Right of jus primae noctis is gross. Not much nightlife. Could not find a bathroom or for that matter a toilet or for that matter a bed or for that matter soap.

I know "Medieval Times" is rated five stars by most Yelp users but honestly there was much less jousting and big turkey legs than I was led to believe and much more fleas and people dying of plague.

User: Sarah
2 Stars

I went here on a Groupon. For what I paid, it was not bad. If you like drawbridges, torchlight, and believing everything that is wrong with your body is because of witchcraft.

Just for future reference: if the selling point of your era is "once a bunch of serfs died of plague, life got a lot better for them," your era is terrible.

Bright side: cheap trip! I've taken cruises that were worse.

User: John
1 Star

Worst Iron Maiden concert ever.

RENAISSANCE

User: Kathleen

4.5 Stars

> LOVE IT. Music scene not the greatest, but if you like perspective in
> your art, this is the first stop. If there were any downsides I would
> say it was that Renaissance men not as well-rounded as I expected.
> As a general note to travelers: everyone's teeth in every era are
> way, way worse than you want them to be.

FRANCE FRANCE REVOLUTION

User: Marie

Zero stars would not recommend.

> WHERE'S THE CAKE?

REGENCY ERA

User: Katie

3.5 Stars

> Fun to visit. Great era for a three-day trip. Would not stay longer
> because no penicillin and also childbirth and arranged marriages.
> If I have to hear one more person delight us with piano playing I
> will draw and quarter something.

CIVIL WAR

User: Johnny

2 Stars

> Wow, I thought it was impossible for politics to be more angry
> and polarized than they are now.
> I was wrong.

VICTORIAN ERA

User: Yelp, Yelp, I'm Being Repressed

3 Stars

Not the biggest fan.

People had put all these little frill things on the bottom of their table legs to keep from being attracted to them, which was weird—like, who sexualizes a table leg? Not this guy.

This era puts the hip in hypocrisy, then removes the I and replaces it with a Y. (This is not a good slogan, but it is about what the era deserves.)

WORLD WAR I

User: Simon

1 Star

Not sure what's so "great" about it. Fast-forwarded several years and everyone was still sitting in the same trenches only muddier and less hopeful-looking.

1960S

User: Kyle

2 Stars

Fine and everything. Was expecting more, given everything the Boomers have been saying about this era for decades and decades. Woodstock was just okay.

1970S

User: Ann
2.5 Stars

> If you remember the seventies, you weren't there.
> One thing I'll say: very cheap trip.

2015

User: Jim
4 Stars

> Basically okay. One of the last nice times before the Yellowstone
> Caldera exploded.

2016

User: Sarah
1 Star

> Ugh. Between the presidential race and that volcano, this was
> a downer of a year. Probably more the volcano's fault than the
> election's, come to think of it.

3038

User: Dan
4 Stars

> If you're not really a "people person," this is the vacation for you.
> Very quiet. I was able to get a lot of reading done. Recommended
> if you're into silence and don't mind inhaling a little drifting ash.

We Are Not a Muse

I.

Being a muse isn't what it's cracked up to be.

Best-case scenario, you wind up with a statue of yourself in a museum, posed at an unflattering angle. Worst-case scenario, someone makes *(500) Days of Summer* about you.

My situation was somewhere between the two. My ex-boyfriend wrote a play about me.

Yup.

It's my go-to crazy ex story. "Yours keeps messaging you on Facebook?" I scoff. "Please. Mine literally wrote a play about me. With a Greek chorus."

His name was David. We'd been friends for years. We met right after arriving at college, at a prefrosh program for artsy people. It concluded with a pageant where I played a Robot King and he played a backpacker who was bad at picking up on social cues. We stayed friends because we kept getting rejected from the same things. It's amazing what that will do to cement a friendship.

When we did get together, it turned into one of those tumultuous relationships you hear about: on-again, off-again, like a defective lamp.

It started cute. He spent a summer abroad. We talked. He missed me, which was . . . novel. I'd never had a guy miss me. I'd been overlooked, sure, but never missed. Every New Year's, I'd spend a week with my grandparents listening to my male cousins call their girlfriends and murmur, "I MISS YOU! I LOVE YOU! NO, I LOVE YOU MORE," into the phone. It seemed like a cruel joke they were playing on me, not an actual thing that happened to people.

When David got back to campus, he informed me that I was the type of girl that he wanted not only to date, but also to cuddle with and take out to dinner in a respectful manner.

I was on board. For once in my life, I really, you know, liked someone. I thought he was cute, and not just in the way that I think every Jewish guy is cute. (I don't undress people with my eyes; I just picture them in yarmulkes.)

For about a week, it went well. Then he realized that dating might ruin our friendship. Why this had not occurred to him before, I have no idea. At any rate, he broke up with me.

No way was that happening.

So I did all the things that you are supposed to do. I took him out for coffee and reasoned with him, using logic. "All relationships," I explained, "end in breakups or in death."

Two months later he had a change of heart and asked me back.

After that he was on board, too.

He listened to me. He laughed at my jokes. He made me watch *Tootsie* and *The Ben Stiller Show* and he recited monologues from *Hamlet* and asked for my feedback on his acting. We had long conversations about his friends and relatives and my friends and relatives and all those daily bits of news that seem so pressing. Shit was getting real.

But when he told me he was in love with me, I was flummoxed.

Everything I had heard about love was terrifying. Love sounded like a diabolical Santa. Love, they said, came for you when you least expected it. Love put all your secrets out in the open. You came home from work one day, and Love was waiting in your garage with a knife, breathing heavily.

Well, I hadn't experienced anything like that. I did give him a watermelon one time. He seemed to appreciate the Happy Administrative Professionals Day card that I bought him—for Valentine's Day. And sure, I'd had the urge to write him a couple of sonnets, but they were casual, ABABCDCDEFEFGG sonnets, nothing formal or Petrarchan or anything. Surely that didn't count.

"Thank you," I said. "Uh. Likewise."

Afterward I went back to my room, feeling both shaken and stirred, like a martini that James Bond would complain about.

Was I supposed to be having feelings for him? I was Scandinavian. I came from a long line of emotionally frigid blond people. To say that we were in touch with our feelings would be a gross exaggeration. At most, they send us a postcard every six to eight years to say that they are enjoying life in the new country. What was I supposed to do with this?

"All relationships," I reminded myself, "end in breakups or in death." I wasn't ready to die!

So I broke up with him.

Turning him into my crazy ex-boyfriend was a snap. I'd barely referred to him as my boyfriend to begin with. To call someone my boyfriend would imply that I was someone's girlfriend. I had gone to an all-girls' school, and I knew better than that. A girlfriend was somebody with a purse who went to your sporting events. I wasn't a purse. I was a PERSON.

And when I read his play, that just sealed the deal.

A few weeks after our split, we were in playwriting class, the Big Fancy Playwriting Class where they perform your play at the end of the semester, and something seemed a little off.

When we read one another's drafts, I realized what it was. There I was, right there on his page.

But he'd started *revising* me.

Every draft came back with my character looking worse. She delivered extended monologues about how she had realized that she was missing out on a good thing. She cried more. David glanced hopefully across the classroom at me.

Who was this girl? Why was she writing sonnets and showing up at his events with watermelon? Why was she telling him that all relationships end in breakups or in death?

With every rewrite, it got worse. "That seems unrealistic, for the character to say a thing like that," I would say, pointing out one of my best lines, transcribed verbatim from one of our GChats.

"Does it?"

"It wasn't like that at all!" I glanced nervously around the classroom. "In this, er, fictional world of the play that you've created."

"Wasn't it?" He frowned. "I think it was."

That's the trouble with being a muse.

It's not what it's cracked up to be at all.

And I hadn't even set out to be a muse. I'd just been mistaken for one, a specific kind of muse: the manic pixie dream girl. Manic pixie dream girls, for the uninitiated—lucky you!—are the lazy man's modern-day muse. They don't have personalities. They have quirks. They wear rain boots and call coffeepots "elf beaneries" and talk about how the stars are God's daisy chain. They descend on nebbishy male writers in search of muses the way seagulls descend on a French fry.

Their hobbies include but are not limited to: running in the rain, dancing in the rain, listening to better bands than you in the rain, playing the ukulele in the rain (it sounds no worse), coming up with twee nicknames for household objects in the rain, and breaking up with nebbishy male writers for reasons that said writers find completely impenetrable, sometimes also in the rain. And then, as the writers sob over their departure, they realize that this heartbreak was just the impetus they needed to create That Elusive Masterwork That Was Always Lurking Just out of Reach.

They're catalysts. They are airy free spirits who, since the dawn of manuscript time, have come waltzing into the lives of nebbishy male writers to urge them to Get Out and Experience Life. They generate plots.

Unfortunately, all the plots are about the same: A young girl sparkling with life, often but not always with erratically colored hair, comes pirouetting into your humdrum existence and teaches you how to feel, love, and throw away whatever medication is keeping you from alarming the neighbors. But then the relationship ends, and you transform your whimsical, credulity-straining romance into a classic work of fiction, and the plaudits come pouring in from all corners.

I never thought of myself as one of them. I hate rain. I hate rain almost as much as I hate ukulele music. Also, they are fictional. So I thought I was safe. It was certainly not my intent to unload turdkilograms of whimsy into anyone's life.

And more than that, I always knew I wanted to tell stories. That's something manic pixies never do. They're not the protagonists of their own lives. They're characters in yours.

II.

Yet David had come to think of me this way. I'm pretty sure it was because of the night I mentioned I was crashing the publication dinner for an International Textbook on Geriatric Care, which is, I confess, the sort of thing these pixie dream girls do in movies.

But I was not motivated by whimsy. I was motivated by food. I have always prided myself on my ability to crash things. I viewed *Wedding Crashers* as a kind of life blueprint. Why would you *not* want to go and get free food among strangers? That's the whole point of human existence: free food. I mean, art, and perpetuating the human race, and everything, but—come now. Tell me you don't want finger cheese.

I was always trying to expand my crash roster. Once, I accidentally wandered from a New York bar into a gallery opening for a Russian artist after someone gave me confusing directions to the bathroom. I walked through one door, then through another door, and—there I was, surrounded by people in fine array, sampling wine and cheese and staring at the art with awe written on their faces. Never one to pass up free champagne, I took a glass and wandered around, trying to look like just one more art appreciator in my natural art-appreciating habitat. I gradually became aware that most of the people around me were speaking Russian. This didn't seem like a problem. I could do a Russian accent. I'd seen *Borat.*

I got another glass of champagne and murmured appreciatively at the canvases. A couple approached me. "Wonderful, isn't it?" they said.

"Yes, yes," I said, trying my Russian accent. "The painting, it is beautiful. Most lovely, yes."

They nodded. Emboldened, I continued. "That, I hear, is the artist there, yes?"

At this point the man began speaking to me in actual Russian. I struggled to maintain my composure. I had no idea what he was saying. This is it, I thought. There goes my cover. They would boot me out unceremoniously and I would not get to try any more of the finger cheeses. I cast desperately about me for a solution.

"Ah ah ah," I said, wagging a finger at him. "I wish to practice my English."

We switched back without incident. I grabbed another glass of champagne. By the time I had worked my way to the bottom of it I was shaking the artist by her gloved hand and repeating the word "beautiful, beautiful" in halting, accented tones. I still have her somewhat bewildered autograph.

Leaving the reception with a belly full of champagne, a guide to the exhibit, and a handful of postcards depicting the art in it, I quite justly felt that I could crash anything on Earth.

Sadly, college life left few opportunities for me to test this hypothesis, until one day, walking through the Harvard Faculty Club, I spotted a sign for the Publication Dinner for an International Textbook on Geriatric Care.

That sounded like a swank time. Nothing says "swank time" like "We've figured out how to care for elderly people so their hips stay intact when they fall over!"

I put on a black dress and showed up during the cocktail hour. One of the nice things about being a white female in your twenties, apart from the VAST MOUNDS OF UNEXAMINED PRIVILEGE, is that if you show up to a nice dinner in a nice cocktail dress, people generally assume you're supposed to be there.

I had a cover story, which was that my boyfriend worked for the publisher. Sadly, he hadn't shown up yet! Oh well! Here I was anyway. Mm, canapés! How do you know Mr. International Textbook?

This was perfect because it required me to have zero knowledge

of or connection to the textbook, and it put the onus on my boyfriend for telling me to come to this dinner, then failing to show up
himself. I wound up talking to the son of one of the scientists who
had contributed a chapter. The scientist had flown in from Korea
and his son spoke limited English, so we communicated mainly by
gesturing and eating the hors d'oeuvres at each other.

I managed to secure a seat at his table, away from the actual people who were responsible for the textbook, and figured I was safe.

But then things started to go downhill. His father came over and
insisted we join the high table. Tonight, he conveyed through words
and gestures, was a great night of celebration, and we should spend
it together.

Then I got a text from David. "Where are you?" he said. "I
thought we were hanging out."

"I'm crashing the Publication Dinner for the International Textbook on Geriatric Care," I typed.

A pause. "I'll be right there!"

I watched in terror as my cover story began collapsing in on itself
like an ill-constructed cake. If he showed up, it would be clear that
he did not work for the publisher and that in fact I knew zero people
involved with this textbook, and then we would be rousted out of
the dinner. And I was already three courses in! This could not pass.
I wanted to make it to coffee, at least.

I glanced up in horror as he walked in.

Remember that David was an actor. He had decided that "My
Boyfriend Who Works for the Textbook Company" was a character,
and that a character required a costume. Accordingly, he had gone
to Urban Outfitters and bought plastic glasses with fake lenses,
which he was now wearing. The fact that he was wearing these
glasses did nothing to change the fact that nobody at the dinner
knew him. My only hope was that we were all too drunk, on wine

and the joy of publishing an International Textbook on Geriatric Care, to notice this fact.

Maybe, I thought, it would be a good idea to greet his arrival by saying, "Oh, this isn't my boyfriend who works for the textbook company! This is my other boyfriend, who complicates things by arriving when he is not expected! My relationship status is complicated, almost as complicated as dealing with bursitis in a septuagenarian, isn't that right, Linda?"

Instead I decided to tough it out. "You made it!" I said.

"Yes!" he said. "I made it! I am Her Boyfriend Seth Aaron Who Works for the Publisher!"

This was when I expected one of the people at the table to say, "You work for Susan?" and David to say, "Who's Susan?" and everyone at the table to start pelting us with dinner rolls. Instead, we pulled up a chair for him.

"Who are you?" one of my dinner companions, a rather drunk lady who had written the chapter on Caring for the Aging Kidney, inquired.

As long as you aren't too obvious about it, you can deflect almost any inquiry by turning it back on the person who asked you and looking like you genuinely care about the answer. "So, where were you on the night of the crime?" a police officer will ask me someday, and I will smile and say, "Well, you know, here and there, but what were *you* up to, Carl?"

Thus my response to Kidney Lady. "He's nobody. TELL US ABOUT THE KIDNEY. YOU WERE SAYING SOMETHING REALLY INTERESTING ABOUT THE KIDNEY," I said.

"Wine is good for the kidney," she said. "Bud naat too mush wine. That's the trick: knowing when to stop with the wine." She swayed a little, gesturing, then lurched into an explanation.

The secret to a good backstory is that nobody actually cares about your backstory. You can let this depress you ("The universe is vast and indifferent and nobody really listens to what you tell them!") or you can get really excited by it ("The universe is vast and indifferent and sometimes this means free cheese!"). I know which option I'd pick.

"Seth Aaron" and I managed to make it all the way through dessert and coffee, and at the end we escaped with the business cards of several of our dining companions and a promise to dine with them the next time we visited Korea.

"That was exhilarating," David said. "I can't believe we did that."

You could see the screenplay writing itself.

III.

When David told the class he had been working on a play about exactly where he was in his life right now, he was not kidding. It was *exactly* where he was in his life right now. Any moment of confusion, pent-up insult, or sharp spike of agony worked its way into the draft. Midway through the rehearsal process, sensing that the play was not "edgy" or "theatrical" enough, David decided that all the female characters should be played by men in drag. Then he changed it back.

There was also a Greek chorus that spoke in verse. Did I mention that there was a Greek chorus that spoke in verse? *There was a Greek chorus that spoke in verse.*

I giggled. After kindergarten, your feelings can't really get hurt too badly by anything that rhymes, unless you make a point of seeking out rap battles.

The play ended with David's character, "Woody," all alone and being lectured by the Greek chorus on his inability to make decisions.

David claimed that some of the play was from his imagination, but even in the play, a character picks up the play, glances at the dialogue, and complains that he is being quoted verbatim.

"He's a composite," Woody tries to argue.

"Composite?" Dick says. "His name sounds exactly like my name and he says the exact same things that I have said to you. He is your roommate, and I am your roommate."

That was the play all over.

As the revisions went on, my character cried a lot more than I remembered crying and delivered a long speech about how rueful she was to lose him. "Enter June," every stage direction would read. "She was hot, but kind of a butterface. She was crying. 'How can you do this to me?' June would say. 'I COULD HAVE HAD YOUR BABIES.' Exit June, sobbing wordlessly."

Sitting there with our classmates and his parents while the actors painstakingly dramatized conversations that he had had with his roommates about his love life was the kind of thing that should have been a nightmare—for him.

I sat next to a friend who kept nudging me. "Did that happen?" he kept asking. "Did that happen?"

"No," I huffed, irritable. "None of it happened. Not like that."

When he broke up with me, in the play, it was extremely dramatic. June cries. June carries on. June brings up children. June is, in short, a psychopath.

The way I actually remember it, we left Au Bon Pain to sit on a scenic footbridge down by the Charles River, and people kept walking between us, and I kept yelling, "Don't mind us—we're just BREAKING UP OVER HERE! YA HEAR ME?"

So maybe it wasn't *un*dramatic.

You know how they say people resemble their pets? Your dog's a psychopath, take a good hard look in the mirror? Exes are like that, too. It takes two to make a "crazy ex" story.

Sure, he wrote a play about me. But me?

I paid a man on the Internet to teach me how to get "your man back, or your money back, in ninety days guaranteed."

Maybe that is how I should have started the story.

IV.

In the play, my character wandered around making jokes constantly and everyone else had to guess her feelings from context clues. One sensed that it was sort of an exhausting process for them.

I did this in real life, too. After a few days of Googling, crying, and Googling while crying, I took prompt, completely logical action: I found T Dub.

I found him the way you find anyone these days: the Google genie. That's not a cutesy way of addressing Google. I just mean the different Google that exists for the dark watches of the night when you have a wish instead of a question. "How do I get him: back/to marry me/to ask me out/to notice me/to kiss me/to propose/to fall in love with me/to love me again/to want me/to like me again?" Google, how? "How do I stop: snoring/coughing/being lazy/eating/drinking/hating myself?" How? Tell me, whatever it is, and I'll do it. I'll do it, Google. Here, have an arm. Have a toe. Have my firstborn.

Usually what happens is you come across a page of Yahoo! Answers people patiently explaining that you can't make anyone love you, but there's always a telltale misspelling that gives you hope. The person can't tell your from you're. What can he possibly know about love? Besides, you've been on there yourself, under an alias, giving people flawed advice about what medicines to give their cats. Maybe you got yourself on the other end by accident. And then there are the people who insist you can do it after all, using "psychological tricks." They, too, have misspellings, but what's a misplaced apostrophe between friends?

And then there's T Dub.

T Dub is on YouTube. He speaks slowly and soothingly and redundantly.

"I've come up with this system," he says, "where you can speed up time so that you don't have to spend months or years healing. You can just do this magic, this healing, and get yourself right there in no time."

Now YouTube's full of people like him. Maybe it was then, too. At any rate T Dub was the first one I found, and I latched on like a bur with dependency issues. No man making videos in his kitchen where he spoke in such a slow, reassuring drawl about getting your ex back could possibly be mistaken about love or psychology, I thought.

After watching a couple of videos in which T Dub extolled the virtues of the complete "Time-Compression Healing" system, I decided to go for it. It was that or drinking to excess and watching *Sherlock Holmes* over and over again. And the latter was going to lead nowhere good—kidney failure or deciding that a deerstalker hat was a good investment.

I paid T Dub the forty dollars he demanded and clicked DOWN-LOAD. Soon I was reading through the accompanying e-pamphlet as I listened to T Dub's words of encouragement. My roommate came home to find me doing sit-ups on the floor as a man's slow drawl encouraged me to "wait sixty days before you contact him."

"What in God's name?" she would have said, once. But this was a full year after the time she'd come home to find a baby pool full of water on the floor and an animatronic Elvis head in the window, so nothing surprised her. "Hi, Petri," she said.

"I'm going to get my man back or my money back," I informed her. "Ninety days, guaranteed."

"That's nice," she said. "Good night."

How none of this made it into his play, I will never know. This, to me, is the real meat of the story. I ate better. I did sit-up(s?). And, more important, I spent a few days really intending to wait sixty days before contacting him.

That was impossible. College is basically a big fish tank. You don't see fish breaking up. Where would they go? How would they avoid each other around the plastic shipwreck? They never break up. They eat each other instead.

At the sixty-day mark, he asked me to come to his house formal with him. I called T Dub to thank him.

"Mailbox full," T Dub's voice mail said.

I was too elated to care.

"Why did you decide it was worth giving this another go?" I asked him.

"Well," he said, "I've been writing this play. About, you know, my life, this fall."

"Oh," I said.

And this time I broke up with him, and all heck broke loose. The revisions began.

The revisions were ugly.

In my defense (this is all in my defense) I didn't know that it was normal. That the moment you attained something it stopped being unattainable and started to pick at its pimples and ramble on too long about subjects that bored you.

In my defense, I kill plants. The first few weeks I'm excited to have them, and I remember that plants need water. Then afterward they slip my mind and I don't notice they've died until a month later when they're sprawled helpless on top of my radiator, frozen in their final gesture of making a desperate play for the window latch.

In my defense, I had been reading Proust, and it had gone to my head. This was what he said would happen. He hated Albertine when he had to spend time with her. She bored him stiff. But when he was without her he was miserable. Proust had his share of issues.

In my defense, this was my first time at this, really.

In my defense—I'm sorry.

When we wound up in the same playwriting class the next semester, I discovered that he had not been kidding about the play. There had been no reason to think he was kidding, but—it was, if anything, *more* faithful to life than I had been capable of imagining.

It was strange seeing myself on the page. I was used to narrating.

"Again, it seems unlikely that the character would actually say a thing like this," I pointed out, flicking my pencil over the portion of the story where June yelled, "HEY, SORRY, FOLKS, NOTHING TO SEE HERE WE'RE JUST HAVING AN ACRIMONIOUS BREAKUP."

David glared daggers at me. I assume. I was studiously trying to avoid eye contact.

"I mean," I continued, emboldened, "who would actually say a thing like that? That doesn't sound like a real person to me."

At least the actress playing me was hot.

"No," David told her, not looking at me. "Gawkier."

"Uh, okay," she said.

"Could you be more of a self-centered bitch?"

"Excuse me?"

"Not you, the character."

"Oh."

Crazy ex stories are hard because they started out as love stories. And the key moment in a love story is the moment when you realize that—of all the improbable things!—there's a person inside someone else! He or she is not just a character in the plotline of your life. You thought you were the only real one. You thought you were alone in the universe, twisting the dials on a radio in a postapocalyptic hut somewhere. Then one day you get a signal back. That's a love story for you.

I'm real. You're real. Now what?

But this isn't a love story.

This is a story about unreliable narrators, about the stories you tell yourself about the people you can't have. In stories like that only one person is ever real. So you don't get to tell this story. I'm the real one; you're a character in my story. I'm the one who gets to tell this.

Turning people into characters does a kind of violence to them. You lose a dimension or two pinning them down to the page. No, you say. Stop. Don't move. This won't work if you move. You are the story I tell about you.

The instant you tell a story it stops being quite true.

"That wasn't how it happened," I said, as June sobbed and the Greek chorus launched into another burst of doggerel.

That wasn't how it happened. Let me tell you how it happened. My crazy ex-boyfriend wrote a play about me. It's a funny story. Not a love story.

Tall Tales

You know the sensation, when you're talking, and you hear yourself talking, and you suddenly drift up above yourself until you are only dimly aware of this person speaking many fathoms below you? And the only sensation that permeates the cloud on which you are sitting as that poor person beneath you rambles on is, "That really isn't going well"? And you watch, in a sort of disinterested horror, as this person keeps speaking and speaking, and things get worse and worse, and you think, "I really should stop talking." And you don't stop. And what seems like geologic ages pass, and you watch everyone around you evolve into higher forms of life, and develop the use of tools. And you're still talking. You know that sensation, where you know you shouldn't be talking but are powerless to stop yourself?

Bertram Wittington has never experienced that sensation.

Bertram Wittington is a friend of my father's. The best way to describe him is as a mine of impressive, obscure, and totally unverifiable information. He used to spend his days riding the bus up and down Wisconsin Avenue, wearing a tuxedo, a carnation in his buttonhole, a top hat, and carrying a cane. He used to come to my home for Thanksgiving dinner. And I was never sure if he had a house.

My father has always adored Bertram, because he has a British accent and the ability to calculate the day of the week for any date in history. When you complain about your lousy day, he will respond with the story of an eminent Panamanian who committed suicide for similar reasons. Tell him that you just ate a sandwich, and he will tell you how President Garfield really died. "Poor man! It was the doctors killed him. Terrible thing."

Probably because of the accent and the top hat, my father is convinced that Bertram Wittington is a great social conquest. "This man has forgotten more about the Schleswig-Holstein question than most people ever knew!" he exclaims.

My mother, on the other hand, did not share his rosy view. This probably dates back to the evening that he came to our house and my father greeted him by plucking her prized orchid and placing it in Bertram's buttonhole. Once, she insists, she saw a centipede crawl out of his collar.

But I've always loved him.

Let me explain. When you're a kid, sometimes you'll be on your way to someone's house and your parents will say, in hushed tones, "Now, just so you know, Gerald is a bit of a character." And you'll think, "Ooh! A character!" You read plenty of books, so you know what a character is. When the car pulls up to the house you're expecting a man to come dashing out in full nineteenth-century garb screaming "DO NOT YOU HEAR IT IN THE WALLS? THE BEATING OF THAT HIDEOUS HEART!" but then it turns out that what your parents meant by "character" was that Gerald thinks way too highly of his dog and says "mmkay?" a lot.

But Bertram actually WAS a character. He could have slipped right into the cast of anything I was reading, completely undetected. If he'd ever wound up at one of those literary parties with Oscar

Wilde, you had the sense that a vicious knock-down, drag-out fight would have ensued over who got to monopolize the conversation.

He also sometimes drank. As a child, I viewed drunkenness as a kind of superpower. I vividly remember the first time I saw a drunk person. I was standing in a line at a church picnic in Wisconsin waiting for an old lady to give me a piece of chicken, a healthy ladling of mashed potatoes, and some runny gray gravy that looked like snail tears, when I became aware that a man farther down the line was speaking loudly and teetering.

"They're gonna beat your butts," he announced, loudly, listing leftward. "TIME will SEE!"

I'd never seen a drunk person before. It was mesmerizing.

This man could say literally ANYTHING! Who knew what would come out of his mouth next?

When I yelled things, my parents said, "Shh!" and "Keep your voice down!" and sometimes they addressed me by my first, middle, and last names, just to show they were serious about it. But this man could just say stuff. Any stuff! As loudly as he wanted! He might as well have flown up into the sky out over the picnic, clad entirely in spandex.

"Come on, Alexandra," my mom said, yanking me in the opposite direction.

The whole ride back I mouthed, "They're gonna beat your butts," to myself, reverently. "Time will SEE!" It didn't even make sense. It was incredible.

Bertram took full advantage of this power. Some nights, you could get a word in edgewise only if he decided to visit the restroom. I was mesmerized.

He sat there with his carnation in his buttonhole, one hand on his cane, holding his audience spellbound. Admittedly, the audience consisted of maybe five people, two of whom had been trying and failing to interrupt his flow all evening, and one of whom was my mother, who thought Bertram was full of it, but one of them was me, and I was riveted. I wanted to do that someday.

His specialty was twofold: 1) sweeping and slightly controversial statements about people, supported by one or two vivid but apocryphal anecdotes, and 2) insisting that current or historical events that people had heard of were better explained by other historical events that no one but Bertram had heard of. "The thing about the financial crisis," he would say, "is that really it resembles *parfaitement* what happened to a man named Herr von Bulow in 1654 in Holland." (I'm making this up. He generally wasn't, although we didn't quite have Google then, so you tended to take his word for it.)

Growing up, every year, I clamored to go to his birthday party. If there was anything stranger than Bertram himself, it was the people who invariably showed up at his birthday parties.

The first year, the hostess was a lady by the name of Elaine who kept going around the party reintroducing herself to everyone under weird aliases. "Hello, I'm Elaine!" she would say. A few minutes would pass, and she would come back around the circle. "Clara!" she'd yell. "It's a pleasure."

Her entire home was covered in blown-up pictures of Bertram at various stages of life. Like the pictures, he had gradually increased in size as time went on. He was holding court in the corner of the party talking about eighteenth-century sailing mishaps, paying no attention to Elaine except at one point in the evening when she wandered over to him and introduced herself as Alice.

"Don't like your hair!" he snapped. "Too yellow!"

She devoted the rest of the night to following us around the house trying to force books on us and then taking them back. My father and I had finally, reluctantly, accepted a book of drawings, only to find her chasing us down the street screaming, "I CAN'T BEAR TO PART WITH IT!"

Strange as these parties were, they were nothing compared to Thanksgiving, one year.

In attendance were Bertram, my parents, myself, my father's college roommate, his daughter Katie—who cared a lot about animal rights—and my mother's friend, who had done some work for the Humane Society.

The evening didn't start too badly. Bertram was in fine form. "The killer wabbit who pursued Jimmy Carter has indeed been, ah, historically substantiated," he was saying. "But never mind *All the King's Men. World Enough and Time* is truly the greatest of the books of Robert Penn Warren."

We were all listening dutifully. Bertram Wittington was a raconteur, and he was going to racont whether you wanted him to or not.

But as we sat down to dinner, the plot thickened.

Bertram had to pause for air from telling us about Bavarian vicomtesses. So the lady who worked at the Humane Society decided to mention her work to Katie.

"Oh," Katie said, stiffening perceptibly. "The Humane Society. How do you feel about killing millions of innocent puppies and kitties every day?"

This was not quiiiite accurate, and I was going to say so, when Bertram jumped in.

"Well, that's nothing compared to what the Bavarian gentry used to do!" he responded. "They used to put eight thousand head of cattle in an enclosure and fire on them with a cannon! Five hundred dead was considered a good day's sport!"

"I don't think that's anyone's idea of sport," said Katie.

"Well, it certainly wasn't the Spanish gentry's!" Bertram said. "They used to hunt gypsy women! With their dogs!"

Bertram paused and became reflective. "But, you know, it wasn't any fun. The gypsy women didn't put up much of a fight, just fell over and died. So do you know what they did?"

Silence. Utter, complete, brittle silence. The only one who didn't notice that everyone was frozen in mortification was Bertram.

I knew that someone had to say something. "What?" I asked.

"They tied their babies to them!"

"I have to leave," Katie said.

"But that was nothing compared to the Roman emperors," Bertram confided to me. "They used to feed their eels on used slaves."

"Ah," I said.

The following year, Bertram was the only one of those guests to return.

When I was younger, mistaking Bertram for a Figure of Some Literary Eminence, my father told me to give him everything I wrote. When I wrote what I thought was my first novel, I printed it out and placed it reverently in his hands. He returned half of it several months later, covered in soup and unintelligible scribbles.

After graduating from college, I gave him my undergraduate thesis, a verse translation of Aristophanes' *Frogs*. For whatever reason, I could not mail him the copy, nor did he have an e-mail address. Instead, he instructed me to drop it off at a Thai restaurant.

"Bangkok Bistro," he said. "They know me there."

I showed up the next morning. "I have a package to leave here," I began, nervously. The man minding the desk looked at me. "For Mr. Bertram?" I said.

"Oh, Mr. Bertram!" the man said, looking reassured. "Sure, sure."

For months thereafter he routinely telephoned my office and said cryptic things like "The Serpent Messenger, perhaps?"

As a kid, I thought of Bertram as a figure like Santa Claus, if Santa were real and showed up at the house twice a year to drop off used books. My father had mentioned I was a Civil War buff, so every few months Bertram would heave his enormous bulk up our front steps, looking like Moby-Dick in a dinner jacket, ring the doorbell, and hand over a large brown paper sack filled to the brim with relevant books, some a little damp.

"He reads everything. That's how he comes to know so much," my father said.

And maybe he did. Every subject I managed to learn about, it seemed he already knew. Whenever I managed to dominate even a small segment of the conversation at dinner, I felt elated. Bertram's conversation veered and leaped so wildly that it was hard to stay on the whole time. If you managed to contribute something to the discussion of the Schleswig-Holstein question, you were left empty-handed when Bertram moved on to the enema that had once been administered to Louis XIV (Bertram had it on good authority). And if you were still on the bucking horse of his conversation even after that, well, he had naughty stories about the recordings that had been made of Martin Luther King Jr. talking about Jackie Kennedy's lips. He generally ladled these opinions out over dessert, as I sat silently, rapt, hoping not to be dismissed from the table to my room upstairs.

"Tell about the killer rabbit," I insisted. "And Jimmy Carter. Tell about Rasputin. Tell about the eels."

His decline and the rise of the Internet coincided nicely. There was not room for both of them.

In the past decade or so, Bertram and I haven't seen each other much. But it's been enough to know that I was right.

Most people seem like characters only from a distance. You get to know them and the mist evaporates and you're left with a person just like all the other people you know. But not Bertram.

He really *was* larger than life.

He even had a show on the History Channel, for a brief time, telling his famous stories from the depths of an enormous chair.

Not that he wasn't also a person. He was. He had numerous friends. I was proud to be on the roster. I went to another party in his honor—a luncheon, a few years ago—and there was a whole long table full of people who wanted to thank him. He'd edited their books or had rescued them from tight spots with his armada of facts or had gotten them through difficulties of one sort or another. The most improbable people always turned up at these parties. (No sign . of Elaine this time, but there was a woman (he'd either flooded or unclogged her sink; I can't remember which) who insistently pressed a CD of her attempt at traditional Indian drumming into my hands. Her instructor, she told me, believed she was the reincarnation of a famous fifteenth-century drum master. If so, she'd lost a little in translation.)

So many things from childhood seem bigger than they are. There is a kind of magic that clings to things when you don't know their backstory. That armchair has always been there. That is the Big Serving Spoon. This is What We Do on Sundays. Things take the definite article. This isn't just a chair. This is the chair. This is the grandmother. This is the house.

Then as you get older you realize that there is no particular magic to any of these items. There was nothing special about this chair. It came from a catalogue. It didn't matter that you had pot roast on Sunday. Those rituals held no special potency. There are no characters, just more people. You see the strings behind the puppets. The movies that once terrified you leave you bemused, at best.

But Bertram was different. If the lines of people waiting to thank him and hanging on his words at long tables attested to anything it was that people had noticed he was something out of the ordinary. He didn't shrink with time, not really.

Yes, he grew older and quieter. He switched to orange juice. He had health problems. Time eats people, always.

But he kept telling stories. Even diminished, he was formidable.

He knew the best way of getting away with being yourself. You could be as odd as you liked, as long as you had something to offer—in his case, a whole arsenal of stories, anecdotes, odds and ends of fact. Once he started to tell a story, nothing could touch him. Not awkwardness, not the silence around the table, not even the thing that might or might not be crawling out of his collar. With him the silence wasn't awkward, just a vacant space to pour a story in. He was a snake charmer of conversations. It was, I realized, possible to live like this.

Awkward? Awkward wasn't in his vocabulary. Sthenolagnia was. Awkward wasn't. He was above all that, floating over the conversation in his luminous cloud, leaving everyone else to scramble below. He just *was*. And maybe, someday, if I learned enough stories, I could make my way up there too.

And one of the first stories that I was able to tell was about him.

One day a girl on my volleyball team announced that she had seen a strange man on the bus.

"Did he have a carnation in his buttonhole?" I asked.

She nodded. "You know him?"

"I know him," I said. "He comes to Thanksgiving every year." I smiled, warming to my theme. "He's a real character."

It's a Trap!

As a general rule, I advise against trying to pick up men at *Star Wars* conventions.

I know it sounds like a great idea.

Conventional wisdom states that a single woman going to a *Star Wars* convention is like an egg cell saying, "Screw it!" and hopping on a plane to go hang out wherever all the sperm cells happen to be. The odds in your favor would seem to be something like 3720 to 1.

But conventional wisdom doesn't know what it's talking about.

Trust me.

Most people have one thing they're deeply, deeply weird about. The moment you find your thing, your world shifts. Something in it just strikes a chord in you. You walk through your whole life like a sleeper agent waiting for someone to whisper the code phrase that activates you, and then you awaken and everything changes: your habits, your priorities, whether or not you have Obi-Wan Kenobi on your toothbrush.

Star Wars was mine. My dad took me to see *A New Hope* in theaters in 1997 when the reissue came out, and from that point, the course of my life was set. I put away former pastimes (good-bye,

Wizard of Oz. It was a nice run) and set out to dedicate my life to the service of this new god. It got so bad that when we bought a new VCR my parents made me sign a contract promising not to watch the trilogy more than thirteen times a year.

Even as it was, I watched the whole trilogy well over two hundred times, until the VHS tape creaked and groaned. Special Edition, 1997, gold box set. I knew certain things about it were lies (Han shot first) but it was the version whose rhythm crept into my bones. I always dutifully and unblinkingly watched all three movies in sequence with all the lights turned out everywhere else in the house, frantically shushing my parents if they tried to interrupt the trance. The outside world did not exist. I was on Tatooine. I was on Dagobah. I was in an X-Wing navigating straight down this trench toward a target shaft just two meters wide. And not once in all this time did I ever skip through the Director's Intro to the Special Edition, so not only do I have the whole trilogy memorized, but I also know every comment Ben Burtt makes about the difficulties of optically compositing snowspeeder cockpits on a white surface so the black line isn't visible. ("It's a constant trade-off. How transparent can we make the cockpit? At what point is the black line more objectionable than the transparency?")

As I said, everyone has something he or she is deeply weird about. This is mine. Maybe you're lucky and yours is football, in which case the whole world is set up to cater to your preferences, or Marvel superheroes, in which case you had a few rough years early in life but now every movie that comes out for the next hundred years is already planned to suit your dearest wishes.

You can tell how mainstream the thing you love is by whether the Big Event You Attend in order to celebrate it is called a "convention" or not. You can tell, too, by how relieved you are when you finally get to turn yourself inside out and wear your deepest passion on your sleeve.

. .   .

I used to think I could pass. Even if, on the inside, I was a large, slug-like Hutt, I could slip into the guise of a passable-looking young lady before anyone spotted me. No one could tell, just by looking at me, that for a while I had contemplated getting a C-3PO tramp stamp. (A friend was going to get an R2-D2. Fortunately we decided against it. Also the tattoo shop shut down. It's amazing what good decisions you can make when you have no alternatives!)

I floated this hypothesis to someone and she started to laugh. "No," she said. "I think people know. You have *Empire Strikes Back* bedsheets. You sleep on those bedsheets under a Darth Maul comforter, underneath a painting of C-3PO in a tweed jacket that you bought off the Internet."

I shrugged. "Mere circumstantial evidence."

"Whenever anyone says *Star Wars* in a restaurant, no matter how far away or how softly they whispered it, you go running over there shouting, "WHAT WHAT TELL ME WHAT THE *STAR WARS* THING WAS.""

I pshawed. "Please. Everyone does that. My point is, I could pass. Take away the sheets and what remains?"

"What about your watch?"

"Take off the watch."

"Everything you say and do."

"Well, other than that."

I love *Star Wars* for so many reasons.

One, because there was never a moment when *Star Wars* hadn't sold out. There are some things you can get a little indignant about when they go commercial—like if there were a big neon madeleine floating in the air just outside the Proust House and an amusement park ride called Trip Down Memory Lane—TASTE! the tea and the madeleine! FEEL! the passion for Albertine! EXPERIENCE! the magic all over again—I guess people might get just the slightest bit upset about it. But part of the charm of *Star Wars* is that Princess Leia has always been on your shampoo bottle. Luke has always been on your bedsheets. Darth has always graced your toaster. You have always been able to get Galactic Bubble Mint toothpaste with Obi-Wan Kenobi on it, brandishing a lightsaber. As I speak I am staring at one of my most prized possessions, a ceramic serving plate for, I guess, chips or dip, on which C-3PO reclines sensually, one arm up, other arm akimbo. They made these things because we bought them!

You can, I guess, map my evolution as a human being as my favorite *Star Wars* character evolved.

First my favorite character was Darth Vader. How could it not be? He was all that I asked for in a man: tall, dark, and breathing.

Then it was Luke. Luke was never cool, but, in a way, that was his charm.

"I'm in it for the money. I expect to be well paid," Han tells the Princess as they escape the first Death Star.

"You needn't worry about your reward. If money is all that you love, then that's what you'll receive," Leia retorts. Luke comes in, and she tells him, somewhat pointedly, "Your friend here's quite a mercenary. I wonder if he really cares about anything—or anybody."

"*I* care!" Luke says.

Yeah, Luke's not cool.

And then I moved on to C-3PO.

I love C-3PO. I love him in part because he's completely useless and very talkative and in a committed relationship with another robot, but also because the one consistent theme of the entire trilogy is that no one ever tells him anything and that no one cares about his problems.

"Secret mission? What plans? What are you talking about? I'm not getting into there," he asks in the opening scenes of the original, as R2-D2 tries to get him to escape the *Tantive IV*, Princess Leia's starship. "I'm going to regret this."

His first lines in *The Empire Strikes Back* consist of telling R2, "Well, don't try to blame me. I didn't ask you to turn on the thermal heater. I merely commented that it was freezing in the Princess' chamber. But it's supposed to be freezing! How we're going to dry out all her clothes, I really don't know! Oh, switch off!"

This problem never comes up again, ever. Although it does explain why the Princess wears only one outfit for pretty much the duration of the movie.

He supplies people with facts and statistics that they do not want. He talks and talks and nobody cares, and none of his skills are relevant to his day-to-day life. He is the galactic equivalent of an English major. He speaks Bocce. He is fluent in well over six million forms of communication.

Here's a list of things that people have said to C-3PO at one point or another:

"Would you just shut up and listen to me?"

"Shut up!"

"Shut him up or shut him down!"

"Shut up, sir."

"Ichota." (the RUDEST)

Return of the Jedi is basically C-3PO's great shining moment because all he's ever wanted to do is have attention paid to him and get to tell stories ("I'm not much more than an interpreter, and not very good at telling stories" in the first film was clearly just Threepio being coy) and now he finally gets his wish. He tells stories—with hand gestures!—he's worshipped as a god, and he gets to do some of that language interpreting that he's claimed to be able to do for the past three movies. "The illustrious Jabba bids you welcome and will gladly pay you the reward of twenty-five thousand!"

My point is: Threepio is great, and I appreciate him more with each passing day. And even more with each passing Jar Jar.

A moment for Jar Jar.

How fondly I remember the spring of 1999, before 9/11 and Jar Jar. In many ways 9/11 is the Jar Jar Binks of history.

This field has been plowed and plowed over again and wept into and plowed a third time.

But put yourself in my shoes.

You are young. You have found something you love. And then you have to somehow reconcile the fact that the thing you expected would bring you only joy has turned up on your doorstep with Jar Jar Binks bawling out, "MEESA CALLED JAR JAR BINKS! MEESA YOUR HUMBLE SERVANT!"

My only weapon was denial. I convinced myself that *The Phantom Menace* was good the same way I convinced myself, for years, that Santa Claus was real: by very carefully ignoring all the facts anyone presented to me. (This also works for things like evolution.) But that could only get you so far. Inevitably you remembered the existence of someone named Nute Gunray and all your defenses collapsed again.

I attended my first *Star Wars* convention right after freshman year of college, when the wounds of the prequels were fresh.

It was a big milestone for me. "Finally," I told my roommate, Svetlana, "I'll get to be myself and go among my people."

"I don't understand," Svetlana said. "Who were you before? Literally the first thing you did on arriving at college was unpack your lightsabers. Do you think you've been hiding? If this is you concealing your love of *Star Wars*, what would it look like if you let it hang out? Would you just dress up as Jabba the Hutt all the time?"

That wasn't a bad idea, I thought. Maybe I should.

I had been saving up all semester to buy autographs.

I'd tried to make money by signing up to do negotiation studies at the business school. This had not been paying off the way I hoped, because I have the business acumen of lettuce.

Once, I tried to buy a cheap knockoff purse on a street corner. "You should haggle down the price," my friends said.

"Sure!" I said. I strode to the corner and picked out a purse. "Pardon me," I said to the man behind the table. "May I haggle with you?"

This, I have since learned, is not how haggling works.

"What?" he said. "No. The price is final."

"Okay," I said, handing him my money. "Forty dollars, wow."

So the negotiation studies were a no-go. Money kept slipping through my fingers like Princess Leia said star systems would if Grand Moff Tarkin tightened his grip. Finally I got a job at the library to push me over the edge.

Nonetheless, I had enough for autographs from all the people I most cherished—the guy who had played Wedge Antilles' gunner in a few shots of *The Empire Strikes Back*. The Imperial officer who yelled, "You rebel scum!" in one shot of *Return of the Jedi*. Several of the rebel pilots exploded during the Battle of Yavin. And Mark Hamill, of course.

I landed in Los Angeles and took a cab over. Walking into the convention center, I felt the way I imagine dogs feel when they visit a dog park for the first time. You've spent months surrounded by hairless beasts who sympathize with but do not understand you. Then suddenly, a hairy stranger has taken your ball and is trying to mate with your leg. No, I'm sorry. What I meant to say was, "Then suddenly, you see that you are not alone of your kind! There are others! All kinds of others! And they wish to frolic with you in an open field." Part of it was just being able to walk into a room and be surrounded with *Star Wars* things—action figures, artwork, tattoo artists doing tattoos while you waited. Part of it was seeing all the people who shared my feelings. I understood the jokes on everyone's T-shirts. Everyone's. That was rare.

With that recognition came relief: I was not alone. This was my tribe.

This was my first time, and it was instant magic. I sat riveted in the hotel bar, chatting with a family of fans. "You built a *Millennium Falcon* in your basement? I DREAM of someday building a *Millennium Falcon* in my basement, sir! Tell me all you know!"

There was a dance party and all the people accustomed to lurking on the edge of the dance floor and shouting over the music about Boba Fett actually got to get up and showcase our moves, waving lightsabers in the air to the dulcet strains of the "Cha Cha Slide." I had no idea life could be like this. There was even a cute guy in a homemade C-3PO suit who vaguely resembled Edward Norton and wanted to dance.

My second convention, I signed up for speed-dating. Midway to the airport, I realized I'd left my Jabba the Hutt suit at home.

Leaving your Jabba the Hutt suit at home on the morning of the *Star Wars* convention is like realizing, the day of prom, that you forgot to buy a dress. "Now I have to fall back on my personality!" you think, as you frantically search through your carry-on one more time. "It can't sustain this!"

My own dating life had not been *Star Wars* dependent. My first kiss was with someone who turned out to be a Trekkie. Not just a Trekkie; an ardent Trekkie who had carefully filmed an entire "new episode" in which he painstakingly reconstructed the setting and vibe of the original series, making all his own effects in Microsoft Paint. Since then, my taste had run more to fans of Woody Allen than George Lucas. Of course, *Star Wars* reared its head now and then, like a space slug emerging from a crater in an asteroid. When a boyfriend suggested we watch *Annie Hall*—"I think it would shed light on our relationship," he argued—I adamantly refused. "That movie stole Best Picture from *Star Wars*," I shot back. "I try not to watch it on principle."

But I was newly single and primed to participate in speed-dating. The odds seemed good, even if the goods were bound to be a bit odd.

I arrived at the hotel and felt immediately at home, dodging R2 units and Darth Mauls, grinning at the pairs of Chewbaccas and Han Solos trying to avoid other pairs, like girls wearing the same dress at prom.

We weren't the only ones in town for love. "I met Ron Paul," a guy told me at the hotel bar. "I *touched* him. Do you understand? It CHANGED my life." (What did I tell you? Everyone's weird about something.)

In another room was the International Yo-Yo Championship. It was impressive. A kid was showcasing his extreme moves in one glove, Michael Jackson–style.

Jedi milled about the lobby. Clearly this was the place to be.

I felt naked without my Jabba suit and, chagrined, wound up buying another one. This, I rationalized, was a long-term investment.

The suit consisted of two parts: an inflatable body and a giant headpiece that fell lightly on my shoulders. You could see out through the nostrils, which were made of mesh. It looked like something the Elephant Man would sport on a fun, casual afternoon out.

Seeing through it was not the easiest thing in the world, but it was worth it. People kept coming up and asking to take pictures with me, even though it deflated slowly until it hung loosely on my frame, as though Jabba had just had horribly botched liposuction. My Jabba Suit was to Actual Jabba as Drew Carey Now is to The Drew Carey We Remember and Love.

Since we were in Orlando, I joined dozens of other fans in the line for the "Star Tours" ride at Disney World and waited dutifully for my turn flying down the Death Star trench and over the Endor jungle. It was dark inside my suit and hard to see, but I bumbled along, panting into the one hundred percent nylon, grunting disapprovingly when people stepped on my tail. The atmosphere was close and sweaty and smelled like a beer I had spilled on the suit earlier.

By the time I made it onto the ride, I had had enough. I was hot. It was hard to see what was going on. I untied the chin strap and took off the head.

"Whoa," said a voice behind me. "Way to RUIN the illusion." I glanced back. A gray-haired man was glowering at me.

"You know what," I wanted to whisper, "there is also NO SANTA." But I refrained.

I should have realized.

In most walks of life, when you pulled off the giant face-obscuring sack to reveal that you were not a large slug but a young woman, it was a net positive. Here, it was a disgrace. This weekend, we were living inside out.

The next day we filed into the speed-dating lounge. The event was hosted by a fat Anakin Skywalker who went by Giganakin. There was also an Obi-Wan Kenobi look-alike DJ and someone called the Scout Trooper of Love who was supposed to facilitate everyone's interactions. He spent most of his time handing out pens.

Someone created a minor disturbance by showing up in a *Star Trek* uniform. "One of the guys asked me to kick him out," Giganakin admitted. To be fair, someone showing up at a *Star Wars* convention dressed as Captain Kirk is like someone showing up at a Marine barbecue dressed as Osama bin Laden's Vengeful Ghost, except that there are international laws that restrain the Marines in such cases.

The dates lasted three minutes each. We were to share no names, no locations. No personally identifying information. We talked *Star Wars*—favorites of the movies, objections to the prequels—complimented each other on our costumes, admitted we'd never been speed-dating before. We compared numbers of conventions. Then the bell rang. We shook hands meaningfully and the men moved on.

The first guy was scruffy-looking, wearing a T-shirt whose meaning I could not immediately discern. Since we were all identified only by number, to me, he will forever remain thirty-four. He seemed squinty. He had several prior conventions to his credit. He was followed in rapid succession by someone labeled forty-two ("You should explain that you're the answer to everything!" I suggested. "You know, forty-two! *Hitchhiker's Guide?*"), a plump guy with a tattoo that permanently affiliated him with Boba Fett's clan, and a fairly normal-seeming fellow in a humorous T-shirt. I thought that we'd hit it off. Just outside the speed-dating room I heard him exclaiming to some friends, "That was *awful*."

Only one guy was flat-out off-putting. He wasn't bad-looking in an Aryan sort of way, but things quickly became so awkward that I wondered whether he might be doing it on purpose, responding to all my questions in monosyllables and bedewing me with spittle.

Darth Vader appeared briefly and declined to participate, although he did volunteer to stay as "eye candy." In any other context, a man standing in the back of a speed-dating event and breathing heavily would have been politely asked to leave. But we were elated. "I want to speed date Darth!" someone shouted. "His last love did not fare so well," DJ Mad Kid Jedi reminded us, sounding crisp and Obi-Wan-like. "I want to date the DJ!" someone else yelled.

The women were attractive. Most were in their twenties, like me, although the participants ranged in age from eighteen to fifty-four. About the men, I can say only that no more than two were openly carrying lightsabers, and that in general they looked less like Wampa ice monsters than I had initially expected.

It turns out that my lack of short-term memory and speed-dating did not combine particularly well. All the numbers began blurring together. Was forty-four the one who said that his favorite parts of *Star Wars* were "the aliens and the explosions" and refused to say anything else? Or was that sixteen?

I got messages from two of the guys I'd put myself down for. One suggested we meet up later in the evening. The other simply provided his contact information.

I ran into a third on the floor of the convention shopping area. He was wearing an ensemble that made him look like a Rastafarian Jedi—a character I assumed I'd missed because I blinked during the eight seconds he was on-screen. He had seemed kind, but sad. He'd said he was going on the speed-dating adventure because his seven-year-old son appeared to think it was time.

When we ran into each other we didn't really have anything to say. "You do look different with the hair," I managed.

"Yeah," he said.

It wasn't quite "I love you—I know" territory.

"I think *Star Wars* is a love story as much as anything," I said to Gigankin after the event was over. From a certain point of view, the series is all about how people are motivated and changed and sometimes twisted by the things they love. For better or for worse. There's Han and Leia. C-3PO and R2-D2. Anakin and Padme. There's familial love—Darth Vader for his kids. Love leads you to the dark side and brings you right back again.

Gigankin seemed to agree. He'd been telling me about how two couples had already made commitments at the Star Wars Commitment Chapel downstairs. Somehow this depressed me. I had been down there earlier; another Obi-Wan impersonator stood under a white awning festooned with lights, cramming as many *Star Wars* references as he possibly could into these "commitment" vows. It was like the Elvis chapel, but without the legally binding effect or pelvic thrusting. ("Remember, in relationships, size matters not," Obi-Wan had said. "Fear not, I sense much love in you.")

I had no such luck. But these weren't the droids I was looking for, anyway.

As it turned out, I'd have gotten more action if I'd stayed inside Jabba.

I learned this for a fact in 2012.

The *Star Wars* Celebration fell right before the Republican National Convention, which I was hoping to cover anyway, so I figured I'd hit Florida a weekend early and get in some good wholesome time with the bounty hunters, assassins, and menacing cloaked figures before wading into the sea of bow ties.

I remembered my Jabba suit this time.

I went to hear Carrie Fisher speak and then wandered into the dance party. The lighting was bad, by which I mean that it was so bright you could actually see the people you were talking to.

I found myself on the outskirts of the dance talking to "Hank" and "Gregor," who had met in the line for Carrie Fisher. They seemed pleasant enough. Hank was bearded and looked nervous. Gregor was young and earnest, if a little on the squinty, spitty side.

"There's going to be an afterparty," he said.

"Oh?" I asked.

"Yeah." Gregor nodded. "I've got a VIP ticket."

"A VIP ticket to the Sith afterparty with Jake Lloyd?" I asked. This was an exciting prospect. Jake Lloyd had portrayed Young Anakin in the first prequel. In interviews he complained that *Star Wars* had ruined his life. The idea of an afterparty with him was intriguing. It seemed like it would be a horrible experience.

"Whoa," Hank said.

"You should come with me!" Gregor said. "I can get us all in."

As we walked from the convention center to the hotel where the afterparty was, we learned more about Gregor. He was, he said, a pundit. His uncle was coming to pick him up at eleven, before he turned back into a pumpkin.

He stopped conversing when his phone rang.

"Hey," Gregor drawled into the phone. "Yeah, I made these cool friends, Hank and Alex. I'm going to stay with one of them. You don't need to pick me up."

"Excuse me?" Hank said.

"What?" I said.

"No, buddy," Hank said. "You need to, um, you need to call him back and say that's not the case, you didn't actually ask us, like, it really would definitely not be cool for you to stay with us."

"Yeah," I said, "me neither. My roommates are pretty big sticklers about that." My roommates consisted of my suitcase, a change of clothes, and several hardcover books by P. G. Wodehouse, but that seemed like unnecessary information to volunteer.

"Oh," Gregor said. "Are you sure?"

"Yes," we said.

"But," Gregor said.

This exchange went on for much longer than this kind of exchange usually goes on when people pick up on social cues.

We reached the line outside the afterparty. Inside, beats throbbed and dancers dressed like Twi'leks* twirled around poles. The line curled around the block in the muggy Florida air. We were behind several Sexy Dark Jedi and Regular Dark Jedi and Sexy People Who Lacked a Jedi Affiliation. I climbed into my Jabba suit.

The closer we got to the front of the line, the shakier Gregor's story became.

"I can't believe you have a ticket to this thing," Hank said.

Gregor pulled out a stiff, laminated red postcard and brandished it proudly.

"That's a ticket?" I asked. It didn't look like a ticket. It looked like a red postcard advertising the event.

Gregor smiled and pointed. "Ian McDiarmid signed it," he said.

"But—" Hank said.

"I'll just show it to the guy at the door," Gregor said. "It's my trump card. He'll understand."

"Will he, though?" Hank asked.

"He'll take it and in exchange, he'll let us in."

"Unless he's a big *Star Wars* collector," Hank said, "I don't see how this will happen. He will just say, 'What is this? This is not a

---

* Sexy aliens with weird head-tentacle things.

ticket. This is a piece of paper with the autograph of someone I have never heard of on it. Why are you giving me this?' And then he will not let us in."

Gregor shook his head. "He'll understand," he said. "Just watch."

We stood in the line some more. If *Star Wars* fans excel at anything, it is standing in lines. Gregor glanced nervously at his watch. It was eleven thirty. "My uncle is coming at midnight to pick me up," he reiterated.

"That's a whole half hour," I said, reassuringly.

He cheered up a little. "That's enough time for, like, six orgasms."

Hank had been growing increasingly nervous the longer this interaction went on. Now he said, "I have to go to the bathroom," and vanished into the night. As it turns out, he was never to return. Later he sent me an apologetic e-mail. ("After being perfectly fine in the Carrie Fisher line, Gregor kept getting stranger by the minute and I'd had enough. I was going to let him use my badge on Sunday, on the condition he mailed it back to me, but he turned and became untrustworthy. I am very sorry I left you there in his company with no explanation until now.")

We arrived at the front of the line with a couple of minutes to spare and Gregor sallied forth, brandishing his postcard with Ian McDiarmid's signature in shiny silver ink. The bouncer took it with a quizzical nod and walked away into the VIP area.

I gazed agog at Gregor through the mesh of my Jabba suit. Had he actually done this? Had all his spittle-spewing bravado paid off? Were we going to get to interact with the embittered Jake Lloyd after all?

The bouncer returned. "I don't know what this is," he said. "Are you Ian McDiarmid?"

"No," Gregor said. The clock struck midnight. He handed me the postcard and made a sudden dive toward me.

It turned out that, in Gregor's mind, this had been a romantic evening.

I don't know if someone has ever attempted to kiss you through the mesh of a Jabba the Hutt suit, but it is definitely a unique experience. Let's just say it's impossible to make any headway. For better results, you could try to tongue-kiss a fully dressed beekeeper. Depending on how soon the other party notices this, it can give you a lot of time to marvel at his tenacity. "Huh?" you think. "I'm alarmed, but at the same time, I'm kind of impressed. Is impressed the word? Maybe it's the word. Should I move? Or just stand here until it's over?"

Several more security personnel appeared. "Sir," they said, "please stop. Please leave."

Outside, a white car with a tired-looking white-haired man in it pulled up. It was Gregor's uncle. Gregor climbed in, still protesting faintly, leaving me with the Ian McDiarmid autograph.

"You okay?" the bouncer asked.

"Oh yeah," I said. "Hey, at least I got a free Ian McDiarmid autograph out of it this time." (Usually, when a guy does something like this, you get nothing! Or blamed.) I handed him my ten dollars and oozed into the regular afterparty.

In the dark bar, the Sexy Twi'lek Dancers gyrated and the beer flowed. If I had actually been Jabba the Hutt, this would have been exactly my jam. As it was, I was about partied out.

Hutts, I reflected, trooping back to my room, were supposed to be asexual anyway. Gregor surely knew that. What did he think he was doing?

Gregor went on to send me hundreds of messages, operating under the misapprehension that, as a fellow pundit, I might be able to get him into the GOP convention in Tampa.

He still follows me on Twitter. (Hi, "Gregor"! Don't kill me!)

So much for meeting people at conventions.

(I feel a little bad for theming this chapter around Nerd Dating, because now it will be impossible to convince Some Nameless Nerds that I am legit. To these fools and trolls, the only real nerd is a male nerd, and lady nerds are dabblers and dilettantes whose passion is skin-deep, and they just pretend to like these things to lure in Eligible Basement-Dwelling Males. This is a slight generalization, but only a slight one.)

I had hoped, in a vague way, that *Star Wars* would perform the office of a mutual friend and set me up with someone. But this wasn't panning out at all. Maybe it was my fault for trying to mix the two.

After all, *Star Wars* was forever. That was even a convention motto.

Things could change in the world. But *Star Wars* endured (even if George Lucas kept doing unspeakable things to the original trilogy in the course of transferring it to DVD, inserting Hayden Christensen where he had no business being and adding more wipes and dissolves.) *Star Wars* was constant.

I always used to recoil when fans marched down the aisle to the evocative strains of "The Imperial March." "Fools," I thought. "What if your marriage ends in divorce and ruins *The Empire Strikes Back* for you? You can't let *Star Wars*, which is unchanging and permanent, get mixed up in something potentially temporary like a lifelong commitment to another person!"

I didn't ever want anything to change things between *Star Wars* and me. I hate change. I hate kumquats and change. And *Star Wars* is my longest relationship to date.

It's had its ups and downs. We fans talk about *Star Wars* the way old sailors talk about the sea—as a harsh mistress whom you cannot help but love, but who mostly has been a lot of trouble and expense.

I think. I'm not, in fact, super tight with any old sailors, but I feel like they squint wistfully out to sea and say, "Ah, aye, all in all, she's been kind, but he who loves her had better watch where he treads, oh, aye."

Star Wars is the only thing that can make us suffer this much. Our love is why some of us were so devastated when we saw Jar Jar for the first time, or heard the tomfoolery about midi-chlorians, or stormed out of the feature-length animated preview of *The Clone Wars* when Jabba the Hutt turned out to have a purple uncle whom George had decided would sound "like Truman Capote." Besides waiting in line, another thing that *Star Wars* fans have an affinity for is dealing with disappointment.

I remember sitting in the dark before *Episode III* began. Please, I murmured, please don't let this ruin it.

There's something terrifying about having that much of yourself invested in anything you can't control. It's weird enough when it's another human being. And it's especially weird when the thing that's capable of doing that to you is something imaginary that a large bearded man came up with in the 1970s.

But I'm less worried about that than I used to be.

Star Wars grew with me, like initials etched into a sapling, or Darth Vader's face carved into a baby pumpkin.

The things we love weave themselves into the framework of our being. They are the trellises on which our thoughts grow; we shape ourselves, our habits, our vocabularies, to accommodate them. If someone asks, "Why do you love this?" the question is as impossible to answer as "Why are you?" You cannot isolate the part of you that loves from the rest of you, or mark its beginning and ending. Old couples grow to look like each other. Old ruins blur into their ivy. *Star Wars* fans name their kids Luke and Leia and show up at conventions dressed as Jabba the Hutt. At first we loved the *Millennium*

Falcon, so we wanted to build a scale replica in our basement. Now we love the *Millennium Falcon* because of the scale replica in our basement.

Every time I watched *Star Wars* I used to hold my breath to see if it felt the same. But now I know it won't. It hasn't moved, but I have.

It's always there. It's magic, still, but a different magic every time.

I turn off all the lights in the house so there's no reflection or glare, shut all the doors and windows, and settle in a chair with my arms folded over my knees and wait for takeoff.

And then it happened.

Not at a convention, of course.

I met a guy who could recite the entire opening credits of *Return of the Jedi*. I mean, among other qualities, obviously. Liking *Star Wars* is not the be-all and end-all in relationships for me. Never mind the fact that every time a friend has met someone she intends to marry, she introduces him to me by saying, "Petri, you'll like him! He loves *Star Wars*." (Seriously, this has happened three times now. People know that I can't disapprove of anyone who likes *Star Wars*. Not entirely. If you told me that Satan was a big *Star Wars* fan I would have to reevaluate eternal damnation. They might have something good showing on the big screen.)

Being in an actual relationship with another *Star Wars* fan still terrifies me a little. On the one hand it's great to have someone who picks up, line by line, what I'm putting down, countering my "Is that legal?"s with "I will MAKE IT legal"s. But on the other hand, when you start sharing the things you love with somebody else, there's a danger. It's no longer private. It's no longer secure. Someone else can walk through and leave muddy footprints on your soul. You get back to your sanctum sanctorum and there are someone else's stray shoes and socks and phone chargers. Once you disclose the actual location of your secret rebel base, you can't retreat there if anything goes wrong. And bases like this are hard to come by.

But that's the whole point of loving something: It means you carry it around with you, and it gets marked and dented and banged up like the rest of you. There's a reason "well-loved" is a euphemism for "looks like crap." You're supposed to Open Yourself Up and Be Vulnerable and Embrace Life, with all the scuffing that entails.

I'm trying to let down my guard, but old habits take a while to die, like someone being shot at by a stormtrooper. We haven't watched it together yet. I don't think we're ready. The new trilogy, the J. J. Abrams effort? Sure. The originals? Maybe later, if this relationship keeps up—say, in a decade or two, after the kids are out of the house. I really don't think we should rush into all of this, as Threepio says.

Dietary Restrictions

As a general rule, don't let your five-year-old self make too many of your life decisions. Otherwise you wind up as a fairy princess who is also a vet, whose entire portfolio is invested in Lisa Frank stickers.

For the most part, I have broken out from under the iron yoke of my five-year-old self. For the most part. She wanted to be surrounded by cats. I am not surrounded by cats. She thought ballet was a good investment of time and energy. I have gotten clear of that. She wanted to be a writer. That one I'm stuck with.

But the toughest pronouncement of hers took me years to wiggle out of. All of elementary school, in fact.

"Chocolate makes me grumpy."

I remember when this resolution formed. It was well after my bedtime one evening. I had just eaten some M&M's, and I was in a foul humor. Perhaps, I pondered, this was not correlation, but causation.

"Chocolate," I announced, "makes me grumpy."

And something clicked.

This was the beginning of a deeply regrettable phase. You think your gluten-free friend is hard to put up with? She might have an actual medical complaint. I had nothing to go on but my intuition.

But I insisted.

I forswore chocolate. Whenever anyone served chocolate at school, I objected. Obstreperously.

They served us chocolate ice-cream bars at lunch.

"Excuse me," I said. "I can't eat this. Chocolate"—I paused ominously—"makes me grumpy."

My teacher frowned at me. She seemed to be searching for some sort of justification. Dogs, she was probably thinking, had problems with chocolate. Maybe I was secretly a dog. You never knew with these private-school kids. They always were coming up with strange ailments. "Okay," she said. It seemed hardly worth the time to argue with a seven-year-old. Maybe this was a real dietary restriction that existed. "Fine." She sent me to the cafeteria kitchens. I explained myself to the cafeteria lady, my confidence swelling. She reached into the depths of the freezer and produced a blue-flavored Popsicle. ("Blue" is a flavor.)

I sucked on it in triumph.

It turned out that if you were firm enough about your preference, people genuinely thought you had a dietary issue.

This became a pattern. Someone would present me with chocolate birthday cupcakes and I would wave them away with all the dismissive authority of a tiny teetotaler. "No," I said. "I can't. My system can't handle the stuff. I know how I get. It's an ugly, ugly sight, and one I wouldn't wish on you—certainly not on a festive occasion like your seventh birthday, Nell."

At Halloween, I sifted moodily through piles and piles of Hershey kisses. I had worked hard to earn them. My costumes were always homemade and, as a consequence, it was hard to tell who I was supposed to be. Part of the Halloween ritual at the Petri house every year was making me practice the spiel I would deliver on the doorstep of each house.

"Don't be fooled by the face paint that makes me resemble the victim of an elevator accident! I am in fact a hobbit, and this is my trusty sword, Sting!"

"Good day, fellow American! I am John Adams, and I am most pleased to make your acquaintance this fine eve!"

"You might be surprised to hear that I am Winston Churchill, but I am."

"I'm Garfield. The cat, not the president."

It was hard going, and at the end of it I felt that I was entitled to the spoils. But most of the spoils were chocolate. This tended to spoil the spoils.

"Here," I said, pouring them out. "I can't eat this. I've been clean three years now. The thought of putting this stuff in your body—" I scowled. "I'm glad I'm not a grump."

"Yeah," said my friend John, who had been trick-or-treating with me, scooping up several handfuls of chocolate, "you're definitely not."

And then came the incident.

I had been so firm for so long. The logic of not eating chocolate became a nightmare creature that ate its own tail, like an ouroboros, which I believe is just a word for a nightmare creature that eats its own tail. (I get a fifty-dollar cut from SAT makers for every word like that I keep in circulation!)

Jane brought chocolate birthday somethings.

"Don't you want one, Alexandra?" she asked.

"I can't," I said. "Chocolate makes me grumpy."

"Are you allergic?"

"No," I said. I was used to this line of questioning. "It makes me grumpy."

Jane's eyes narrowed. "I don't believe you."

This blunt response took the wind out of me. I had never needed to defend myself before. Everyone took it on faith.

"You can give it to me," I said. "But I warn you, you will not like what you see. Chocolate makes me grumpy. I know."

"Really?"

This could not pass. I would not abide this questioning.

Resolute, I took a bite. And another bite. I ate the whole thing.

I sat there like Jekyll about to turn into Hyde, waiting for the change to come upon me. At this point I had swallowed my own press releases, hook, line, and sinker, like a credulous fish. I was convinced that something horrible was about to happen. I would go rampaging through the countryside and eat a villager. There was no telling. Years of not building up any tolerance to the stuff had probably taken their toll. I would be a menace to myself and everyone I loved. They would have to put me down like a rabid dog who had also eaten chocolate.

Everyone else watched nervously, expecting something similar. And waited.

"Stay back," I warned.

I didn't feel anything. That couldn't be right. I had to feel something. I was in too deep. I had to feel something. I had been so committed for so long. Maybe you had to let yourself feel it.

This set the pattern for all of my experiences with controlled substances. Years later, the first time I tried beer, I drank a tiny Dixie cup full and convinced myself that I was inebriated. This is what it feels like! I told myself. "Kid, don't you feel your coordination leaving you and your confidence building? That is what drinking does." To prove a point to myself, I walked a zigzag down the sidewalk, singing an old drinking song. (It turns out that this was not actually what being drunk was like at all, as I discovered to my chagrin a few weeks later, kneeling over a toilet, having consumed four beers in quick succession.) The same thing my first time with marijuana. I failed to inhale properly (Bill Clinton would have been proud) but nonetheless spent the rest of the night insisting that I had "the munchies" and that "man, time's just, just so deep, right, man?" When I actually figured out how to inhale correctly, I spent the entire evening convinced that my soul was leaving my body and frantically bargaining with God.

No, I thought. This was what grumpy felt like. I just hadn't felt grumpy in so long that I didn't remember.

Everyone was still looking at me, waiting for me to make a move, the way we looked at ants in the science classroom after someone placed a big obstacle in their paths.

I had to do something.

I climbed up unsteadily onto a chair. I climbed from the chair onto the table. "I'm grumpy!" I announced. "I'm grumpy!" I stamped my foot for emphasis. "I'm grumpy!"

Apparently this incident left more of an impression on those who witnessed it than I thought. In eighth grade, when I went to my elementary school reunion (yes, it was the kind of elementary school that had a reunion), I stood there in a skirt trying to look approachable and cool.

"Third grade," I murmured, to Jane. "Whoa, can you believe how LONG ago that was? Like a lifetime. How are you? You still studying to be a vet-princess?"

"Ha-ha," Jane laughed. Her claws came out. "Does chocolate still make you grumpy?"

"Ha-ha," I laughed, with as much nonchalance as I could muster. "That was so long ago. We've all changed so much. We're totally unrecognizable."

"Did you say grumpy?" someone else said, joining the conversation. "I remember the time you were so grumpy you stood on a chair."

"I don't remember that at all," I lied, unconvincingly.

"Because you had chocolate!" Jane added.

"Are you still grumpy?" someone else asked, joining the circle.

I swallowed. "Well, I haven't had chocolate in so long, who can really say?"

Then I made up an excuse to leave the room and sat in the bathroom for a very long time.

Reputations are hard to keep up.

Under the Dome

I don't usually tell people this, but we've been getting to know each other for two hundred pages now (unless you're skimming!), and I think you're ready to hear it. My dad was a congressman.

I was never someone who walked around announcing this fact. "Do you know who my father is?" are words that have never left my lips. "What does your dad do?" people would ask. "Um," I would say. "He's a civil servant. Works in government."

I tried to make sure that people had some idea of who I was before they figured out who he was. Because not only was my father in Congress—he was a Republican. A moderate, admittedly. But for most people in places like College Campuses and Coastal Cities and Hip Hangouts of the Young, the word "Republican" came wrapped in a horrifying miasma. I might as well have walked in and announced that my family liked to grill and eat kittens. "You were raised by Republicans?" people asked. "Poor girl. If it had been wolves, you might have had a chance."

"No," I tried to explain. "He's a moderate. He's okay. You don't need to start the reparative therapy on me. Please, put away those prongs and flashcards." It took some time to subdue them, during which I would have to insist repeatedly that we believed in history and women, understood that science was real, and did not conduct pagan sacrifices to Ronald Reagan under the light of the full moon.

Once I had satisfied them on this front, they kept circling. "Well," they asked, eyes sparkling, closing in, "what's it like?"

I think when people ask, "What's it like being a congressman's daughter?" they picture something like this.

A large black SUV pulls up outside a building. A woman in perfect designer clothes gets out of it.

She approaches a man with a big flag pin and expensive shoes. He is wearing a suit jacket lined with the broken dreams of the American people that was given to him by The Sinister Billionaire Who Owns the Senate.

"Hello, Harold dear," she says. She is calling him "dear" only in case there are cameras around. For the past eight years he has been leading a secret double life in a relationship with a flight attendant named Dave Hypocrisy. Everyone knows this except the American people, who are having the wool pulled over their eyes.

Harold's Most Trusted Staffer, Marley, approaches. Marley is a short, sinister-looking bald man in a robotic headpiece who resembles Lando Calrissian's assistant Lobot in The Empire Strikes Back.

Marley has just killed a rabbit with his bare hands for no good reason. He wipes his bloody hands on a wad of dollar bills from Big Oil.

"Thank God we have our connections to Big Oil," one of the other staffers says. This staffer has been walking and talking in the background the whole time. "Did you know that six pigeons die by flying into oil rigs every week?"

(The staff can only communicate by referencing obscure and dubious facts that Aaron Sorkin found on the Internet somewhere. Staff members are also required to walk up and down hallways whenever they speak.)

Marley gets an important e-mail on all nine of his Black-Berrys. "Sir," he says, "the press are closing in on the trail of that prostitute you killed."

"I don't have time for this!" Harold yells.

His wife stiffens. "Marley, go take the big black SUV with tinted windows and pick up our daughter from cheerleading practice."

It turns out that this daughter is nowhere to be found. She is running amok because she was always expected to be perfect and now she is sick of it. She sees her father only once a year, when the family Christmas card photo is taken, but has gotten a dim sense of her father's personality from his publicity materials. ("I think he is very into shaking hands with hopeful-looking elderly people, and also combating wasteful government projects.")

Now she has numerous piercings, one for each important school event that Harold missed during her formative years. "I'm becoming a terrorist," she recently informed him. "I'm doing it just to hurt you, because you used me as a prop in all your campaigns, and I never had my freedom."

"Over my dead body," Harold responded. "Now smile for the camera."

I regret to say that this was not my experience.

There was no staffer picking me up in a black SUV with tinted windows.

My dad rolled up outside school in a big green '77 Chevy Zephyr. When we replaced the Zephyr, instead of getting a car from a year when I had actually been alive, we got another Chevy, a '79. It was giant, blue, and had only two doors.

My mother gave it a long, hard look. "I guess it'll build character," she said.

It didn't have air-conditioning that worked either. It did, however, have a functioning AM radio.

By the time we finally replaced it with a used Malibu, which was when I was in about eighth grade, I was just overflowing with character. I had so much character I was basically an entire Dickens novel.

The difficulty with telling people what it was like to be the daughter of a congressman is that I don't know what it was like to be the daughter of anyone else.

Childhood, especially when you're an only child, is like being plunked down on an isolated human outpost in deep space for the first eighteen years of your life. Everything you know of Earth and its customs you hear from the humans charged with your rearing, or pick up by chance from the TV. "We'll have a nice traditional Fourth of July," my parents informed me, "where we all pretend we're Founding Fathers and discuss the course we hope the nation will take."

"But," I said timidly, "I don't think that's what other people do on the Fourth. At least, that wasn't what the people in the Home Depot commercial looked like they were doing. Shouldn't we be repainting a room very confidently?"

"Don't worry," they reassured me, as I donned my vest and ruffled shirt, "this is completely normal."

And then one day you make the mistake of asking if this is what other people do, and it turns out that, no, this is not what other people do at all.

It's like learning you've been pronouncing a word wrong half your life. You now have to question *everything*. It's suddenly possible that your normal is strange. You have to go back over your whole life, underlining relevant passages from your diary and scrawling question marks in the margin.

"Giving your pets middle names is a thing, right? Ginger Growl-tiger Petri? Ketcham Tape-Recorder Petri?"

"Did you have to play electric piano in a corner at your dad's fund-raisers?" you ask, nervously.

"Everyone else's mom was extremely fond of George Washington, right? And every Christmas, your family rewatched the 1984 *George Washington* miniseries starring Barry Bostwick, and your mother got very emotional about it?"

"No," everyone says, "that is not what you so glibly term 'a thing.' In fact, most people don't do that at all."

But as a child I thought all of it was normal.

To me, the Capitol was just a place I sometimes hung out in after school. It might have been a little heavy on the marble and the symbolism compared to other dads' offices, but who was I to judge?

If you like allegorical paintings or sculptures at all, hoo boy, this is the building for you. George Washington in a toga, being taken up into Heaven? Check. Big statues of Vague Nouns like Freedom? Heck yes. Paintings of people surveying new lands or generals dying on battlefields or oddly contented-looking Native Americans signing over large tracts of land? Look no further.

Sometimes when there was a vote well into the night, my mother and I would drive to the Capitol and eat a family dinner in the House Dining Room, with its big gold plush chairs, blue and gold carpet and a large waitress with blond hair pulled back into a too-tight bun, who brought me my thick-cut fries.

I thought this was just what you did.

I even voted.

Fun fact: Until you're twelve, they let you vote. (At least they used to.)

Members of the House voted by selecting the appropriate button and then swiping their voting cards, and until you were twelve you were allowed to walk onto the floor with your mother or father and press the vote button. There were four buttons: green for yes, red for no, yellow for abstain, blue for present, if memory serves.

They were a lot of fun to push. I'd cycle through the colors, watching the vote change color on the wall. "Stop on 'Yes,' " my dad would say, looking a little uneasy.

Sometimes, I just waited in the cloakroom until he was done. I was fascinated by the congressional pages, college students in fancy blue jackets who looked so grown up and worldly and important as they filed in and out. The cloakroom had raspberry Popsicles with little seeds and large comfortable chairs, and there were plenty of members who would shake my hand and ask me when I planned to run. (If you like being asked when you plan to run, being a congressional kid is definitely for you!)

I would tell them in an authoritative eight-year-old manner that "I would only touch politics with a long-handled spoon" (a line that got some bewildered laughs) or tell them fun facts about cats. Cats, I assured them, were my passion, not public policy.

My dad's office was in the Rayburn Building. Like most congressional offices, it had a big American flag, a big state flag, and lots of pictures of the Wonders of the District, such as the OshKosh B'gosh headquarters, which was represented by a poster of two toddlers in fetching overalls sharing a watermelon. There were posters from wildlife preserves. There was cheese paraphernalia.

There were Christmas cards. Every year on the squintiest, brightest day of summer, my family went and stood in front of a scenic Wisconsin landmark and took a picture in which only one of the three of us (two at the absolute most) ever looked good. This became our Christmas card, which my dad then mailed out to everyone he could. Framed versions of these cards sat all around the office. Whenever I visited, I could see myself as a plump baby, propped on my mother's lap in holiday colors; then as a toddler; then sitting in a swing; then indoors in my holiday best, trying to hold the squirming family cat long enough for the picture to take.

How long ago that had been, eight-year-old me mused, rising up on tiptoe to peer over the top of the desk. I barely recognized myself.

In the picture it looked so orderly, but I knew that the moment after the flash had gone off the cat had gotten away and it had been mayhem. Pictures were funny like that.

My favorite place in the Capitol was Statuary Hall.

Everyone who was *anyone* was there—or standing in bronze or marble just down the hall. My dad pointed them out. There was Father Marquette, one of Wisconsin's own, and Bob La Follette, just getting up from his chair to say hello. There was Will Rogers. "Will Rogers," my dad told me, "said he never met a man he didn't like."

I frowned. Will Rogers, I thought, must not have met a lot of people. By age nine I'd already met several people I disliked. Some of them were men. Some of them were girls my age. Some of them were just people who didn't want to hear fun facts about cats.

Apart from Will and Bob, my favorites were the statues from Hawaii—the big statue of King Kamehameha with gold trim that was always garlanded in leis, and the big boxy statue of someone called Father Damien who looked like a deranged refrigerator.

There was even a place in Statuary Hall where you could stand and make your words echo across the chamber, if you whispered just right. This had been a big advantage to John Quincy Adams, back when Congress used to meet in this room. He would lie on his desk pretending to be asleep, but secretly, he would hear everything.

I liked the Rotunda too, but not as much as Statuary Hall. It was a little too heavy on the allegory, even for me, and I got a crick in my neck from staring up at the ceiling where George Washington sat wrapped in a sheet communing with similarly draped symbolic figures. What was it, I wondered, about symbolic figures and sheets? Couldn't you be symbolic while keeping your pants on?

The other great thing about Capitol Hill was how many things there were to ride.

Under the Capitol ran a variety of trains. On the Senate side, an automatic train opened and closed its doors every few minutes in exactly the orderly manner that trains under fascist regimes are supposed to.

It filled with people in sensible black suits or pantsuits. Spewed them back out. Filled again. Spewed them back out.

There was also another train that was old-fashioned and upholstered in brown leather. It had no ceiling and resembled two restaurant booths settled back to back on a rolling track. In it a conductor sat all day pushing the lever. Push, and the train went from the House Floor to the office buildings. Pull, and it went back from the office buildings to the House Floor.

There was also an elevator, complete with attendant. She sat smiling in the elevator, pushing the buttons for everyone, like a very personable vestigial limb.

I thought that was just what you did.

Elections came and went.

I was in a couple of ads. I was always annoyed that I didn't get to say much of anything during them. "That's why I'd like your vote," my dad would say, as the camera rolled, and from my mother's lap in my Sunday best I would murmur, "I'd definitely vote for him!" and then they'd have to tape the whole thing over.

And in summer, there were parades.

We pulled a big metal sign out from the trunk and attached it to the roof of the car. PETRI FOR CONGRESS, the sign read. Like all our campaign materials, it was half blue and half green and said PETRI in big white letters.

It had suction cups on the bottom, and four strings with a little hook at the end that we secured at the top of each of the car's windows by rolling the window up to keep it in place.

My dad and I walked to the front of the parade to see what we could see.

I could never make up my mind whether my dad was good at hobnobbing or not. He carried a pocketful of Packer schedules with his face on them, printed out in blue ink. He would sidle up to a fire truck.

"Rah rah!" he'd say, waving a fist.

"Hello, Congressman," the fire truck driver would say.

"Looking good up there," my dad would say. He would extend a hand with a Packer schedule in it. "Have a thing."

Then we would walk away from the truck. He would turn to me, looking authoritative.

"I always find that if you say 'Have a thing,' they don't know what it is, so they take it!"

I nodded, absorbing this information. I never said "Have a thing." Sometimes I would say "There you go!" just to spice things up, but usually my spiel went, "Have a Packer schedule! Have a Packer football schedule! Have a Packer schedule! Have a Packer schedule from my dad!" I started adding "from my dad" because people tended not to yell at you as much if they knew you were personally connected to the politician peddling the schedules. Usually. The other trick was not to make it a question, because if you asked, people could say, "No."

There were a lot of parades. A *lot* of parades. Parades with Shriners and Lions and Rotarians and Elks riding motor scooters in their little maroon fezzes, tassels floating in the wind. Parades with clubs dressed up as slightly dingy Peanuts characters. Parades where it rained. Parades where it didn't. Parades where you were allowed to throw candy and parades where throwing candy was absolutely forbidden. Parades where everyone watching was drunk and had been so since approximately nine in the morning. Parades that went past convents at the tops of hills, where you could sit with the nuns in the shade.

Some parades had one guy dressed up in an inflatable suit to look like an ice-cream cone. It always rained on those parades. There is nothing sadder than a man dressed as a giant inflatable ice-cream cone walking slowly through the rain, deflating a little with every step.

Some parades had someone dressed in a plush pig suit, pushing a shopping cart, to represent Piggly Wiggly. The parades with the heaviest plush suits were always on the hottest days.

There were generally a couple of big floats—the county Republicans, say, with a large plaster elephant statue on it—or a local church with all the Sunday school kids dressed up as animals who did or did not make it onto the Ark.

There was a dance team that was good. There was a dance team that was not so good, doing exuberant choreography to "Black Hole Sun" all the way home.

There were singers with microphones and speakers blasting country rock, riding behind a truck in a big cage.

There was a beer float playing "Spirit in the Sky" on loop.

There were bagpipers.

There was a long line of fire trucks with sirens going slow and loud, tossing handfuls of Tootsie Rolls out the window onto the hot sidewalk.

There was usually one float handing out sticks of flavored ice.

The best place to be, my dad informed me, was behind the band. The worst place was behind the horses. The horses left plenty of evidence of their opinion of the proceedings that was very easy to step in.

Often we were behind the fire trucks. Sometimes we were behind the vintage cars, honking and misfiring, with or without Fairests of the (County or State) Fair waving demurely from the backseats.

Once, my father reported with great excitement that we would be marching behind the "ballet dancers."

Ballet dancers! I thought, in excitement. I took ballet! I was excited to see what they had in store for us. Wouldn't they be afraid they'd ruin their shoes?

We heard a faint jingling in the distance as the dancers approached.

It turned out that my father had misheard, and that these were belly dancers. It was some sort of class from the local rec center.

They all wore bells on their feet and shook what their mothers had given them. (Their mothers had not been stingy.)

As I got older I started to play "Guess Who's Leaving Town Immediately After High School Ends." The only male member of the dance team, doggedly lip-syncing to P!nk on the back of a float? Probably a safe bet, given the fact that he was bracketed by floats embracing sentiments like "Noah Knew What to Do About Climate Change." Maybe that guy dressed up as an ice-cream cone? It was difficult to tell whether he had dreams under the inflatable cone suit.

My role in the parades evolved as I aged. First my job was just to walk along holding my favorite stuffed animal and wave and be a blond six-year-old with curly hair who didn't really understand what was going on but appreciated the applause.

Then I got a pair of stilts and my job was to walk through the parade on stilts, first small yellow ones, then a bigger pink pair. We finally stopped doing this after I had a growth spurt because when I stood up on the stilts I was taller than my dad.

Then my job was to hand out the Packer schedules.

Sometimes we had staff in the parade to drive the car while my mom and I passed out schedules and waved, but usually it was just the three of us. My mother drove. My father walked, waved, and handed out the occasional schedule. I ran down one side of the sidewalk frantically canvassing for all I was worth. Sometimes I canvassed too quickly and got tangled up with another candidate's team, also handing out football schedules, and we had to rumble. "These are also MAGNETS!" I would shout, nearly toppling an old lady out of her lawn chair.

When you handed someone a Packer schedule, one of six things would happen. The person would either say, "Thanks," and take it, say, "Thanks, and can I get one for my husband, too?" say, "Thanks! Tell him he's doing good work!" say, "No, thanks, I've got one," say,

"NOPE! He's ruining the country!" or withdraw his hand as if burned and shout, "VIKINGS FAN! VIKINGS FAN!"

At the end of each parade, we pulled over to the side of the road in the midst of a ruck of sweaty marching band members holding their tall hats, took down the sign from the roof of the car, and got rapidly back on the highway to hit the next one. "Do you think that crowd liked us?" my mother would ask.

"They were fine," I said.

"They said, 'I don't want your schedules!'"

"That was one guy," I said. "And it was because he was a Vikings fan and had nothing to do with politics."

I also had to help out at fund-raisers.

When you think of fund-raisers you probably picture some kind of large gala where a talented musician wails away on a sax and everyone is wearing floor-length gowns and there are dozens of Sinister Oilmen lurking about. The Congressman stands at the front of the room giving an eloquent speech about America and hinting at his larger national aspirations, and his wife and child stand within the spotlight and beam supportively.

My father did not employ a saxophonist.

Instead, I sat at an electric piano in the corner of a room with a big lunch buffet.

My services were very cheap, but you got what you paid for. In a far corner of the room, behind the flagpole, I played the electric keyboard as quietly as possible, because my mother began each fund-raiser by rushing over to turn the volume of the electric keyboard as low as it would go.

Then my father would come barreling over and turn the volume all the way up. "We can't hear you on the other side of the room!"

A few moments later, my mother would come rushing back. "We can HEAR you on the OTHER SIDE OF THE ROOM!"

They ping-ponged back and forth all afternoon until we sat down for lunch.

I played imperturbably throughout.

As the years went by, it seemed odder and odder that I was doing this. I had stopped taking lessons after the sixth grade. Why, the constituents probably wondered, was a seventeen-year-old sitting there playing "Joe's New Haircut" by Nancy and Randall Faber, a piece that required only the black keys on one hand, concentrating with such intensity that her tongue protruded slightly from one corner of her mouth?

But they were too polite to say so. "How nice it sounds!" an old lady would tell me, very loudly.

"Thank you!" I would shout back.

"What?" she would say. "What's that?"

"THANK YOU!" I yelled back, in all caps.

"MY HUSBAND USED TO PLAY LIKE THAT UNTIL HE DIED! IT IS A WONDERFUL GIFT!" the woman would yell, midway through my sentence.

People who could actually hear were a little less effusive in their praise.

We usually had other musical entertainment that was better than I was, though I set the bar pretty low. The high point was a guy with a guitar who had written a song about the town of Hazelhurst and its business professionals. "Mr. Smith will stuff your vulture/If you want taxi-der-my! Hazelhurst! Hazelhurst!" is an actual lyric from this song, which you can download online!

Maybe someone's idea of a good time is listening to me play the piano badly; then hearing my mother tell rambling stories about

George Washington that were not exactly related to the speaker she was introducing; then eating some dubious-looking chicken with a red sauce on it. *Someone* must have thought this was a good idea, or we would not have done it exactly like this every year.

I kept trying to be helpful. One day in my father's office I volunteered to answer the phone. It was a lot harder than I was expecting. People actually had serious concerns, and I was not sure what to tell them. Finally I decided to get around it by pretending I was the answering machine. "You have reached the office of Congressman Petri," I said, hitting a button. "Beeeeep." Then I wrote down everything that the person said afterward, as quickly as I could. I even caught the number! Sometimes.

There are six or eight people wandering around the district now who I really hope got the constituent services they wanted, and all I can say is, I'm sorry; I could not write fast enough. I hope you called back.

I also tried to help by double-checking all the phone numbers of DC landmarks that we gave to touring constituents. This was how we discovered that the number we had listed for the Newseum was a recorded advertisement for a sex hotline.

When I called it, a sexy recording answered in a low breathy voice. Did I want to TALK, she wanted to know. Because she certainly wanted to TALK to me. All I had to do was call the following 900-number. Could I please give her a long, hard talking-to?

I froze in terror and tried to back away. The phone had a cord, so my range was a little limited. It did not sound like the Newseum, exactly. But the woman said she wasn't wearing pants, so maybe it was an allegory.

I handed the phone to an actual staffer. "I don't think this is the Newseum," I said.

She listened for a few moments. "Odd that no one's complained."

. . .

I also want to apologize to anyone I ever gave a tour of the Capitol to, constituent or otherwise.

That thing we stopped under on the way to the Old Senate Chamber was not the biggest chandelier in North America. Nor was it a chandelier that the architect of the Capitol "just happened to find at a garage sale and bought for a mere dollar." Nor was it made of more pieces of glass than any other chandelier south of Canada. It was just an ordinary chandelier.

I'm sorry. It seemed like a good idea to say something.

I spent a lot of time on tours getting lost and having to fill the time with erroneous statements.

"This hallway here," I would say, "is something special that not a lot of tourists get to see." We would walk past several locked rooms to what I realized was a dead end, and I would have to turn us around. "But first, take a look at this plaque," I would say, pointing to a piece of paper that certified the building was up to fire code. "Not a lot of people get to see this plaque. This was where Tip O'Neill would come when he needed to get some quiet thinking done."

"He would crouch next to this filing cabinet?" the tourists would ask, sounding impressed but uncertain.

"Oh yeah. Sometimes Robert Byrd would join him. That was when Congress was Congress."

One of the group would try to take a picture and I'd hurry us along so that she would not be able to post this online and label it "Tip O'Neill's Thinking Spot."

"Notice the hallway," I would add. "This floor is real American linoleum. You will also see a lot of doorknobs as we walk and I invite you to think about those doorknobs. I think it was Will Rogers who said, 'Never trust a representative whose doorknob don't shine like a well-worn buffalo nickel, because that means nobody's been coming to pay him a call, boy howdy.'"

Finally we would get back on the beaten path, sometimes after several more wrong turns. If we got really off track we started to pass staffers going to and from the Remote Siberian Mailroom. Staffers would turn quizzical stares on the dutiful file of visitors marching along behind me, like ducklings who had made a horrible mistake when imprinting.

Then we would get back in sight of the Chandelier of Lies and I would suppress a sigh of relief. "Oh, here we are!" I would exclaim. "Just where I knew we would be all along, after I showed you Tip O'Neill's thinking place. This here is the *Statue of Plenty*."

"It looks like the *Statue of Freedom*."

"Um, it is that also. In fact most people call it that. But its sculptor, Constantino Brumidi—"

"I thought you said he painted the rotunda before falling off a ladder to his death."

"This was a different Constantino Brumidi."

It was not quite that bad, but it was dang close.

I don't want you thinking that I never got to do anything cool because of who my dad was. His job taught me a lot of cool vocabulary. One afternoon I was having difficulty distinguishing between "obdurate" (stubborn) and "obfuscate" (to make unclear).

"Just think of my colleagues," my dad said. "Obdurate is what they are and obfuscate is what they do."

I never had a problem again.

And I got admission to some pretty exclusive events—like for instance, when I was in the eighth grade and my dad entered me into a milking contest. It was at a Breakfast on the Farm event and the organizers had wanted him to compete. "My daughter will do it," he suggested, urging me forward. I went. It did not seem that hard.

My father always said the definition of intelligence was the ability to adapt to your surroundings. I took this to heart. So far I had had to adapt to nothing more challenging than constituents who wanted to rant to someone. It turned out that if you listened to anybody long enough, you could find something you agreed with and work from there. Sometimes you had to listen a long time, though. ("I agree," I would say, finally. "I do not think the government should take away all our guns so that they can do exactly what Hitler did, either. That seems like a bad plan, if anyone is doing that.")

So surely I could adapt to this circumstance.

There was an udder. I gazed at it.

When you gaze into an udder, the udder gazes also into you.

The other person stationed at an udder was wearing some kind of ribbon to mark her as Fairest of the Fair or Most Eligible of the Farm Breakfast or something. She looked lean and efficient, like someone who'd been on nodding terms with an udder before.

Conceptually, I understood what was involved in milking a cow. I was supposed to squeeze the udder so that the milk would go into the bucket at my feet. It seemed deceptively straightforward. Like childbirth.

I settled on my stool.

Then came the command to milk.

I aimed for the bucket. I thought I aimed for the bucket. The milk went everywhere but the bucket. It got on my fleece. It got on my hands. It trickled up my arm. It was warm and milky.

Meanwhile the Fairest of the Fair was just getting warmed up. She was hitting her target with pinpoint precision. Soon, it looked like, she was going to need another bucket. Her cow seemed pleased and sated. Mine didn't move, but you got the feeling from the udder side of things that she knew I was no expert and felt a little embarrassed by the whole display.

By the time the other milker had handily won, I had finally figured out how to aim at the bucket.

Small victories.

Whenever I tried to talk to other congressional kids about the perks of being a congressional child, they gave me an odd look.

"Oh yeah," I told them. "I get to walk on stilts in parades. And I got to visit the 'Great Wall of China.'"

"In China?"

"No," I said, shaking my head. "In Wisconsin, where they manufacture the toilets! It's a wall at the Kohler plant in our district covered entirely in toilets."

I knew life wasn't normal, but I'd thought it was at least normal for Congress.

But there was that look again. Like I was visiting from space.

Maybe I wasn't old enough yet. Maybe that was it.

The TV suggested that when I got to high school, the privileged circle of other Children of Congressmen would go around in black SUVs doing designer drugs and wrecking one another's pool tables. Also we would spend a lot of time mocking the one girl at school whose dad was only Secretary of the Interior. "We don't even know what the Interior IS!" we would yell, pelting her house with Fabergé eggs. "How does it feel not to come from the Halls of Power?"

But no. The most exciting thing that happened was that I was in a play with the son of the Senate Majority Leader. He played a giant baby. The son, that is. The Senate Majority Leader only played a giant baby during his TV appearances.

I did get to hobnob occasionally.

There is a picnic every summer for Congressional Families on the White House lawn. The Bush years had the best food. The Obama years had a dunk tank.

The Clinton years saw the lawn transformed into a carnival where you could win large bears stuffed with sawdust.

I shook hands with Bill.

"Wash your hands!" my mother hissed, afterward. "You don't know where that hand has been!"

In her defense, this was at the height of the Lewinsky Scandal, which I mostly remember as That Time in Fifth Grade When My Mother Had to Give Me a Slow, Halting Explanation of Oral Sex. This was a time when no parent felt positively inclined towards the commander-in-chief.

Also, I got to go to the White House Christmas Party a couple of times. There, there are photo ops with the President and First Lady. Congressmen wait in a long penguin line of black suits and tuxedos and stand next to the First Couple while someone snaps a picture. Then it's back to the long table of hors d'oeuvres, ham sandwiches, asparagus, the occasional fondue, desserts, and the champagne bar.

I always really enjoyed this. It was one of the few occasions when my actual experience of being a Congressional Family Member lined up with what everyone said it was supposed to be like. I stood under the paintings of Abraham Lincoln and John Quincy Adams, watching men hobnob in suits while waiters passed trays and a band played. "Ah, yes," I thought, "here *there* is."

I left reluctantly.

Outside, as we walked to the car, we'd see a line of limos with tinted windows disgorging men with headsets and BlackBerrys, yelling urgently at men with flag pins.

I had an awful thought. Maybe it wasn't that TV was getting it wrong.

Maybe we were.

If my experience wasn't quite what you picture, maybe it was because my dad wasn't either.

He looked the part, of course. He was a tall man with gray hair and Allen Edmonds shoes. He'd been in the Peace Corps, gone to Harvard, walked all the way across the state for his first campaign.

He and my mother had met in a kind of cheese-ball romantic way that you never expect when your parents are the people in question. Her date for the evening stood her up and she wound up at a party her cousin was throwing. He was there. He went home and told his roommate, "I've just met the woman I'm going to marry! I'm going to call her and tell her!"

"Yikes," his roommate said. "Don't do that."

Thanks to his roommate's patient coaching, it took my mother years to discover how socially awkward my dad actually was, and by then they had already been married for a while and she had gotten attached.

When my mother was in labor, he hastened to the hospital with a big stack of *Economists* to read in the waiting room. "That was probably better," my mother said. "It gave him something to do besides offer verbal encouragement."

He loved to read. When I was old enough he read me *The Hobbit*. Then *The Fellowship of the Ring*. Then *The Two Towers*. All of the Hardy Boys and most of Nancy Drew.

He wore suits to everything. Once, we were driving through Montana and got a flat tire and he sallied out to change it when a total stranger pulled up alongside. "Oh no," the man said. "Don't ruin your nice suit. I'll do it."

"Nice suit?" my dad asked, sounding baffled. "This is my most casual outfit."

My father had the erroneous idea that he had grown up during the Great Depression. Sometimes we drove past a stand selling bags of potatoes for a dollar. "Dear, pull over!" he would shout to my mother. "This will feed us for a year!"

He often came home from Dollar Stores with bags full of SPAM, cases of expired shampoo, and other bulk items that we did not want. "All set for winter!"

He hoarded soaps from airplanes and hotels in a big basket in the bathroom. Whenever he flew, he would come home carrying the little single-serving pats of airplane butter in one pocket, partly melted.

It's not that he didn't spend money, though. Every so often he would find some large household item that nobody needed and buy it, no questions asked. Once, we came home and discovered that he had installed gutter covers because a salesman had pointed out that they would stop things from getting in the gutters. "Isn't that the point of gutters?" we asked, timidly. But there was no reasoning with him.

Whenever my mother was out of town, the two of us went to a restaurant called Martin's Tavern for dinner. We went there on 9/11 after he picked me up from school and drove slowly through an hours-long tangle of traffic with the horror blasting through the radio over and over again.

"If it's the end of the world," he said, "we might as well have lunch."

Maybe he was doing it wrong.

Or maybe there's never a there there. Maybe that's the thing that is impossible to get people to believe. People expect that there's a

Great Something past the gate, that you get admission to fancy restaurants and tickets to galas and your picture in the paper all the time.

You sit there with your family on your asteroid wondering whether you're doing it right. The funny thing is that the fact that there is no "there" there in your particular case never quite stops you from believing that someone somewhere might have one. You just haven't walked under the right velvet ropes yet.

All you can see is the pictures people send, and those always look so perfect. The family beams out of the Christmas card in color-coordinated ensembles. Your friends pose with celebrities or at the tops of photogenic rock formations or stand proudly in front of home-cooked latticework pies. You begin to worry that everyone else's life is an endless procession of these moments, strung together like colored lights on their Instagram-ready Christmas trees.

"There" is like a stage set. It's not a real place, but you can take pictures on it and send them home. You look at your own pictures and see: Well, that was the second before the cat got away, and the cake immediately collapsed, and those shoes were torture and none of us knew that old man standing in the back.

With other people's pictures you can never tell. Maybe they're doing it right. Maybe for them the cat stood still and the cake held up.

This shambolic reality always seems especially disappointing when it comes to politics. Politics is one of the last realms where the imagination runs free. Behind the curtain, you can conjure up whatever vision you like. Sinister puppet-masters, making deals, greasing palms, pulling strings. You want the people with whom you disagree to be hypocrites or idiots or monsters, a little less or more than real, so that you can hate them without guilt.

But that would be too easy.

Behind those curtains is just more of the same.

If I've learned one thing growing up like this it's that conspiracy theorists are full of hooey. (If I've learned two things it's that the best place to be in a parade is in front of the horses and behind the band.)

Spend even a little time behind the scenes and you realize that if something goes wrong, it's almost always incompetence, never malice.

You can see why these theories catch on, though. There's something incredibly reassuring about the idea that behind the scenes, all our awkward fumbling is being guided by an invisible hand, even if that hand is sinister and comes out of a long dark sleeve. Don't worry. Top men in wood-paneled rooms have got things Under Control. Go to sleep. The lidless eye of the Illuminati will keep watch.

I once went to several days of hearings held by UFO enthusiasts who kept insisting that The Government Knew Things We Didn't. They sounded upset, but, in a way, relieved. There were solutions to all the world's problems—fossil fuels, the environment, sudden horrors that wipe out innocent people—it was just that the solutions came from alien technology that the government was Keeping from Us.

I tried to argue with a woman who was so eager to hear this news that she had trekked across the country and was sleeping on a stranger's couch. "Look, I mean," I said, "does this strike you as likely? I really—just"—I spluttered, then recovered—"you've met people in your life. Have they ever struck you as exceptionally competent at keeping secrets? Could they really have seen a thing like this and kept it to themselves?"

"Oh, no, they're out there," she said. "I've seen them myself. Out in the desert. There were lights moving in the sky."

"Oh," I said. "Oh. Well. Good."

We sat in silence for a brief time. Quite brief. Conspiracy theorists tend not to allow very long gaps in the conversation.

But we've all seen them, if not to that degree. The lights in the sky that we read to mean what we wanted them to mean. The picture where it looked like everything was under control.

I'm sorry to report that behind the small section of curtain I got to occupy there wasn't much there, there. This was just the usual mess of a childhood, with parades and allegorical statues thrown in.

There were undeniable perks. I got to tour a cheese factory and meet a man whose ENTIRE job was tasting wheels of cheese after they came off the line to see if they passed muster.

I got to hear from a man in a clown costume who came pounding over in his big shoes to tell my father why Congress absolutely needed a backup plan against terrorism (why you would decide to share your policy preferences while still wearing full clown makeup and the shoes never quite made sense to me).

I got to sit in the corner at fund-raisers plinking away at a dinky electric piano.

I got to milk that cow.

My father put up a picture of me staring at the udder in his office, next to the toddlers in overalls and the family squinting and the cheese paraphernalia.

It wasn't the greatest picture ever. No picture taken of you in eighth grade is. In the picture, if you squinted, it almost looked like I was doing it right.

You know how pictures are.

Self-Defense Tips for Fairy-Tale Girls

Many things are awkward, but one of the most awkward, in my book, is the advice they give to young ladies about Avoiding Trouble. Also, fairy tales.

To illustrate this point, I have combined the two. Here is what the crowd of advice givers and finger pointers and armchair quarterbacks would no doubt say the girls in these fairy tales should have done differently.

Snow White

What did I tell you? Never leave your apple unattended at a party.

Little Red Riding Hood

What were you wearing? Red? You should have known better than to go out in red like that. You know what red does to a wolf. You were basically a neon sign. A sign that said, "Eat Me and Then Eat My Grandmother." He couldn't help himself. That's how wolves are. It's a primal thing.

Sleeping Beauty

If you get in a position like that near a spindle, whose fault is it, really, if you fall into a sleep like death? You should have known better than to go upstairs with someone you didn't know. And you were asking him to kiss you. Forest of thorn, guards, tower, dragon—try putting up some actual resistance next time.

Gretel

Kidnapped by a witch? Well, what did you think would happen when you started eating all those *carbs*? Gingerbread is a sometimes food, especially the kind you find in people's walls. It's full of the wrong kind of saturated fats. To be frank, the witch is really the least of your problems.

The Little Mermaid

You did good. You really get what appeals to men: legs, and a woman who can't complain.

Rapunzel

Of course he climbed up your hair. What did you think would happen? That's on you. You don't want princes climbing your hair up to your tower, try not having hair. Or a tower, come to think of it. They seem to find their way there anyway.

Belle

What were you thinking? Why did you stay? If it'd been me, I'd have walked right out of there, you bet. Day one. He's a monster, and furniture doesn't talk.

Cinderella

You're the one who left the shoe. What did you think would happen? A prince sees that, he sees an invitation to follow you to your house and force your family to try on footwear. Look, I didn't make the rules. That's just how the male brain works.

Internet Bitch

As a small child I used to keep a detailed mental list of naughty words. It was my personal version of Ariel's chamber of Thingama-bobs and Whatsits, carefully culled from conversational shipwrecks in the world above. I cobbled them together and ordered them based on the things that saying them made the people around me do. There was "damn," which made my mother look sheepish, "ass," which had gotten me a stern talking-to from my second-grade teacher, "shit," which someone got into trouble for writing on a piece of our classroom furniture, "turd," which got my mother to look disapprovingly at my aunt, "bitch," "hell," "dickcicle," a word from a funny story about a man who had gone out to retrieve his newspaper on a cold morning without wearing enough layers, which my relatives had all laughed at and then, when they noticed me, insisted was a type of bird, and "krup," which I thought was bad because of its placement in the *West Side Story* song "Gee, Officer Krupke." I ran through these unsayable words in my head after bed-time, like counting black sheep. I ran through them until they were meaningless noises and I didn't see what the trouble was at all.

From there I branched out to a second collection: odd old exple-tives. Gadzooks! Egads! Dagnabbit! Odds bodkins! I came up with phrases and translated them into Norwegian online. "Dra liger tjaerliget til en sau. De erren sonnen au en moose!" (Go make love to a pig! You are the son of a moose!) Why, I thought, limit yourself to certain lumpy monosyllables when so many things were so much more fun to shout? My mother had a college roommate who had shouted something along the lines of "Grilled cheese that lands on the floor on the wrong side!" in moments of deep rage, so I knew there were levels beyond this that I could dream of attaining someday.

You could mark sea changes in my life by the phrase that I used when I was upset. Blast! gave way to Uff da! gave way to Zounds! Once, some of these words had been fearsome. A century or three ago, if I'd gone downstairs grumpy and mumbled "Zounds" into my oatmeal, I would have been stuck spending the rest of my life in an oubliette without Wi-Fi. Now I could casually throw it around on the playground, and the only consequences were to my social life. These fangless words became my constant companions.

Actual bad words, meanwhile, retained their incantatory power. To me, they were unsayable in a way my exclamations weren't. When I finally came to use them, I found myself glancing around, nervous, for someone to crawl out of the woodwork and ask for my dollar for the swear jar. If not that, then something worse. A kraken, an octopus, a birthday clown. Something bad was bound to come. You couldn't just *say* them and get away with it.

I've come to appreciate certain bad words. For the most part, bad words are funny. Just listen to them.

Fuck has a jolly sound. It is the little black dress of curses. You can dress it up or down as the occasion requires. You can wear it discreetly at work under a tailored jacket and then bring it out at the end of the evening in a more private setting.

Shit, on the other hand, I've never liked. It's too close to Sith, and those folks were evil.

Turd has a rotund companionableness to it. If you say it right, you get the sense that Turd meant something beautiful in its original language. Perhaps this is overstating Turd's case. Let's say, rather, you get the sense that the person bestowing the name had an old Auntie Turd whom he loved very much.

Asshole always seems to be driving a fancy car.

Dickcicle. Heh.

Now I know which words pack a punch and which don't. I've been on the receiving end, and it's different than you think.

Take slut.

Slut. It begins with the slick insidious "sl-" that launches a thousand insults: slippery, slimy, slough, slattern, slump, slithering, slug. Nothing good starts with that noise, that vigorous pursing of the lips. Lolita would not have gotten very far if her name started with a "sl." It does not go trippingly off the tongue. You have to uproot it somewhere deep. It pulls itself out of your mouth like a layer of dead skin, like a condom being rolled off and chucked into a trash can. Slime. Slick. Slip. Slid. Slop. Slytherin. Slurp. Slut.

It's a discouraging word. A cowboy would never call another cowboy a slut.

Slut. Say it enough times and it—never quite sounds pleasant, the way "fuck" and "turd" do, like things you would call your Viking comrades in the mead hall.

Take bitch.

Bitch never makes it into the merry Anglo-Saxon camaraderie of Turd and Fuck. Perhaps it's the missing U. Perhaps it's the unfortunate rhyme. (Witch? Itch? Fitch? Sandwich?)

Of course bitch is fine on television. Shit's a no-go, but bitch? Who's that going to bother? Not even dogs. Just, you know, ladies.

For half the Earth, we take a lot of guff.

Guff's another funny word. Not ugly, just funny.

Cursing on the Internet has always struck me as a waste of time. Half the fun is saying the word out loud.

But it has never stopped anyone.

I spend my days writing on the Internet. Writing a column is like dropping a rose petal into the Grand Canyon and waiting for the echo.

Most days, nothing.

Some days, boom.

The echoes go flapping around your head like bats, and when you wake up in the morning there's guano everywhere.

(Guano's a funny word.)

My most memorable encounter with "bitch" was in the middle of all that excitement with Sandra Fluke.

In case you don't remember this story, Sandra Fluke was a Georgetown law student who was supposed to testify before a Senate panel on the need for insurance plans to cover birth control, but the panel said no because she wasn't an elderly clergyman, and when someone pointed out that it was weird that elderly clergymen were the only people being consulted about contraception, the answer was, "Hey, when was the last time you saw an elderly clergyman get pregnant? Something must be working."

Contraception might seem like an issue both men and women could get behind, but that's a misconception. (Life, for lots of people, seems to begin at misconception.) When you're a man, you are at a much greater risk of becoming a Supreme Court justice than of getting pregnant. Lightning will strike you—twice—and you will be elected president well before any such thing happens.

By far the most effective method of contraception is carrying a Y chromosome around with you at all times. Failing that, I don't know what to tell you. It was your fault for leaving home without it.

Fluke testified to the Democrats on the panel anyway, and then Rush Limbaugh called her a slut.

I wrote a piece pointing out that the only advertisers who seemed eager to get themselves associated with Mr. Limbaugh's program were advertisers who targeted the Jerk Market—Web sites for people seeking affairs and sugar daddies, which had all been eagerly putting out press releases saying "We'll still advertise with you!"

Limbaugh called me out about it on the air—they weren't *actually* advertising with him, he said; they just *wanted* to. In the course of this—because one of the rules of criticizing female writers is that you can't just disagree with what they've written; you have to personally insult them—he called me B-I-ITCHY.

It really wasn't that big a deal. He didn't even say the whole word!

Not being an avid talk-radio listener myself, I totally missed this. (I am a little outside the age sample. The average age of the Rush Limbaugh listener is deceased.)

I'd gone to bed without giving it much thought, and then I woke up and there was guano everywhere.

I knew it was bad when I got into the office and a colleague hugged me, unprompted. I had more voice mail than the characters in *RENT*.

I made the mistake of answering one and somehow the conversation went off in the direction of AIDS and how many people had it because they wanted to have it.

"That's very interesting," I said. "I've never heard that."

"Oh yes," he said. "They're called bug hunters. The lady who teaches health at my community center explained all about it."

"Fascinating."

At least I knew I didn't have to pay attention. There are phrases like that. After you hear them, you can put the phone on mute. "Ah, good," you can say. "I can be sure nothing you say from here on out matters."

It was also International Women's Day.

Of course it would have been International Women's Day. Think piece holidays always attract this kind of thing. I even wound up on cable news. I called my mom, who told me not to wiggle my arms too much. I called my old babysitter, who was old but still very much alive, which meant that I had to explain who Rush Limbaugh was. By the time I had finished, she was irate. "Don't waste your time on him!" she told me. "He doesn't like you? Who wouldn't like you? The man must not be right in the head. Something's wrong with him. Put him from your mind. A better one will come along." "No, he's on the radio," I tried, worried that she thought he had broken up with me. "Don't worry with him," she repeated. "He must be a scamp."

Encouraged, I sat down in front of the camera.

"I mean how do you feel on International Women's Day being called and your work being referred to in such a manner by Rush Limbaugh?" Al Sharpton asked me.

I swallowed. "I would say it's a weird thing to be referred to as that on a *Thursday*," I said.

(It was also a Thursday.)

I wrote a response, too, in which I offered Rush an olive branch and a sandwich. Speaking of rhyming words.

(He has yet to take me up on that sandwich.)

It was amazing, the response. People from all corners of the Internet came rushing to attack or defend. "I don't know who you are or what you said," they said, "but Rush despises you, so you're okay in my book." Or, alternatively, "I don't know who you are or what you said, but Rush despises you, and that's enough for me."

I've been called worse things by better people. And better things by worse people. And worse things by worse people. And better things by better people. And sometimes nobody calls at all.

All I know is that if you want to know exactly what you are doing wrong in your life, just write something on the Internet and wait for the comments to roll in.

Your nose is wrong.

You look like a "female Mark Zuckerberg."

You look like a "turkey in heat." (Never having seen or spent much time with any turkeys in heat myself, I had to take that person's word for it.)

Once, an angry commenter called me a "blond bimbo" and I was absolutely elated. "A bimbo!" I told my friends. "A blond bimbo! I didn't think any of the online pictures of me were that good!"

It was not supposed to be like this.

The Internet was where we were supposed to be brains in jars, communing on a level of pure thought. No longer did it matter what you looked like. You were words on a screen, thoughts transferred directly from mind to mind. But somehow before they can decide whether what you've said is valid, they have to decide if you're attractive or not.

Not if you're male, though. Guys can go straight to "idiot" without passing through "bimbo" or stopping to pay a toll at "definitely wouldn't fuck her." (Why do we have to stop there, anyway? That's a complex negotiation between two people. Probably your reason for concluding that you definitely wouldn't fuck me would be that you had seen me doing a spastic dance move I call "inoculate the herd" and would have nothing to do with any of my opinions on the Internet.)

Speaking of which, a Web site exists that began with the premise that a guy didn't think I was fuckworthy, then finally concluded, after several pictures, that he would do so "grudgingly" and would probably not enjoy it. Thanks, guy! Did you ever consider whether *I* would fuck *you*? No, of course not.

Of course you didn't. That's part of the problem.

If I can get on my high horse for a second here—whoa, a horse! This sentence is off to a dangerous start—I always knew I was a feminist. I didn't know I *needed* to be a feminist.

I had the erroneous idea that feminism was something that had been taken care of, already—if not in the first wave, then certainly in the second. All the obvious obstacles seemed to have passed from view. No hoop skirts. Whenever my parents said anything about arranging a marriage, it was safe to assume they were joking. Nobody was standing on the bridge to any professions saying, "YOU SHALL NOT PASS!" Tina Fey existed. So did Princess Leia.

You could, I thought, just go out into the world with your eyes on exactly what you wanted to be and just BE the pants off whatever that was. Which was great news, because I had plans.

But then I tried it. Try being a person when everyone keeps insisting that, no, no, you're not a person, you're a *woman*. And there are ways and words to shut you up.

And I've still got it comparatively easy. If it weren't for a certain "fe," I'd be in the single most privileged American category, White Male, the category where your only problem is that you never knew what adversity was and you feel like if you had it would have made you a better writer.

As long as you are forced to be a woman first instead of a person, by default, you need to be a feminist. That's it. Men are people, women are women? Screw that. Screw that.

I am sick of having words aimed to shut me up. I am sick of having to be anything other than a person first. Zounds!

I enjoy being a girl, whatever that means. For me, that meant *Star Wars* figurines, mounds of books, skirts and flats. It meant Civil War reenacting and best girlfriends I'd give a kidney to and best guy friends I'd ruin a liver with and making messes and cleaning up some of them and still not knowing how to apply eye shadow. That's being a girl. That's being a person. It's the same damn thing.

I wish Rush had just called me an idiot. I'm happy to be called an idiot! On the day when someone on the Internet calls me an idiot first and ugly second, I will set down my feminist battle flag and heave a great sigh.

Then I will pick it back up and keep climbing. There are many more mountains to overcome. (Try walking down a sidewalk at night when you're a lady! Just try it. Try running for office as a woman! Look how nicely Michele Bachmann had to dress in order to NOT be taken seriously as a candidate. Try being blamed for the worst thing that's ever happened to you.)

I can't wait until women writers are just writers and woman CEOs are just CEOs and women politicians are just more double-dealing spawn of darkness.

I like the Rush Limbaugh story because there's a sandwich in it, but I have others. We all do. And if you don't believe me, just ask, especially if your day has been going too well and you feel that, all things considered, you have more hope and confidence in humanity than you would like. I can tell you about the night I was walking home from work and a stranger told me I was pretty and I said thanks and he grabbed me and tried to kiss me and I had to fend him off with an umbrella and fortunately other people were coming down the sidewalk so I didn't have to find out what happened next. I was fine. I apologized to him. ("Sorry!" I said. "I'm really sorry.")

That part was only almost funny. "Sorry!" I'm sure it put a damper on his evening. I'm sure he had plans.

But I don't like to tell that story. I prefer stories where I'm the protagonist. I prefer stories that might end in a sandwich.

Words are just words. And yet. If I were world president (as if we'd ever elect a lady world president!) I'd ditch certain words. I'd retire them to a farm upstate with turkeys in heat and the little red A's that you sew on your bodice when you adulter. I want them to be a MUTE button that works only on the person who utters them. Like that guy with his AIDS bug hunters, or one of those trilby hats—a way of flagging people you don't have to keep listening to.

Take slut. Take bitch. Please.

Right now they survive, thanks to deft handling.

You know those people who think they can talk to large predatory animals—tigers, bears, overindulged cats? ("Pumpkin gets me. Pumpkin would never hurt me. We understand each other, don't we, Pumpkin?")

Maybe it won't bite you. But you're keeping it around.

Words can be like that, if you let them.

You can seize them. You can appropriate them. You can sing them. You can dress them up and make the best of them. You can bedazzle them onto your velour tracksuits. You can Take Them Back, set them off on purpose like fireworks instead of waiting for them to be shot at you. But that's because they still pack such a wallop. You don't see people having to appropriate "tree" or "delight." ("Hot Delight in Charge." "Yeah, I'm a total tree.")

Send them to the country and let them stay there. Release them next to "cuckold," safely defanged and retired on whatever the op-

posite of a stud farm is for centuries now, with the occasional appearance among consenting adults. Let it roam free with "bawd"
and "ribald" and "Uranian" the noun.

I'm not saying we round up the words and tear them out of sentences and put them into a van and send them away with sirens blar-
ing. That doesn't work with words. I'm not even saying we stop
using them when we want to.

Words are an atlas to our thought. They map out our understanding of the world. They mean less only when we stop spending
time in the places they denote. Ancient Greek insults are remote,
not just because they're Greek to us but because the things they
thought of to insult would not be the things that would leap instantly to our minds. "FEW-CATTLE-HAVING MAN!" "INSUFFI-
CIENTLY OILY WRESTLER!" "HUBRIS GUY!"

"Zounds" lost its blasphemy when we stopped swearing by God's
Wounds. I haven't heard a Polish joke in years. It ceased to be a dis-
tinction that mattered. Suddenly you looked and just saw people
and the word seemed pointless. The word pointed to a place that no
longer existed in your mind.

And that kind of change is harder. Time does it, and effort. The
way out of it is simple: You have to stop thinking that it's an insult.
("Yeah, all right, I'm not an oily wrestler and I have zero cattle, but
actually I think this is progress.")

It's possible. It happens all the time. It happens with the names of
people—first you say "John" like it has a foul aftertaste, and then
you meet him for drinks a time or two and it's just "John," flat, and
then gradually he's your good friend "John!" and the word comes to
occupy a new position with regard to your thoughts, not by any particular virtue in the word but because your thoughts have shifted
around it.

These things happen slowly. You can't legislate it. You can't do

anything other than leave the words to fight it out, gruelingly, painfully, until people know which way it really points, that it silences
the speaker and not the target.

You can't call someone a "slattern" and expect it to sting.

I wonder who was the last person to say "slattern" and mean it.
Or "zounds."

I wonder who the last person will be to say "bitch" that way. Or
"slut." When they will settle fangless in the back of the dictionary
with the other retirees, blankets over their knees, reminiscing about
when they used to shut people right up. When they will be harmless
enough to turn up on the second list, edges sanded off, safe for the
playground.

"People used to call one another that," other Word-Ariels will
marvel. "And it used to hurt. But that was a long time ago."

The Dog in the Manger

Right after I turned sixteen, two awful things happened. I got my driver's license. And we got a dog.

I don't like dogs.

Maybe this is too strong. Put it this way: I hate all dogs, except yours. Yours is fine. It's other people's dogs that are the problem. (This goes for your baby as well. Yours is nice and smart and just bursting with potential. Other people's create disturbances on public transit.)

I was not one of those kids who saw puppies and lit up.

I knew that such kids existed. I carpooled with them: first a family with a van and a big gray wolfish dog that matched the gray fuzzy seats; then a family with a gangly golden retriever that clashed with their Volvo's faux-leather interior and left it stippled with fine long hairs. Both cars smelled about the same, one "dog with undertones of crushed Cheerios," the other "dog with leather and a hint of something sweet."

I don't have a good sense of smell, but you don't need a strong sense of smell to know a place smells like dog, just as you don't need to be a wine expert to successfully identify rubbing alcohol. There is no way of describing that smell except to say "dog." It's one of the primary colors of smells—clean laundry, grass, new car, silent fart, dead body, dog, wet dog. There are smells that are tastes—funnel cake, lemon, barbecue—but of the smells that are just smells, dog is primary, like "red." Say it, and you know.

I didn't like the smell. I never wanted a dog.

On the day I took the SAT, we got a dog. I got into the car, and there was a bulldog in it.

It sat in the back panting ominously, like an unidentified caller late at night.

I knew, in theory, that we were planning to get a dog. We had voted on a name for the putative puppy over Christmas vacation. But I had been secretly hoping nothing would come of it. I hated change. A dog meant change.

I suspected that the dog was supposed to fill my parents' impending empty nest. This was just the tiniest bit awkward, since I was still in the nest. "Hi," I said. "Remember me? I have not gotten into college yet, and I still live here."

"Oh, good!" my mother said. "Another householder! I was wondering who would feed the dog in the evenings if I was running late from work!"

I grumbled to myself. This had not been the point of my remark.

The puppy was brown and white and wrinkled and stumpy-tailed, like a cheerful egg roll covered in hair.

Of course the puppy seemed to like me. Dogs always seem to like me. It is because I am not comfortable around them. Dogs and nudists (my experience with nudists is more limited, but I think the rule holds) flock toward you the instant they sense discomfort. It seems to be a matter of principle. "You're uncomfortable?" they ask, stepping closer and looking guilelessly up at you. "Well, that's on you.

That's something you have to work through on your own. I'm just being me, and I want to share my love and acceptance with you." (Dogs sometimes emphasize this point by humping your leg, although nudists don't.)

The dog's name was Ketcham.

This was the result of a family vote. The winner was "Humphrey." A close second was "Tape Recorder." This name was my suggestion. I figured that as long as we were going to bring a dog into the family, we might as well look as crazy as possible when we tried to call it. "Think of it!" I told my grandfather. "We'll say, 'Hey, Tape Recorder! Sit, Tape Recorder! Come, Tape Recorder!' And everyone around us will be confused and alarmed!"

My grandfather appreciated the fine logic of this suggestion, so Tape Recorder got two votes. Humphrey just narrowly edged it out.

Ketcham, my mother's suggestion, got just one vote: my mother. But that was the vote that counted. Still, it was nice to feel that we'd had a hand in the process. "Tape Recorder can be his middle name," she suggested, placatingly.

Probably the only thing weirder than a dog named Tape Recorder Petri is a dog named Ketcham Tape Recorder Petri, but that was the name that wound up on the dog's certificate, helpfully abbreviated to Ketcham T. R. for future vet visits.

When Ketcham (Tape Recorder) arrived, my mother suddenly pulled out a big pile of books on the Care and Maintenance of Bulldogs that dated back to 1987. "Wait a second," I said. "1987. I was born in 1988. Were you deciding between me or a bulldog?"

"Of course not," my mother said. This would have been more reassuring if she had not continued, "Anyway, your father didn't want a dog."

I frowned. Replacing me, were they? Not if I had anything to say about it. I stalked off to my room.

The puppy made a point of systematically chewing his way through everything we owned. Nothing was safe. Not shoes, not chairs. Not legs. Not pieces of wood. The only things he didn't want to chew were the chew toys we bought him expressly for that purpose. It was no good trying to explain the situation. There was no reasoning with him. The only words he understood were "dinner," "walk," and "car ride." You couldn't really assemble a good sentence out of those.

"No" was outside of his vocabulary.

We tried training him, of course. At least, my mother took him to a trainer for a summer, and he emerged with a certificate of participation. That seemed good enough. He learned how to sit if he felt like it, stay when he was in the mood, and shake spontaneously when you had not instructed him to. My mother was especially proud of having taught him to "spin around."

"Ketcham," she said, holding a treat directly overhead and moving it in a counterclockwise fashion, "spin around!" Ketcham obediently followed the treat in an enthusiastic semicircle. "Good boy!"

I don't think it helped, training-wise, that he was probably never sure what his actual name was. We got pretty nickname-happy, pretty quickly. "Hey there, Bonzo!" "Hiya, pooper!" "Hello, fatso!" "Stay, booger-bear."

I don't blame him for not answering to booger-bear. I certainly wouldn't have.

I spent most of his first year with us secluding myself in my room and typing up manifestos against The Bulldog As an Institution. "First," I wrote, "bulldogs must be born by caesarean section! Were there no humans, bulldogs would cease to exist. (Indeed, this is the best argument for the annihilation of humanity.) Bulldogs are abominations who have persisted too long!"

My friends generally agreed. The other dogs in our friend circle put Ketcham to shame. They had self-control. Ketcham, on the other hand, turned into a star-struck Romeo the second he spotted an unfamiliar leg, bounding across a crowded room on winged feet. "Hey, leg," he would say, sidling nearer and positioning himself. "This is crazy, but I feel like I've known you my whole life, and we should go all the way! We may never see each other again, right? Who knows what the morrow may hold? Gather ye roses while ye may! That's right. Just like that."

"Ketcham, please, stop humping Caro's leg," I bellowed.

He ignored me.

We had had a falling-out after he had gotten wise that the "invisible treats" I kept throwing him weren't actually treats. It had come as quite a blow to him. His entire portfolio was wrapped up in invisible treats. He kept expecting to find one under the carpet any day now. Then my mother caught wind of it. "That's cruel, Alexandra," she said. "The poor dog doesn't know any better!"

My father shrugged. "Look at the savings," he said. The only way you could get Ketcham to obey you was by bribing him heavily with treats, and these were starting to run into the double digits.

Other dogs understood such commands as "stay" and "sit" and "don't jump up on the sofa when Mrs. Vangilderstern from the garden club is there." But Ketcham was not other dogs. Ketcham understood these commands only when you had a treat in your hand. And sometimes not even then.

My mother still insisted on having dinner parties. For years she had complained that the house was bad for dinner parties because of its lack of "flow." This seemed like less of a problem than the fact that there was a bulldog trying to mate with the legs of the guests and tables, barking when he was denied immediate access to food.

In typical Petri style, she figured that if we could not avoid the problem of a large dog who would make it impossible to hear what the speaker was saying by barking the whole meal, the next best thing was to insist that this was part of the plan.

"We are lucky tonight to have a tableau vivant!" she said, pointing to the dog, who yipped and jumped against the thin dog barrier that was the only thing between him and steak. "A chorus, if you will! A Greek chorus!"

(I apologize to anyone who had to eat dinner at our house between 2005 and 2013.)

"If you had indulged me like this," I informed my mother, icily, after the guests left, "I would not have turned out well at all. I would be lying on the carpet drooling and eating your shoes."

The dog glanced up from where he lay on the carpet, drooling and eating a shoe.

"Perhaps," my mother said. "But we held you to a higher standard."

Maybe pets resemble their people. In that case we are exuberant, overfriendly, just a little out of shape, and very, very, well potty-trained. (He had that going for him, at least.)

"How could you say no to a face like that?" my mother asked, ruffling his fur while he woofled contentedly.

"Easily," I said, removing my shoes and placing them on the window ledge where he could not get at them. "He looks like Winston Churchill under a terrible enchantment."

My father and I felt some solidarity in this. Ketcham was clearly my mom's dog. We were both never quite sure where we stood. My father approached him like a constituent. "Hello, hound. Good to be seeing you," he said, thumping his hand on the dog's bewildered head. "Good to be seeing you."

"Hi, pooper," I addressed Ketcham, putting his food and concatenation of pills (all carefully concealed in cream cheese) into his bowl. I had read a story once by James Thurber that said if you looked into a dog's eyes for too long, you would deprogram the dog and it would attack you with everything it had, so I addressed most of my remarks to the dog's lower left flank. "Hi. There's your food. Too bad you don't speak English and it makes no sense for me to converse with you." (Our chats tended to get pretty meta pretty quickly.)

"All you understand is tone, anyway," I added, moving my voice into the pitch reserved for baby talk and greetings to dogs. "Aw, yes, boy, I really, *really* resent your presence in this house! *Who's*-outstayed-his-welcome? *Who's*-outstayed-his-welcome! You have! That's right, boy! You have!"

Just before Ketcham came to join us, I got something else. My driver's license.

This was also a change for the worse.

I learned to drive in Wisconsin, which was an experience.

The driver's ed instructor had lots of homey wisdom to share. "This trick for parallel parking is easy as snot off a doornail," he informed us.

Never having removed snot from a doornail, I was not sure what this meant.

Based on my skill at parallel parking, I assume he meant "a long involved process that generally does not result in the outcome you want and gets a lot of people to yell at you."

"The trick about deer crossing signs," he said, "is that's a great place to go and set up your blind."

Everyone else in the class nodded.

We watched an instructional video about the dangers of drunk driving. The central incident of this video was an encounter between Sister Ruth Ann ("Sister Ruth Ann was an angel of mercy to those who knew her. When she was not taking food to nursing homes, she was suckling orphans in her bosom and healing the sick with her gentle touch.") and someone the video described only as "Pacho, the illegal immigrant." ("It was Sister Ruth Ann's birthday, and she was having a wonderful day. She was just driving home after sharing her cake with some orphans. But Pacho, the illegal immigrant, was not having a wonderful day. Pacho was drunk. He hit Sister Ruth Ann, killing her instantly.")

Fortunately this did not come up on the road test.

Which I passed. I'm not sure how.

They should have known something was up when I spectacularly failed to yield to oncoming traffic, slowly parked my way two feet up onto a curb, and left my bright headlights on for the entire drive even though it was eight in the morning. But I passed. I think it was because I always meticulously covered the brake at train crossings, and there were a lot of train crossings on our route. You could rack up points that way.

I haven't improved much since then. I am in no way exaggerating when I say that sometimes, simply watching me try to park a car has summoned total strangers out of buildings to offer pointers and shout encouragement. ("Turn the wheel the other way! No! The other way! Here, I'll do it.")

I have dented cars by wrapping them very slowly around concrete pillars when there are no other cars nearby.

I am at the awkward phase between your teens (when it is clear that you are just learning) and your mid-eighties (when someone finally, FINALLY comes and takes the car keys away) when no one knows quite what to do about your tendency to screech to a halt at intersections, turn your entire head to see if someone is coming from an abandoned field where no cars are, then speed out into six lanes of oncoming traffic without looking at all.

My friends do not let me drive, not since the time two of them got stuck in the backseat as I drove with my mother. This was calculated to bring out the worst in me as a driver. My mother liked to scream and clutch the upholstery and strike the dashboard with her hands, emitting loud cries, like a woman in a Shakespeare tragedy who had just received terrible news. "Ohhhhh," she wailed. "Slow doooooooown! Do you see the stoplight?"

"Of course I see it," I said, noticing the stoplight for the first time and screeching to a halt. "Please, stop yelling. You are making me nervous and jittery."

"Do you see that pedestrian?"

"YES I SEE THE PEDESTRIAN!" I said. "HE'S ALL THE WAY UP ON THE SIDEWALK! STOP YELLING!"

"Stay in the middle of the lane," my mother added. "You're all the way in the middle of the road."

"I *am* in the middle of the lane," I said, swerving quickly back into the lane.

"There's a stop sign."

"YES!" I yelled. (This time I had seen the stop sign.) We screeched to another halt. "I SEE THE STOP SIGN! I SEE ALL THE STOP SIGNS!"

I was a defensive driver, all right. Very defensive.

"DRIVE MORE SMOOTHLY AND CALMLY!" my mother yelled.

"I CAN'T!" I yelled, swerving wildly around. "YOU ARE MAKING ME UPSET AND I AM UNABLE TO CONCENTRATE! IF I HIT ANYTHING, IT IS ON YOUR HEAD!"

My friends in the backseat exchanged a terrified look. (I could tell because I had not adjusted the rearview mirror properly.) If they made it out of this alive, their glances seemed to say, they would amend their lives. Primarily they would be certain never to travel in the same car with me again—and to make certain no one else we knew did, either.

My trouble wasn't that I was just a bad driver. If only. I knew plenty of people who were bad drivers and always made it where they were going very rapidly and with minimal incident. What they had that I lacked was a certain confidence, the unswerving belief (unlike their driving, which involved a great deal of swerving) that all the other cars on the road would somehow get out of their way. And somehow the other cars did. When you got into my friend Haley's car it was like Mr. Toad's Wild Ride, but at the end you were several hours early and the experience was fairly pleasant, if you had not lost your lunch.

No, my trouble was that I knew that I was bad. I was the world's most timid driver. Like Gatsby, I could spend hours staring at a green light in complete bewilderment. Then, like Daisy, I could speed carelessly through an intersection and strike a pedestrian. Even when the light was green and everyone behind me was honking, I was never quite sure it was for me. I knew that my tendency was to look the wrong way at intersections, so to compensate I swiveled my head all the way around, like a thoughtful owl.

My parents did little to make matters better. "You are a terrible driver," they told me. "Also, remember, you are our sole reproductive investment. Are you sure you need to drive there? Are you sure you need to go there at all? Why not stay here, where it's safe, and we can have fun laying some more Styrofoam padding at the foot of the stairs?"

"I need the car to drive to a comedy show near Baltimore," I told my mother.

"That's okay," she said. "Sure. Fine. Do you mind if I crouch in the backseat? I won't even come inside to watch the show." She clutched my wrist. "I just want you to live."

And she did, too. I could not dissuade her. I was, at the time, twenty-two years old.

It was around that time that I decided I should perhaps sign up for a Zipcar. The monthly fee was steep, but it seemed cheap in comparison to the price I was currently paying every time I wanted to borrow the car.

The Zipcars were great. There was no one in the car but me, my crippling self-doubt, and my poor sense of direction. With the combination of these three things, I was always certain to make it where I was going, usually sometime within the same day that I set out, seldom more than five hours late, often with my brights on the whole way.

The whole country was my oyster, at least in the sense that an oyster is not a thing you should be driving on.

I'm not going to say that I overused the Zipcar service. But once, on Valentine's Day, I got a bouquet of flowers delivered to my office.

"Aw," I told my boyfriend. "You shouldn't have."

"I didn't," he said.

I opened the card on the flowers. They were addressed to me from a Zipcar I had once driven all the way to North Carolina, thinking it would be cheaper than renting a car. Evidently it had not been. I don't know if you've ever gotten flowers from something you've left a half-eaten slice of quiche inside? It makes you feel a little odd.

My parents always reminded me not to drive with the radio on so that I would be better able to concentrate on the road. This did not work out quite as they hoped. I would get behind the wheel. For the first several minutes, I focused admirably on the road. There were cars! I was careful not to hit the other cars. There were trees! I was careful not to hit the trees. There were pedestrians! I stopped to let them pass. There were lights and signs. I was careful to be aware of the lights and signs! This driving thing, I felt, was a cinch. One could do it in one's sleep.

Not that I would sleep while driving. Of course not. I began to think about my Sunday school teacher, who said that she had nearly fallen asleep at the wheel and had only managed to stay awake the whole drive through the power of prayer. God, I reflected, seemed to visit lots of people while they drove from place to place. Someone my parents knew said he'd been visited by God while driving. God had a book idea for him. The book, God said, was going to explain once and for all what God had really meant by starting all those different religions. Was now, God wondered, a good time to share this idea? Sure! the guy said, pulling the car over to the side of the road. Now was great. Nothing else too pressing. (You couldn't really tell God that you had plans to see *The Curious Case of Benjamin Button* and could God come back later when you had a pen handy?) It seemed a little odd that God would not choose someone with a bigger social media presence to share this revelation, I mused, but God had always moved in mysterious ways. Or maybe the guy just had a brain tumor—

At this point, honking and swerving drew me from my reverie and I realized I had barreled through a red light.

I berated myself. This, kid, I told myself—I always address myself as "kid." I take a pretty avuncular tone when I talk to myself, more so if I have been drinking—is exactly what your parents feared. This is why you don't drive. Because you might die. You will get distracted while driving and die. Look at you, getting distracted.

What if I die, I began to worry. What if I die right now? I haven't finished writing anything! I haven't even designated a literary executor. Maybe I should stop at this red light and text my friend Martin to designate him my literary executor. But he might think that was weird. I mean, you can't not talk to somebody for months and text him suddenly out of the blue that he's your literary executor. He might worry that something was up. Anyway, your laptop isn't password protected. Your mom can be your literary executor. She will be able to read everything. Oh God. Everything. Maybe I can stop at this red light and text my mother that, in the event of my death, she should disregard everything in the folder labeled "Erotic Fanfiction" because that folder was put there as a joke by a stranger. (Gee, kid, that folder's a little on the nose, huh? Maybe you should just relabel the folder when you get home. But that assumes you live.)

While you're at it you should probably erase your browser history.

Man, if you die right now on this car trip, you're never going to write that series about a magical high school in space that was going to be this generation's *Harry Potter*. That's going to be sad. The world will never know what you had in you. Sure, you had made a couple of notes but they will be completely indecipherable to anyone but you and people will just think your mind was going.

Also you'll, you know, never find love, and stuff. And George Lucas will never meet you and shake you by the hand and look into your eyes and say that he really respects you as a creator and thinks of you as a peer.

Damn, that's sad. If you had only lived. The things that were inside you! The things you had to say! To George Lucas particularly.

(More honking. I screeched to a halt, narrowly avoiding several pedestrians who had just entered a crosswalk directly ahead of me. A woman slapped the hood of the car and shouted something rude.)

This is it for you, I thought, my knuckles whitening on the steering wheel at ten and four. What a shame. What a waste. What a shaste. (Wame?) If you'd known you were going to die, you would definitely have made it a priority this morning to write a poignant and tear-jerking essay about how beautiful life was and how much you still hoped to share with the world. With dew in it, probably. Dew and the warmth of people's eyes and smiles. Well, not that. That didn't sound like the kind of thing that people would read and regret your premature passing. "All things considered," people would say, "she was only a moderate talent, and the world is no worse off."

No, you should have said something really powerful. Something that would really get people in the gut. Something with insight in it. Real, genuine, heart-jerking insight into the world that you had wrung out of your own rich life experience. You would have titled it—Think, kid! Think!—"Nobody's Literally Hitler (Except, of Course, Hitler)." No, not that. Dammit. It would serve you right if you did die just now.

Well, you would come up with something. And it would be meaningful. And also you would have left a note on your secret on-line fanfiction account explaining that you were probably never going to finish that story where the Romantic poets could control metal with their minds, but very sexily.

How much you had left unfinished. And the world would never know what it had lost!

Dagfuckit.

(At this point you discovered that you had driven the car up several feet onto the curb and overturned a trash can.)

So you see my difficulty.

This is why I am not a good driver. I think too much. Well, "think" might be generous. I—get distracted.

Instead, I started turning the radio on. The worst that would happen while the radio was on would be that I would thump the brake cheerily in time with the rhythm. And that seldom led to any deaths.

Which brings me back to the dog.

When I came back from college, he was still there and seemed pleased to see me. I took him on more walks.

I had not really warmed to him. "Warmed" would be strong. I lukewarmed to him. I grew tepid. I tolerated him exactly the way that the posters in my school counselor's office warned me didn't count as real tolerance. That is to say, I disapproved of him, but silently, and if he'd sought to marry my daughter, we would have had words.

He had, I noticed, retained his old habit of barking urgently at the door in the middle of rainstorms so that you would take him out. Once out, he browsed leisurely around the yard as though he didn't have a care in the world. He squinted at the sky. He sniffed each tree and bush. "DO YOUR BUSINESS, POOPER!" I shouted, to no avail. "Go wee-wee! Do whatever it is you came for! Pee! Urinate! Use the facilities! Go see a man about a dog! Whatever the verb is! Do it!"

Nothing.

"Fine," I said. "Let's go back indoors."

That was not acceptable either. Once the door shut behind him, he started barking again, and back out we went.

Only when I was soaked through and Ketcham felt like a moist settee did anything in his demeanor shift. "Ah," he seemed to say. "I remember now. There was something that I came out here to do." He sniffed carefully through the bushes again with the air of a man skimming through a book for a particular passage that had spoken to him.

"Ketcham, wee-wee," I said. "Please? Please wee-wee? (Yes, kid. This is where we stand. Out in a rainstorm, remonstrating with a dog in English as though he spoke the language.)"

He bolted for the dampest bush and squatted contemplatively under it. Then, his business at last complete, he went sprinting back indoors to dry himself by rubbing his wet haunches on whatever piece of furniture I valued most.

It was our little ritual.

I also walked him around the neighborhood.

In theory, one of the advantages of walking a dog is that you get to make friends around the neighborhood. They see you out walking your dog in your glamorous yet practical dog-walking ensemble, the dog gives them a conversational opening, and things flow naturally from there. The next thing you know, true love has bitten you on the ankle. At any rate something has bitten you on the ankle. Or maybe the stranger's leash gets tangled up with yours, and —wham! bam! thank you, sir/ma'am!—you have moved in together, Pongo and Perdita have hit it off, and you are raising enough Dalmatian puppies to make a really fetching coat. Basically the sky's the limit. As a way of meeting people, dog-walking offers all the advantages of riding public transit and making excessive suggestive eye contact with the person across the aisle without any of the dread that, at the next stop, this person will be replaced by a large sweaty man in a mesh shirt while your thoughts are elsewhere.

This would have been easier to pull off if I didn't insist on keeping up a running dialogue with the dog. The dog didn't know we were having a running dialogue. He thought I was just making more of those mouth-sounds with which he had come to associate me.

"Great," I would say. "Yes. Let's stop and lick that gray substance off the sidewalk. That's a great idea. Wonderful. Oh, a tree. Good. Wouldn't want to pass a single tree without urinating on it, would we? No. Of course not. Great. Oh good, tinfoil. Yes. That does seem like it would be good to eat. No, I'm sorry. There was sarcasm in my tone just now. Please don't eat the tinfoil, boy. Oh, come on. Oh, what good is it reasoning with you? You don't understand any words that aren't 'dinner.' No, I didn't mean 'dinner.' Don't give me that hopeful, trustful, reproachful look."

Oddly enough, few people came up to introduce themselves while this was going on.

He was, by bulldog standards, cute. Which is to say that he looked like Disney Quasimodo, not Regular Quasimodo, so people were always stopping to pet him.

"Oh yes," I told them. "Go right ahead. He's very friendly. Just loves people. Don't you, boy?"

They all petted him and let him lick their faces. I tried to look like this was what I was looking forward to doing when I got home.

"Hello there," I said, awkwardly poking the dog on the head in what I hoped looked like a companionable manner. "We sure get along, huh, buddy? What a lifelike interaction we're having!" Surely they could see right through me. I felt like Mitt Romney.

"What a great dog you have," the petters said.

"Oh yes," I said. "The greatest."

I would try to make a tactical retreat at this point, but Ketcham wouldn't budge. Sometimes, without warning, he would sit down in the middle of a walk and refuse to continue. You would have to pull him home by sheer force of will. Try dragging a bulldog eight blocks by his leash and see how tenderly you feel toward him afterward. It's like trying to drag a drunk boulder out of a party, while the boulder whines that it was having a good time and didn't want to leave yet.

My mother referred to these moments of recalcitrance as "sit-down strikes." To her, they were just another piece of evidence of Ketcham's rich inner life.

It was amazing what a rich inner life the dog had. "Look at him," my mother said. (The dog had just farted and was staring behind him with an expression of horror and alarm.) "Look, he's mortified."

If my mother was to be believed, the dog always had a lot on his mind. In fact, his thinking generally aligned itself pretty well with hers. "I don't think it makes sense for you to drive all the way to Caroline's," she would say, as Ketcham pursued a blue soccer ball around the yard, panting contentedly. "Do you? You'll have to turn right around, anyway." At this point the ball rolled out of Ketcham's reach behind a bush. He emitted a frustrated yelp.

"Ketcham says he agrees."

"Why are we listening to him?" I asked, a little testily. "He's a dog."

"Ketcham is an experienced traveler," my mother said.

This was true. The one thing Ketcham really did well was travel by car. On car trips, I sat in the backseat, feet wedged on top of several bags of kibble, spare bowls for water, special bulldog powders and ointments, Ketcham's favorite blankets, a spare bed that had some of the stuffing coming out at the seams, a squeaky rubber George W. Bush, some bitter spray we had purchased to dissuade him from eating wooden table legs—a spray that had had no impact whatsoever other than to make him look much less happy while he chewed through the same table legs as before—and several bottles of water in case he became dehydrated. Ketcham generally sat next to me, sprawled lavishly atop his favorite mat, or resting in his travel cage. We had tried putting him in the front, but he had interfered with steering.

He was a good traveler. He barked only when he needed to go outside to do some business, and only just before, like the alarm on the dashboard that dings when you have twenty miles left to refuel.

Other than that, all he did was sleep for hours and hours on end, snoring noisily, no matter who was at the wheel. This was more than could be said of any other member of the family.

Even when I drove, he was unfazed. He slept placidly as I drove very slowly on the shoulder of the road, signaling the wrong way. I felt my frozen heart expand a little.

"Ketcham has the right idea," I told my mother, glowering at the passenger seat, where she perched up against the dashboard emitting loud shrieks. "Why can't you be more like him?"

Even when I almost barreled through an intersection and had to bring the car screeching to a halt, toppling him into the seat well, he barely complained.

"Woorrrf," he muttered, a little reproachfully, trying to heave his sizable hindquarters back up onto the seat.

"Look what you've done!" my mother said. "The poor dog! Don't you know he has sensitive hips?"

"He's fine," I said.

"You don't know that," she said. "Bulldogs never express pain. They suffer in silence. You never know that something's wrong until it's too late."

"Where are you reading this?" I asked. "Are you sure these are bulldogs and not the heroines of tragic Victorian novels?"

"Pay attention to the road."

The poet Hart Crane said that "some are twisted with the love of things irreconcilable" and this described pretty well how Ketcham felt about swimming. If anything could melt my frozen heart where the dog was concerned, it was watching his futile attempts at dog-paddling. He resembled a T. Rex trying to scratch its nose. Put him on a lake, and he bolted for the water within moments and plunged in. For a little while he would remain buoyant, kicking with all he had, and then his prow would dip lower and lower in the water and we would have to wade in and bring him back to shore before he was entirely submerged. That was the trouble with being built like a bulldog. You were built like a bulldog: all head and wrinkles and protruding tongue and splayed, squat legs. No structural integrity. And not particularly streamlined or aerodynamic.

Still, he had big dreams. I respected that.

I was beginning to see what my mother saw in him.

In theory, you can learn a lot about yourself from the empty-nest purchases your parents make to replace you. I knew a guy whose parents bought a grand piano and a car. But he's now a law professor, so maybe they knew what they were doing.

Mine just got the dog.

And the dog got a kind of indulgence I hadn't known was an option in my family. "Man," I told my friends, "if I'd known this setting was available, I would have selected it years ago."

I watched as my mother tenderly rubbed ointment into the dog's posterior as he chewed his way through her favorite shoes.

"Don't eat the shoe, Ketcham," I said.

"Leave him alone," my mother said. "He's had a rough day. Haven't you, booger?"

Ketcham panted amiably at her.

"You know," I said, unable to come up with anything else, "I never ate any of your shoes. Not a single one."

Ketcham farted and looked behind him to see what the terrifying noise was.

My mother smiled. "He takes after your father."

My mother was always worried that something was Horribly Wrong with the Dog.

One of her favorite techniques of parenting was to sift through big books of Medical Ailments That Could Seize upon Your Family Members at Any Time. This was in the days before WebMD, which, naturally, she took to like a hypochondriac fish to water (hypochondriac fish need water too). The book had a handy flowchart that would tell you whether or not you were having a stroke. It didn't have any immediate application, but I looked forward to running down several flights of stairs and turning to page six eighty-three if the moment ever did come.

Before the dog, we had a cat. Whenever the cat stared at the wall too long, my mother would be overwhelmed with concern. "It's kidney failure," she said, sadly, shaking her head. "That's what it means when a cat stares at the wall too long."

"I think she's asleep," I said.

My father and I tried to allay her concerns when it came to the dog. We had different techniques. Neither was particularly effective.

"Does Ketcham look unnaturally bloated to you?" she would ask, cocking her head nervously to one side.

"No," I said. The dog looked exactly the same as he ever looked. He was chewing pensively on a first edition of something. "If anything, he looks slimmer than usual."

My mother dismissed me with a wave. "You don't pay attention," she said. "How would you know?" She walked into the living room where my father was. "Does Ketcham look bloated to you, dear?"

"Oh yes," he said, not looking up from his crossword. "Hideously bloated."

"Thank you!" my mother said. "You see, Alexandra? Your father thinks—"

"It's monstrous, really," my father went on, warming to his theme. "The poor creature. He looks about ready to croak to me. 'I'm bloated,' he said to me earlier. 'I am not long for this world.' He's a blimp. He's five times his original size. Horrible thing."

"De-ar," my mother said, realizing what was going on. "That isn't helpful."

She walked back into the sunroom and stared at the dog again, this time cocking her head to the other side. "I think he does look bloated," she announced, to the room.

"Well, good," I said. "I'm glad we got to have this discussion."

"Ketcham," my mother announced. "Car ride!"

Ketcham perked right up. He loved car rides, regardless of destination.

Then she would take him into the vet. "They said he didn't seem bloated to them," my mother would report, returning home with the bill. "But if he wants to have dog LASIK surgery or a dog spinal fusion, they gave us a brochure."

"Why don't we just pay for the dog to have an Ivy League education instead?" my father asked, frowning at the receipt. "We might save some money, and afterward, he could support himself."

When he finally did take a turn for the worse, we didn't notice. His head grew a little larger, but I assumed that was just my mother's praise finally taking effect. We took him to the vet a couple of times to see why he was just sitting around the house all the time looking, depending on whom you listened to, wistful and definitely sick in the kidney (my mother), completely fine, if anything better than usual (me), like he was definitely dying and probably setting his affairs in order with Bulldog God as we spoke (my father). They didn't know what it was.

And then he started going steadily downhill. The circuit of his walks contracted. His get-up-and-go got up and went.

"Aw, c'mon, buddy," I said, dragging him down the street. "You sure you don't want to urinate on this tree? Hey, look, some tinfoil. Your favorite. You always did like a good piece of tinfoil." He came to a halt near a tree, looking uncertainly at it. "Come on," I said. "The neighbors won't mind. Here. I'll get into the tree box with you. It'll be a party. See? Easy as snot off a doornail." I squatted near the tree in question, raising my leg in an encouraging manner. "Hup, Ketcham! Hup!"

(All the attractive men whom I had hoped to encounter on my walks before chose this precise moment to walk by.)

Ketcham shot me a reproachful look, as if to say that such joys were now behind him.

He went fast. In retrospect we should have seen. But it's hard to see from up close. Travel a year at the speed of light and you don't change at all, but when you return home the whole planet's full of strangers and your feet turn to dust when you touch shore.

After graduating from college, I noticed things I hadn't spotted when I lived at home, hiding my shoes just out of reach. My father favored one leg when he walked. My mother was getting her first gray hairs. She displayed them with excitement. ("Finally!" she crowed. "My hairdresser thought I was dyeing it in secret!")

The house was beginning to reshape itself so that you didn't notice where the hole had been. Change. This was how change looked.

Empty-nest dogs take the shapes of their containers.

When you have a kid you get into the groove of asking—Are you eating enough? Are you warm enough? Are you getting enough fiber? Are you getting enough sleep? Worrying is a hard habit to break. They had done it for eighteen years. They were not about to stop now.

They needed to give all this love to someone. I packed up and went to college. I packed up again and moved into my own apartment. They stood there with their hands full of all this love and nowhere to put it. There is nothing more awkward than love.

And Ketcham was there, panting, more than happy to receive it. He was easy to please, uncomplaining, loved to ride in cars. He never asked to drive.

I don't wish I had a time machine to go back and tell anything to the girl getting into the car after taking her SAT, a little too self-serious and not kind enough, to whom eight years of a bulldog was an eternity. If I had a time machine I would certainly not waste it on that. But I do regret it, a little.

I wish I'd understood what they were doing. They weren't replacing anyone. The empty-nest dog is what you hold on to so you can let go.

Regret is like a time machine you carry with you all the time that doesn't work. It gives you perfect coordinates, though.

"I think the dog's dying," my mother said. "Could you come to the house and take a look at him?"

I came by and found him lying under a large bush.

"Do you think he seems like he's dying?" my mother asked, cocking her head to one side. "Your father seems to think so."

"Well," I hedged, "who among us isn't dying?" I frowned at the bush. "You okay in there?"

The dog didn't say anything. I don't know why I had been expecting him to.

"Well," I said, "I'm not an expert."

None of us were.

He seemed to be getting worse. My mother feared the dog was going to die in the night. We sat there for hours listening to see if he was still breathing. Something was the matter but we didn't know what.

And then one afternoon when we were debating his status the dog heaved himself up from his favorite resting mat and began hyperventilating, lurching forward several feet, panting, gasping, and stumbling. We didn't know what to do. We called the vet. They said to bring him in. He was a sizable dog and since it was only my mother and me, and getting him to the car would require going down several flights of stairs, we loaded him onto a makeshift stretcher and started the journey down. There is nothing heavier than a sick bulldog. I don't know how we made it down.

The car was in the driveway.

"Hurry," my mother said, as we loaded the dog into the back hatch. "Hurry."

My mother handed me the keys. "I'll sit in the back with him," she said. "You drive."

This was unusual.

I stared down at the keys in my hand, trying to remember how to drive. It had something to do with the car, I reasoned, or we wouldn't be standing next to the car. I got somewhat unsteadily into the driver's seat.

"Be sure to adjust the mirrors," my mother said.

In the back of the car, the bulldog wheezed.

"Don't worry," I said, adjusting the mirror the wrong way, then putting it back the way it had been. "It's going to be fine."

"Quickly," my mother said, "but safely. Drive smoothly."

Ketcham wheezed.

"Ohh," my mother said. "Ohhh."

I thought it had something to do with my driving and braked instinctively, then realized we were still parked in the driveway.

I turned the car on and put it in drive. We oozed slowly out into traffic, like nervous molasses.

"Smoothly," my mother said. I tried to imagine what driving smoothly would be like, in the hopes that I might just start doing it spontaneously. This was a technique I had. It had never worked before, but that didn't mean it wasn't worth trying.

"Don't worry," I said. "Don't worry."

"Hold on, Ketcham."

Ketcham wheezed.

"Ketcham loves a car ride," I said, encouragingly.

"He's going," my mother said. "Ohhhh."

I glanced nervously from left to right in case any cars were coming. We were driving down a side street and were not yet near the intersection, but it was important to be safe. What if cars started spontaneously shooting out of houses?

There was a stop sign. I stopped just in time. Ketcham and my mother lurched a little.

"Smoothly," my mother said.

"I am!" I said.

Ketcham wheezed. He did love a good car ride.

"Just keep driving smoothly. Ohhhh. Buddy. Ohhh Ketcham. Ketcham old buddy, it's all right."

The route we had chosen had something like sixteen stop signs along it. I have never driven more slowly in my life. We oozed from stop sign to stop sign. Drive well, I thought. Drive with urgency, but with caution. We progressed very slowly to the top of the hill, where this road intersected the main road.

Given that I was driving, everyone seemed remarkably calm. Ketcham had stopped wheezing.

"Ohhhh," said my mother. "I think he's dead."

At this, my foot sprang almost spontaneously onto the gas and we shot through a red light.

"Sorry!" I said, coming to a rapid halt. "Sorry. My foot hit the wrong pedal."

"He's dead," my mother said. "He's not breathing."

"Are you sure?" I asked. "We're almost there. Is it possible he's just relaxed?"

We arrived at the vet's office and I began attempting to park. I was agitated. It was not easy as snot off a doornail. After a couple of halfhearted spins of the wheel, I gave it up.

"I will park," my mother said. "You go inside."

I went in to tell the vet what had happened. They went to the car and took him out and did all the official things you do to a dog when the dog's time is up. Yes, they agreed, Ketcham was no longer with us. They supposed dog eye surgery was out of the question now, which was a shame because the procedure would have been so expensive. But did we want to get a commemorative plaster mold of his paw? That would be plenty costly, and would last longer.

"Sure," we said.

We paid the bill. *Ketcham T. R.?* they asked. *Yes, Ketcham T. R.,* we said. Of course the joke was the last thing to go.

We got back to the car and there wasn't a bulldog in it.

The ride home was quiet.

"I will drive," my mother said.

"Are you sure?" I asked. "I can."

"It's fine."

The car felt empty. Her eyes were damp. Air whistled past the window.

"It was my driving that did him in," I suggested, trying to get her to smile. "I frightened him to death."

"No," she said. "You were fine."

So Far, So Good

"When we got into office," John F. Kennedy said, "the thing that surprised me most was to find that things were just as bad as we'd been saying they were."

That sums up how I feel about adulthood pretty nicely. All the things that I thought they had made up to lend excitement to romantic comedies turned out to be real.

Weddings, it turns out, are real. All of it is real.

For instance, if you are at a David's Bridal, and a bride there finds a dress, they will actually ring a bell. This terrifies me. There is a certain special kind of horror reserved for the realization that the things that happen in reality shows also happen in reality. If all the bell-ringing and fervent saying "yes yes I will yes" to the dress is real, then nothing is impossible. Honey Boo Boo must exist.

You actually see registries for hundred-dollar toilet brushes—which is a lot to ask for something that you will definitely put into the toilet. Most hundred-dollar purchases are things you desperately try to keep out of the toilet.

I was standing at a David's Bridal in Chicago, wondering how we'd come to this. Here was the gang—well, a number of us, anyway—

trying on bridesmaid dresses. This seemed far too adult a thing to be happening to us.

But my friend Joan was getting married, so there we were.

"They seem to be letting me," she joked.

I had known these girls for a grotesque amount of time. As far as having embarrassing stories to tell, it was mutually assured destruction all the way around. The only trouble was that most of the stories implicated all of us.

There were a few that implicated just me. The first time my friend Hannah met any of us was when I'd gone up to her and said, "Greetings, Earthling!" (This was during my "greetings, Earthling" phase. Come on. Everyone had one of those.) Later I met her at the airport in Wisconsin holding an accordion, wearing a cow hat (complete with udders), and playing a polka. Look, it seemed like the thing to do at the time.

In sixth grade, we all got really into the Trojan War. We had read about it for class, and something in it had spoken to us. That year, for Halloween, a number of us dressed up as Trojans. We turned our old school uniforms into white chitons, donned crested helmets, and carried swords. I was unable to understand why everyone who came to the door was laughing and making references to condoms. "Is your friend a Durex?" some teenagers shouted, running past.

"My friend is the warrior Hector after Achilles dragged him around the walls of Troy!" I yelled after them. (This was in fact true, but she just looked like a ghost who had gotten into a fight on the way over.)

Then there was Menelaus.

I don't think most people give Menelaus any thought. Why would you? He's a minor character in Greek mythology, the husband of Helen of Troy back when she was Helen of Sparta, before the Trojan prince Paris abducted her and started that whole Trojan War thing.

He's a footnote to history, really. A footnote to mythology. Okay, he was in the *Iliad* and the *Odyssey*, but he wasn't really the person you came away with strong feelings about.

The gang did, though. We came away with strong feelings about everyone.

And we had an ongoing feud about Menelaus' weight. "Menelaus," I insisted, "was fat."

"He was not," my friend Angie said. "He was big-boned."

"Nope," I said.

I even went so far as to create a "Trojan War Homework Help Web Site" to add weight to my claims. The only tangible result of this was that a fourteen-year-old Canadian boy began e-mailing me requests for homework help on topics ranging from "Write a story about Achilles" to "Feminism in *King Lear*." I haven't heard from him since graduating from high school. I hope he's figured out how to write papers on his own, or his life's going to be difficult!

We were the ones who liked books and Monty Python and (to our chagrin) LiveJournal and (even more to our chagrin) Hot Topic. One year we performed the Monty Python sketch "How Do You Tell a Witch" on the class camping trip. Nobody laughed. We realized, after we sat down, that this was because anyone in our class who would have enjoyed this skit was onstage performing it.

One night, completely sober, we were transfixed by an ad for a milk shake called a SONIC Cookie Dough Blast. We had to have one, we decided. At all costs. The nearest SONIC was in Delaware? Fine. We would drive to Delaware. We would drive to Delaware right now.

(We drove all the way to Delaware.)

When we arrived it was midnight and they were just closing up, but we patiently explained that we had driven across several state lines on this mission, so the employee took pity on us and prepared our Cookie Dough Blasts. We sipped them, in triumph, at a picnic table, feeling that we'd gotten away with something.

We went to the high school that *Mean Girls* was based on. (Well, one of the many high schools that claim this title. High schools like to claim this title because it makes you imagine that our dialogue was much snappier than it in fact was. And I was quoted in the book *Queen Bees and Wannabes*, so I think our case had merit.)

The gang was girls. But we weren't mean. Not on purpose, anyway. We expanded or contracted as the years went by and people came or went, insta-friends joined the circle, old friends migrated off to join the Cool Girls or the Girls Who Cooked. We were sort of a bro-y, eclectic gaggle of theater geeks and regular geeks and sci-fi nuts and regular nuts. When we made it to high school we took up residence in an area of school called the Pit. It was formerly the Sex Pit, but when we got there, any sexual activity ceased, unless you counted putting up a big poster of Orlando Bloom.

We watched *The Rocky Horror Picture Show.* "Stay sane inside insanity," we sang. The gang covered for me.

"What's the Rocky Mountain Horror Show?" my mother asked.

"Don't worry," Joan said. "It's definitely wholesome."

We went to see *RENT*.

"What's this?" my mother asked.

"It's a musical," I told her. "It's based on *La Bohème*, by Puccini."

My friends tried not to snicker too loudly.

Even by then we knew our function: We were there to Talk About It in the Car. Everything around us was ridiculous. But at least we were there to make eye contact with one another and say— "Yes. I notice it too."

We spent a lot of time together in our parents' cars, not just driving to Delaware. There was the Black Pearl, a Volvo so named be-

cause "What a car is . . . what the Black Pearl is . . . is freedom." There
was the Purple Eggplant, a large purple minivan with sliding doors.
There were others, mainly minivans, but those had the best names.

"Shotgun," everyone shouted, always a beat before me.

"Backseat," I would shout, lamely, as we approached the car—or
"Bitch seat," if there were five of us—just to make it clear that if I
always got the worst seat in the car, it was because I had planned it
all along. At this point it was an assumption, just as it was assumed
that I would not be the one in the driver's seat (they had paid dearly
for this knowledge) or the one controlling the music (no one else
was quite as eager to rock out to Songs of World War I.)

The summer after ninth grade, on the lake in Wisconsin, three of us
were out in a canoe lighting sparklers. A voice shouted across the
lake, "Hey!"

"Hey!" we said.

"How old are you?"

We paused. "Seventeen," we said. This was a lie. Clearly. It was
both untrue and completely pointless. There was nothing you could
do at seventeen that you could not do at fourteen, except, oh, have a
driver's license and see R-rated movies. But that wasn't exactly relevant in the middle of a lake.

Still, we paddled giddily back to the shore, feeling as if we'd gotten away with something.

We ate Ethiopian food together, visited one another at college,
moved from couches to air mattresses and back again.

"I love all of you and I'm glad we're friends," Hannah remarked,
sagaciously, as we drove from someone's house to someone else's
house one winter break from college, "but you're not the same girls
I became friends with."

We went from bar mitzvahs to bars.

We started figuring out how to drink. There were dates with people who weren't one another. Slumber parties where we played Risk and The Sims and stayed up talking for hours turned into slumber parties where we played beer pong and trekked out to the nearest diner in the wee hours of the morning to coat our stomachs liberally with grease.

We left town. We came back again.

We went to Atlantic City and I won a hundred dollars playing blackjack and a seagull pooped on me.

For a while we got into the habit of ringing in the New Year, too, in clumps. The exact composition of the clumps varied. Friendship is an island but sometimes people catch ships to the mainland and aren't seen for years, then wash back up onshore as though nothing happened. There were pictures of all of us on one another's walls, in varying combinations. It took three or four pictures before you pieced the whole gang together, so those same three or four pictures showed up on everyone's walls.

Sophomore year of college we drove up to New York City for New Year's Eve and crashed in Amy's dorm, because we were convinced you could drink there. We went to an Irish pub where they couldn't have cared less, but we were absolutely wild with excitement. We were getting away with it!

We glanced significantly at one another, as if to say as much.

The next year it was one of the usual basements. Then it was Philadelphia. Then it was a basement again. I joked that every year we wound up somewhere worse. At the rate we were going we would be ringing in 2016 in Detroit in an abandoned warehouse.

It is very hard to describe something that has never been more than an arm's length away. It's like when the machine to test your vision is on the wrong setting: Everything's large and blurry and just that little bit too close that makes it impossible to see what it is. You know that something is there. At some point along the line the person whose locker was next to yours and had the same bowl cut for years and liked *Star Wars* as much as you sprouted up taller and started to wear jewelry and you watched as her bangs grew out slowly.

We grew older.

The scariest moment is not when they card you that first time and say, sorry, not you, not yet. The scariest moment is when they check the card and the card is real and you're actually allowed to be drinking.

Like the people in *The Hunger Games*, we heard the engagement cannons sound and watched as the names and pictures of our married classmates were plastered across the Facebook sky. They fell one by one, with dignity.

We'd been expecting Joan to fall for a while.

"Dave's a college graduate," she told us.

"Wow, Joan!" I said. "That's great!"

Ice formed on her upper slopes.

"Whoa. There's no need to be sarcastic," she said.

"What?" I said. "No, Joan, that was my sincere voice. I'm genuinely excited."

She gave me a look. This was a problem I'd had for years. It reared its head at the worst times, like when I was trying to give Amy a sincere compliment at the stage door.

"You were just great in that show," I would say. "I loved when you walked off the stage." (I had heard somewhere that more specific compliments were better.) "Not in the sense that I was glad you left the stage," I would add, hastily. "I just thought you did a really good job with that exit. And also with everything else, of course.

Actually. You were great. No. Really. There are bad performances, but this was not a bad performance. Sometimes you see a performance and you're like, that was awful, but that was not how I felt at all this time. Not to say that I felt that way at other times."

This got less and less reassuring the longer it went.

"My dad's sick," someone would say.

"Oh no," I'd say. "That's AWFUL."

"Whoa, Zandra."

"Haven't you noticed I'm NEVER sarcastic?" I would plead, looking desperately from one friend to another. "Guys, come on. You know me."

And fortunately they did. Joan shook her head and we moved on to what kind of ring Dave would probably get her.

And now we were standing in a David's Bridal, shopping for dresses like Real People. Didn't they know this was the gang? Didn't they know how recently we'd been standing in our uniform dresses with the sleeves cut off, insisting we were Trojans with no irony whatsoever? Why were they letting us do this whole Adult thing?

What you want, David's Bridal, is a real wedding party of real, official bridesmaids and a fire-breathing bridezilla. Do I look like a real adult to you?

It was a beautiful wedding.

They broke a glass and signed the ketubah. There's a picture of us standing there with our bouquets in hand, with the happiest expression any of our faces knew how to make. This is how As Happy As Possible looks on me. There's how it looks on Angie. It's like watching the same tune played on different instruments, moving from tuba to cello to zither. (If any of you are reading this, I am not saying that anyone looks like a tuba or a zither, I swear. I picked bad instruments.)

As a frequent wedding guest—if I go to one more, I'm entitled to a free soda!—I can state for a fact that weddings are intensely one-size-fits-all.

The rituals are potent.

Everything you have ever heard about weddings is true. Everyone cries when you expect. The bride looks beautiful. Everyone dances, especially the drunk uncle.

All these tropes are tropes for a reason.

Things you only played at when you were a kid are actually suddenly acutely real. You know the person gently forking a large hunk of cake into a new spouse's face. You know these people. Death and birth are things that happen to people you've met. You start to recognize names in the wedding announcements in the paper

That is what is so terrifying.

Apparently this is legit.

This is one of those perennial surprises of twentysomething life. You are always operating under the unstated assumption that this is some kind of enormous joke that everyone is in on. My friends, whom I remember as the people trying to get out of class on the grounds that *The O.C.* said it was Chrismukkah, are actually having babies or practicing law or instructing other people's children. How is this okay?

One of the most terrifying moments in any young adult's life is the moment when your friends' parents and your old teachers start casually asking you to address them as "Randy" and "Gretchen" as though this weren't a HORRIBLE ANATHEMA THAT would bring on THE END OF WORLDS.

The odd thing is that nobody stops you. I can rent a car. I can vote and walk into an office and—doesn't anyone notice that I am secretly twelve?

We have business cards?

Who do they think we are, adults?

Oh God.

Adulthood always felt like something we were sneaking into together.

Can't everyone see that, as far as these things go, I am a series of cats standing on one another's shoulders inside a big coat? If you could just sit in your apartment all day being a bunch of cats, it would not be so bad. But you have to go outside and pass among people. And you never feel that you are doing a very convincing job. You get back indoors and peel off the coat, gasping with relief. "Whew," you say. "Fooled them again."

It always feels like a near thing, though. It's the same furtive, panicked feeling I always get when somebody asks me for directions. I am a competent human being getting through my day and navigating my city just fine until the second someone asks me for directions. That is when I lose all spatial sense and everything I say becomes a horrible lie.

"How would I get to the Cathedral?" someone asks.

"Uh," I say. I glance around in the desperate hope that they were really asking someone else. (There is never anyone else.) "There's no Cathedral here," I suggest. "They tore it down a while ago."

"The Washington National Cathedral?"

"Oh," I say, feeling increasingly hopeless. "Well, uh, just keep going left until you can't go left any longer? It's at—Massachusetts Avenue and Jujamcyn." The instant these words leave my mouth I know they are wrong. Jujamcyn was a theater company where I once delivered a package in the summer of 2008. I have no idea how this name came into my mind at all.

"Thanks," they say. They give me a hopeful, uncertain look like a dog about to go on a car ride. ("You wouldn't steer me wrong, good buddy!") I look back sadly with a sort of pained expression.

("I'm unworthy of your trust and where you're going they may attempt to neuter you.")

The one reassuring thing about moments like this is that I know I am not alone. It doesn't matter how long you've lived in a place or how well you know it. Direction panic strikes just the same. My father, on the phone, once confidently told visiting friends that we lived "on Estabrook Road," even though he'd grown up in the house and not only was it not on Estabrook Road, but as we listened to him hang up the phone we were not sure that Estabrook Road was in fact a road that existed. We thought he might have just made it up out of thin air. This is the kind of thing you do when giving directions. You panic. You blurt out anything.

Joan was not embarrassed about this.

"You're looking for the Cathedral?" she'd say when tourists asked her for directions directly in front of the cathedral in question. "Oh, that's miles down the road. You have to turn on Wisconsin and cut over to Kalorama. Hurry or it'll close!" The tourists would dart away, and she would shrug. "What? They should know better than to ask me."

That's how I feel about adulthood.

I've always had the dim sense that I missed orientation.

I've always thought someone would notice. At some point—last night, say, around ten, when I was sitting outside Safeway on a bench by myself eating an entire take-out pizza straight out of the box—someone would tap me on the shoulder and gently whisper, "You missed orientation, didn't you?"

I would nod, my eyes filling with tears of gratitude.

And then the next day I would have to show up at a chilly conference room in a convention center (coffee would be provided). Among the group would be the guy I'd seen clipping his toenails on the subway and the woman I encountered in the same subway station turning slowly around in a circle looking bewildered and alarmed, before getting on the train, then jumping off again at the last minute, then standing there as several trains came and went, looking like a deer in headlights whose cell phone had just died.

A panel of patient-looking people in business attire would tell us how everything is done. How to iron. How to want to iron. How to respond to important e-mails promptly instead of saying to yourself, "That e-mail seems important, and I need to think up a good response" and then letting three years go by.

Human beings have been doing all these things for so long, someone must know how we've managed.

Then they'd send a guy to check on you every few months— "Hey, Alexandra, we noticed you've eaten 'dinner' at 7-Eleven three times this week—at three in the morning. Is everything okay? Do you need a refresher?" Periodically they'd offer special classes on things like Parenting Like a Normal Human and Not Finding Poop Funny After Age Eleven.

There had to be orientation sometime, surely.

We went to a lot of assemblies together, the gang. Assemblies about how to avoid drugs and assemblies about how Melanie's dad had gone to the Amazon and had some very trippy experiences and assemblies about work-life balance and assemblies about friendship.

But no one ever stood up in front of us and said, "At one point— maybe not now, but soon, and for the rest of your life—people will start mistaking you for an actual adult. Nothing you say will dissuade them. You will have to live out your days surrounded by people who assume you know what you are doing. They won't just ask you for directions. They'll let you rent cars, own land and property, and represent them in courts of law!"

That's the advantage of having friends who remember you from Before, as a spindly twelve-year-old who never cursed and always wore vests. The gang who taught you how to put on eye makeup, who talked you through your first crushes on real and fictional humans. They know what a lie this is.

Not that you aren't just as good at being an adult as everyone else.

That life doesn't come with an instruction manual is hardly news. Nothing comes with an instruction manual anymore. But usually you can look up what to do online.

This works so well for electronics that I have been trying to apply it to life.

"Is it okay to eat this ham I just found?" I type into Google. I'm not sure why I think Google will know what ham I'm talking about, but this has never stopped me.

And thanks to that lovely Autofill feature, I know there are plenty of people with even more basic concerns, like "is it okay to cry?" There's a guy earnestly Googling "can my cat get mad at me" and another guy frantically Googling "can my cat get high."

Clearly we have no idea what we're doing.

The Internet is great when it comes to putting everyone's soft mortifying underbelly within easy reach. It is a mirror where we see what we want, and what we want is gross and porny and covered in bacon and needs to take a shower. It runs on id. What makes it tick is the stuff we really want, not the stuff we say we want or want to look like we want. Puppies running into walls. Quizzes. Weird niche porn. Mortified admissions under pseudonyms. One of the most popular Reddit posts of all time is entitled "What's your secret that could literally ruin your life if it came out?" And it's got more than forty-five thousand comments. Ah, the Internet, home of the rueful admission.

Except when it's not.

Yes, it has its dressy side. That's Facebook. Facebook is where your friends proudly display all the accomplishments and milestones they are too polite to inflict on you in actual life. In actual life if someone did any of the things that they do on Facebook, you'd disembowel them within minutes.

With new parents, this can't be helped. They would do this anyway. It's in their nature. I think we recently defrosted the frozen remains of a caveman from 64,000 BCE who was gored from behind while showing another caveman a rudimentary stick figure drawing he had made of his toddler enjoying a carrot. This is just what parenting does to you. It's the other things. Even people you know are lovable, thoughtful, and self-effacing in actual life turn into perpetual promotion machines on social media. Great meal. Hot car. Awesome vacation. New necklace. New baby. New job. New house.

You stare at all the photos of New Houses and New Babies and Artfully Crafted Salads and Friends Hanging Out Without You Doing Something Tasteful.

And you can't tell that a few seconds after they sat there looking like something out of Norman Rockwell their cute children shoved sticky fingers into those impeccable red velvet cupcakes and cried under their perfect sunhats until their faces were splotchy and red. You suspect as much. But you don't KNOW.

Everyone sees this competent-looking thing walking around, but that is just the tip of the iceberg, while for the purposes of this metaphor under the iceberg is not more ice but instead a crowd of really nervous penguins frantically trying to hold the ice in place and feeling that they aren't quite up to the task.

The times you feel this most acutely are the times when you look most like you know what you're doing. Like graduations. Like weddings.

Like most milestones, weddings are days of frantic scrambling around asking what's going on and where Cathy is and where you're supposed to stand. Only one person ever knows the correct answer to those things, and that person is never there when you are trying to find out. Instead, other people cheerfully volunteer answers that are wrong. "I think Cathy disappeared behind the barn," the lady doing everyone's makeup says. "She said not to bother her. Also you should definitely stand in a semicircle behind the groom."

You'd think by now we would realize what's going on. But accustomed as we are to the idea that we personally are cats in raincoats, it is always hard to believe this of others, even if the others in question are trying to apply false lashes to you while visibly intoxicated. "She must know something I don't," you think.

But then it looks beautiful, and for a few moments, it is. Those decorative gift boxes that a moment ago you were scrambling to fold fit perfectly with the tablecloths. You figure out where to stand just in time.

And every so often, not too often, but just enough, we wind up together again. It's a bachelorette party, or Hannah's just been through a breakup, or Margo's graduating. And everyone piles onto a bed or a couch or into a car (the Black Pearl is gone, but the Purple Eggplant survives) and heaves a sigh of relief. Here we are. In this together. We've managed to sneak by this far. I guess they're letting us slide.

Acknowledgments

If you're in this thing at all, it is because I love you. If you are not, it is for the same reason.

There we go, Mom! Wasn't that bad, was it?

Thank you to Fred and everyone at the *Post* for being almost comically understanding and terrific throughout this process. Thank you, Tracy, for being a swell and patient editor, and Anna for being a rad agent and human.

Thanks to all the businesses where I crouched or ate while typing this, including: Baked & Wired, Starbucks, 7-Eleven, Barnes & Noble, Chinatown Coffee, Soho Tea and Coffee.

Warmest, most carminative thanks to my folks, my grandparents, the great states of Indiana and Wisconsin, the Food Brigade, team trivia, team Pudding, BMI, the Love Nest, Team J-Golds, the Pun Community, my wonderful neighbors, Dagmar, Jesus (not that one, the other one), Jesus (you), Jesus (Luke Skywalker), Actual Real-Life Carl, Poop, the Sensorium, Curtis Lemuel, Passengers Housman and Jackson, Jesus (P. G. Wodehouse), Marcel, that lady on the bus once who would not stop talking to me about her idea for a TV show, Reuben, "Carl," Jesus (that guy on the Internet who said the mean thing), Oscar, Grover, and the woman who let me onto the dog agility course, for believing in me.

And Madeleine, always.